THE GROWTH OF GOVERNMENT IN DEVELOPED ECONOMIES

To my children

Johanna
Magdalena
Carl August
Carl Mikael
Carolina
Carl Johan

The Growth of Government in Developed Economies

JOHAN A. LYBECK

Gower

Published by
Gower Publishing Company Limited
Gower House
Croft Road
Aldershot
Hants GU11 3HR
England

Gower Publishing Company
Old Post Road
Brookfield
Vermont 05036
USA

British Library Cataloguing in Publication Data

Lybeck, Johan A.
The growth of government in developed economies
1. Political science
I. Title
350 JF201

Library of Congress Cataloguing-in-Publication Data

Lybeck, Johan A., 1944–
The growth of government in developed economies
Includes bibliographies and index
1. Expenditures, Public
2. Government spending policy
I. Title
HJ2019.L93 1986 339.5'22'091722 86–14827

ISBN 0 566 05178 8

Printed and bound in Great Britain by
Biddles Ltd, Guildford and King's Lynn

Contents

Figures

Tables

Preface

As a macro-economist schooled in the ultra Keynesian tradition of the Stockholm School of Economics and the University of Michigan in the 1960s, I, as many others, have become increasingly dissatisfied with the way economics treats policymaking. What is the purpose in assuming that the policymaking agents in government and Parliament minimise a quadratic loss function with unemployment and inflation as its main arguments, when this simply is not true. Policymaking is frequently not performed for the benefit of those affected by the policy but for those deciding on it! A second criticism that can be made of most policy studies in economics is the overly aggregative nature.

My dissatisfaction gradually turned me to political science and parts of this book are also presented as a doctoral thesis in that field. Political science frequently assumes exactly the opposite of traditional economics: policymaking units are openly self-serving and the object of study is often highly disaggregated: a small policy area or even an individual policy decision.

However, political science lacks two advantages of economics. Firstly, and most importantly, it often lacks a clear concept of exactly what model is proposed. An economist coming to political science cannot help but feel that many of the ideas advanced are simply *ad hoc* and cannot be derived from any underlying behaviour or functions, neither of policymaking individuals nor of households or firms. The second comparative disadvantage is its lack of good statistical tools. With deplorable frequency, analyses are still performed in terms of simple correlation coefficients.

The present study is an attempt to combine what is best of economics and of political science. The theoretical chapters will deal with explicit models, derivable or derived from explicit maximising behaviour of economic agents. The statistical problems will be those suited to account for simultaneity aspects and disequilibrium phenomena of those decisions. However, while the approach is still at a very high aggregate level, the whole approach to the growth of government is more in the political-science tradition than in the economics tradition. The growth of government is viewed as a result of several interactions in society: between voters, elected bodies at various levels, the government, and interest organisations such as labour unions. The normative part of the book, treating rules that may put an end to the ever-increasing relative size of government, is also firmly rooted in the tradition of the fields of political science and government as they existed before the Second World War, before the field was beset by the behavioural revolution.

Several of the chapters in this book have been published previously in another form. Chapter 3, describing the growth of government, is a summary of a textbook in Swedish that appeared in 1984. Chapter 4, which is largely a criticism of short-run causes for the growth of government in the form of so-called politico–economic models, was published in the *European Journal for Political Research* in 1985. Finally, Chapters 6, 7 and 8 are a rewrite in a more scientific form of a White Paper written for the Swedish Treasury. With the exception of Chapter 4 they have however been completely rewritten for this book. Chapter 5, which proposes a new model to explain the long-run expenditure growth, has been written specifically for this book.

Previous versions of separate chapters have been presented at many institutions. I wish to thank in particular the Departments of Economics and Political Science at the University of Gothenburg, the Department of Economics at the University of Uppsala, the Institute for International Economic Studies at the University of Stockholm, the Department of Economics at the University of Umeå, the 1983 annual meeting of the Swedish Political Science Association in Uppsala, and finally the Symposium on the Constitution and the Growth of Government arranged by the Swedish Study Group for Cooperation between Business and Society (SNS) and the European Public Choice meeting.

Several individuals should also be singled out for specific thanks, namely Arne Bigsten, Gunnar Biörck, Mats Dahlkvist, Klas Eklund, Nils Elvander, Bill Fransson, Bruno S. Frey, Hans Garke, Axel Hadenius, Magnus Henrekson, Douglas A. Hibbs Jr., Ake Hjalmarsson, Sören Holmberg, Jan-Erik Lane, Leif Lewin, Rutger Lindahl, Bengt Metelius, Lennart Nilsson, Gustaf Petrén, Bo Sandelin, Bo Särlvik, Nils Stjernquist,

Daniel Tarschys, Gordon Tullock and Aaron Wildavsky.

Obviously I remain solely responsible for remaining errors and misinterpretations.

For help with data and literature in the country survey in Chapter 6, I also want to thank Professor Krister Ståhlberg, Åbo Academy; Professor Jean-Dominique Lafay, University of Poitiers; Dr Hans-Dieter Stolper, University of Bonn; and Professor Alice Rivlin, Congressional Budget Office of the United States.

Diligent and skilful assistance has been rendered by Magnus Henrekson (Chapter 5) and Arne Karyd (Chapter 4). Most of the several versions in Swedish and English have been typed by Anne-Marie Brisman. I remain heavily in their debt.

Finally, I want to thank the Nordic Economic Council and the Gothenburg Business School for financial assistance.

1 Introduction

Since the Second World War the public sector has expanded drastically in all OECD countries. The increase has been especially noticeable in the ten years that have passed since the first oil crisis of 1973. For the OECD area as a whole the share of the public sector in gross domestic product (GDP) or gross national product (GNP) has increased from 33 to 43 per cent in ten years. The increase has been somewhat faster in the small OECD countries than in the larger ones, 13 as compared to 7 percentage points. The increase in the Swedish public sector is without exception in comparison with other countries: from total expenditure in comparison to GDP at 31 per cent in 1960 to 45 per cent in 1973 and 68 per cent in 1982.

There are many different ways of measuring the relative size in an economy of the public sector: public employment as a fraction of total employment, public production as a share of total production, public demand (consumption and investment) as a share of total GDP, total public expenditures including transfers in relation to national income or GDP, public saving as a share of total saving, and so forth. No measure is the right one to use in all instances in measuring the size and influence of the public sector in society. The different measures answer different questions. This will be discussed further in Chapter 3.

An interesting observation is that as late as 1960 total expenditures, including transfers in relationship to GDP, were relatively similar in most developed OECD countries. Sweden, The Netherlands, Luxembourg, Denmark, Belgium, Italy, France, Norway, Germany, the UK,

Finland, and the United States, all had expenditure ratios of GDP between 25 and 35 per cent. When the focus is shifted to 1982, a completely different picture appears. While the public sector has grown in relation to GDP in all OECD countries, the size of the increase is remarkably different, as noticed above.

What this implies is that the focus of most investigations of the growth of the public sector has been erroneous. Instead of studying why the public sector has grown, it is better to study why the growth of the public sector is different in countries that have after all a relatively similar economic and institutional set-up.

At a conference in 1977 Daniel Tarschys expressed his dissatisfaction with the then existing explanations of the growth of the public sector. Firstly, he found few empirical studies. He was also dissatisfied because he found the existing studies very simplistic. The studies either took a demand perspective and assumed that the growth of the public sector could be ascribed to various factors stimulating the demand for goods and redistributions from the public sector or focused on the mechanisms that supply the public sector, for example, voting mechanisms in Parliaments or the power of bureaucrats. A third group of studies treated the growth of government as conditioned by financing aspects. However, in Tarschys's view, all the three categories must be integrated into a common study, since all factors are at work simultaneously.

As will be seen in later chapters, Tarschys's lamentations are still unfortunately true. There simply does not exist any study (to my knowledge) that has attempted a simultaneous and integrated approach to the problem. Either the various studies have tested one theory after the other with no respect taken to their simultaneity, or all explanatory factors have simply been aggregated into one giant estimated relationship with no regard taken to cause and effect. What is needed is an explicit model of supply and demand of public sector services. Without such a model, it is difficult to be as optimistic as, for instance, Musgrave who writes: 'a realistic appraisal does not sustain the hypothesis that distortions in the fiscal process have been the primary cause of fiscal growth; nor does it sustain the proposition that bias must necessarily be towards excess. Quite possibly the public, by and large, and subject to correction over time, gets what it wants.' (Musgrave 1985, p.306). How do we know?

Since the public sector in relationship to the total economy has grown in all OECD countries the subject of this study should be of interest to students of government in all these countries. However, the starting point in this study is Sweden. Naturally my origin biases me in this respect, but I think that Sweden in other respects also provides an interesting example. Not only has the growth of public expenditures been most remarkable but Sweden has frequently been singled out as a test case for various social and economic experiments. However, while the starting point is frequently Sweden, the discussion certainly treats the experiences of other countries as well. In Chapter 3 the size of the public sector on various measures in various countries will be studied. In Chapter 4 a survey is made of politico–economic models of several countries. In Chapter 5 a time series model for the long-run growth of expenditures of Sweden is contrasted with a mixed time-series cross-section study where most developed countries are included. In Chapter 6 a survey is made of constitutional constraints in several interesting countries. Finally, and most evidently, the chapter on alternative constitutional constraints, Chapter 8, takes as its starting point in several instances the United States' discussion and proposals.

The institutional arrangements surrounding the relative powers of the government and the Parliament is at the centre of focus in this study. In Sweden as in other democratic societies Parliament alone decides in principle on the level of taxation and the use of public funds. However, in a parliamentary democracy of the Swedish type it is natural that the division of powers between the government and Parliament has been given constitutional form only to a very limited extent. The most important rule is that the government cannot without authorisation from Parliament borrow or otherwise bind the state to economic liabilities (the Constitution, Chapter 9, § 10).[1] In this way the government is also bound to parliamentary decision regarding expenditures. Parliament can however give the government some freedom of action for a longer period than the fiscal year. Chapter 9, § 7 in the Constitution specifies that 'Parliament can provide guide-lines for certain activities for the state for a longer period than means are allocated'. Chapter 3, § 2 states however that 'A bill that includes a new or a substantially raised grant should contain an evaluation of future costs for the purpose stated'.

The rules that exist in the Constitution as well as in the act prescribing rules for the activities of Parliament are however related to form and do not impose any limitations on the actions of the political organs. Despite a successively larger share for the public sector in society, independently of how one measures it, and despite a larger and larger deficit in the public budget, no serious discussion has been undertaken at all in Sweden of the desirability and the possibility of binding the state budgetary process by certain constitutional means.

In some countries, and most particularly in the United States, there has been an abundant discussion throughout the post-war period of the need to limit Parliament's ability to underbalance the budget and to increase the public sector in society. However, one can clearly distinguish two separate strands in the analyses. One concerns politicians' behaviour over the business cycle. Does the economic business cycle arise because politicians stimulate the economy with lowered taxes and increased expenditures just before an election in order to be re-elected? The four-year business cycle that has been observed in the OECD area throughout the post-war period would thus be explained by the fact that the election periods have also been around four years.

A more interesting proposition concerns the long-run process. Why has the public sector grown in relation to the national product in all industrial countries? Should it be ascribed to deficiencies in the whole democratic process? Is the increasing share of the public sector and the ensuing inflation generated by the fact that government and Parliament tend to yield to various pressure groups? (Burton, Hawkins and Hughes 1981.) Some students of the problem of democracy have wanted to take the analysis even further, for instance Crozier, Huntington and Watanuki. They find that the democratic goals of equality and individual self-attainment tend to lead to diminished authority of government and Parliament, at the same time as the large participation on the part of the public in decision-making in society leads to great strains on the government apparatus. According to this analysis a mature democracy is unable to handle the increasingly stronger claims that various interest groups in society make.[2]

The Keynesian revolution of the 1930s has indubitably made it more difficult for the economist to understand the political process. Economists in the Keynesian tradition have drawn two conclusions on economic policy. The first is that economies do not have a built-in equilibrating tendency in the sense that low inflation and low unemployment are automatically maintained. The government must intervene to fulfil these targets. The second is that the government also possesses the means to steer the economy over the business cycle. In this way Keynesianism acquired a tendency to try to do too much ('an interventionist bias' according to Brunner). But at the same time the Keynesians have had an overly simplified view of the political decision-making process. A typical study of the economy and economic policy starts from certain objective goals for society in the form of inflation, unemployment, growth, income equality, etc. Economists then ask themselves what instruments should be used and how much in order to attain these goals. There has never been any doubt about the fact that reality sometimes imposes restrictions on the possibility to attain the goals, nor that lag effects create problems for economic policy. But it has been taken for granted that politicians and economists have the same set of goals and view instruments in a similar manner.

In the public-choice tradition this naïve view of politicians has come to be questioned more and more. Instead of viewing politicians as altruistic one presumes the same type of utility functions for the politicians as for other agents in society, namely maximisation of own welfare. In this welfare function for a politician may be included the possibility of re-election or for the bureaucrat to acquire a larger number of subordinates. Even if these beliefs are frequently overstated, so are the Keynesian ones of the all-knowledgeable, altruistic politician. For these reasons the question to be taken up in this book on the growth of government is in the border area between economics and political science. One cannot analyse economic policy and the growth of the public sector without also including institutional and political aspects. This has been clearly described by two of the main pretendents of the public-choice school, Buchanan and Wagner (1977), p.93:

> Whether they like it or not, those who seek to understand and ultimately to influence the political economy must become political economists. Analysis that is divorced from institutional reality is, at best, interesting intellectual exercise. And policy principles based on such analysis may be applied perversely to to the world that is, a world that may not be at all like the one postulated by the theorists. Serious and possibly irreversible damage may be done to the institutions of the political economy by the teaching of irrelevant principles to generations of potential decision makers. Has the teaching of Keynesian economics had this effect? The question is at least worthy of consideration.

Chapter 2 provides a starting point for the analysis. Wherein lies the problem of the successively larger relative size of the public sector? Is it the budget deficits that constitute the main problem or is it the rise of the public sector itself? Is it the excessive use of instruments over a business cycle and hence the excessive swings in such variables as inflation and unemployment that constitute the main problem or is it the more long-run growth of the size and influence of the public sector? These questions are then taken up in greater detail in later chapters.

Chapter 3 provides a background for the later theoretical and empirical discussion. It tries to explain what is meant or should be meant by the public sector and how different measures of the size of the public sector should be used to answer different questions. The growth of the public sector in Sweden and other countries on several measures is also shown.

Chapter 4 treats the short-run problem, namely the so-called politico–economic models. Do voters in the evaluations of political parties include economic factors in their decision-making? And has the incumbent government consciously manipulated the economy before the election in order to increase the possibility to become re-elected? If this is the case, the implications for how constitutional limitations on the powers of government should be constructed are quite different from those that arise if the growth of government is a more long-run phenomenon.

In Chapter 5 the cyclical variations in the growth of the economy and of the public sector is essentially ignored. The focus is instead on the growth of the public sector in the last 30 years in Sweden and other developed economies. A brief survey is first made of some earlier and recent empirical studies. An attempt is then made to formulate a model that accounts simultaneously for the demand and for the supply perspective of the growth of government. This model is then estimated on time-series data for Sweden and for a mixed time-series cross-section data for other developed economies.

In Chapter 6, existing constitutional constraints on the growth of government in some interesting countries are surveyed. The recent constitutional debate in the United States looms importantly in this chapter, but Finland with its unique qualified majority for tax decisions in Parliament is also studied. The specific allocation of powers between government and Parliament in the UK, Germany and France is also taken up.

The fundamental principle in any democracy is majority rule. A total 50.1 per cent of the population (Parliament) is given the right to suppress the other 49.9 per cent. As an introduction to the later discussion on qualified majority rule, Chapter 7 provides a preliminary and more theoretical discussion of decision rules in economic theory. What advantages and disadvantages are really connected with simple majority rule?

Chapter 8 is the normative kernel of the book. It draws upon the results of earlier chapters, namely that the growth of government simply cannot be ascribed to politico–economic cycles nor to demand for more public goods and services. Instead, by default, the explanation is shifted to areas that can be measured only with great difficulty, such as competition between interest groups in society and collusion between various groups and decision-making bodies. With this in mind the chapter takes up various norms that could be used to stop the further growth of the role and size of the public sector.

The first norm treated concerns an exchange-rate norm, that is a fixed exchange rate prescribed by the Constitution. Until the new 1974 Constitution the gold standard was actually written into the Swedish Constitution, albeit that the rule was suspended since 1931. Another occasionally advanced norm connected with the name of Milton Friedman is a monetary norm. According to this norm the money supply must not increase more than at a specified rate of growth independent of the state of the business cycle. In a closed economy where money is created by state borrowing in the central bank the monetary norm is in many aspects similar to a norm prescribing budgetary balance. In an open economy the two norms will however be different. The growth of the public sector can however also be held back by various ceilings for government expenditures or for the share of taxes in national income.

In particular the last two mentioned norms have of course been extensively discussed. The chapter will however also take up and analyse some other norms that could be given a constitutional status. One possibility is qualified majority rule, another is limitation of what the government can and cannot do. The instrument of popular referenda could also be used to circumscribe the powers of government. Finally, one could attempt to increase the powers of the executive *vis-à-vis* the Parliament by various means.

The area covered by this book is thus enormous. On the positive side, it summarises the growth of government and tries to explain the causes for that growth. On the normative side it tries to give recommendations for what constitutional means could be used to put a stop to the ever-growing size of the public sector. It cannot possibly be the task of this book to say the final word on any of the matters discussed. However, given the American domination in the field of the study and the relative meagre contributions from the European side so far, perhaps the book can provide an impetus and starting point for the debate also necessary in the open economies of Europe.

Notes

1 The Swedish Constitution really consists of three parts: the main one directing the form of government (Regeringsform) and two subsidiary ones relating to the succession of the royal house and to the freedom of the press. All references in this book are to the main Constitution. The rules regulating the internal working arrangements of Parliament (Riksdagsordning) no longer have the status of a constitutional law under the 1974 Constitution Act.

2 Mancur Olson's recent book *The Rise and Decline of Nations* is a further step on this path of analysis.

References

Brunner, K. (1970), 'Knowledge, Values and the Choice of Economic Organization', *Kyklos*, 23 (no. 3).

Buchanan, J.M. and Wagner, R.E. (1977), *Democracy in Deficit: The Political Legacy of Lord Keynes* (New York: Academic Press).

Burton, J., Hawkins, M.J. and Hughes, G.L. (1981), 'Is Liberal Democracy Especially Prone to Inflation' in D.A. Hibbs and H.

Fassbender, eds, *Contemporary Political Economy* (Amsterdam: North Holland).
Crozier, M., Huntington, S.P. and Watanuki, J. (1973), *The Crisis of Democracy* (New York: New York University Press for the Trilateral Commission).
Musgrave, R.A. (1985), 'Excess Bias and the Nature of Budget Growth', *Journal of Public Economics*, 28 (December).
Olson, M. (1982), *The Rise and Decline of Nations, Economic Growth, Stagflation and Social Rigidities* (New Haven: Yale University Press).
Tarschys, D. (1977), 'Forskning om den offentliga sektorns expansion', in B. Gustafsson, ed., *Den offentliga sektorns expansion* (Uppsala: Almqvist & Wiksell).

2 Wherein lies the problem?

The causes for the rapidly growing public sector can be found not only in the political or the economic spheres. They are founded on the interaction between the polity, the economy, the administration, and various organisations. One simply cannot find the reasons why the public sector has grown within one sector of the society in isolation. However, very few studies have taken this integrated point of view. From the political science perspective, researches have to my mind focused too heavily on the concept of power. Irrespective of how one defines the concept – as a function of position in society or as a function of decision-making or even non-decisions – one lacks a suitable frame for reference. How can one say that one person has too much power without referring to an ideal state where all persons have equal amounts of power or an extreme perversion where one person has all power?

Economists long ago developed one answer to the question of how one can compare an actual situation with an ideal or with an extreme perversion. Economists focus on the mechanisms that guide the economy. What signal does the market give and how do various economic agents react to these signals? When the steering system is used as a starting point for the analysis, the suitable frame of reference is immediately available. When economists posit the perfect market as a starting point it is not because they believe that reality is perfect but that a starting point is required, a frame of reference, to be compared with reality.

Within the Norwegian 'power' investigation (*maktutredningen*) Hernes (1978) has been able to create a similar frame of reference for four different spheres in society by studying the mechanisms that guide decisions in the spheres: the economy, the polity, the administration, and various interest organisations.[1] Hernes's discussion starts from an ideal condition in each of the four spheres. He then goes on to consider interactions between the spheres that could lead to improvements or to distortions in the characteristics of the guidance systems, for instance when political decisions counteract imperfections in the economic mechanism.

The starting point then is the perfect market, the perfect democracy, the perfect administration and the perfect interest organisations. These are represented in Figure 2.1. On the ideal market the consumer rules. There are many small and independent firms and consumers. Both sides have perfect information. The price system gives the information that both buyer and seller need and serves as a co-ordinator of individual decentralised decisions. The constitutional foundation is given in the form of freedom of ownership, freedom of profession, freedom to conduct any business of one's liking and freedom of contract. These imply that the state has the responsibility to maintain law and order and guarantee that contracts are fulfilled.

The perfect democracy has many similarities with the perfect market. Voters rule supremely and politicians adjust to their opinions. Voters are independent of one another and equally strong, since power exists exclusively in the right to vote. Voters and politicians both have full information. The foundation for political decision is guaranteed by certain constitutional principles in the form of the traditional bill of rights. Since the politicians always know exactly what the voters want, political decisions are representative of voters' opinions.

The third sphere is the perfect administration. In these the bureaucrats obediently follow political decisions from above, lacking own ambitions in other respects than advancing up the career ladder in line with their own competence. The centralised administrative decisions become co-ordinated since they follow centrally-given rules and directives. Since everybody has perfect information the outcome of an administrative decision is given and known. The constitution grants freedom of appeal and guarantees impartiality and equal treatment for all.

The fourth sphere contains the various organisations in society.[2] In similarity to the parties their task is to articulate members' interests. The leadership of an organisation follow members' opinions, of which they have full information. All interests become organised and are equally treated. The constitutional foundation is the freedom of negotiation and of contract, together with the political freedoms

	The perfect market	The perfect democracy	The perfect administration	The perfect interest organisation
1	The sovereign consumer initiates	The sovereign voter votes	The political leadership instructs	The sovereign member of a group demands
2	The producer adjusts to demand	Politicians adjust to voters' opinions	Administrations follow rules impartially	Organisations articulate members' interests
3	Prices provide buyer and seller with full information	Voters and politicians have full information on all alternatives and their consequences	Administrations possess the necessary knowledge	Organisations are fully informed of members' interests
4	What is demanded is also produced	All opinions become represented	What is required is also performed	All interests are fully organised and articulated
5	Prices depend on free competition	Political decisions depend on competition among parties	Career advancement through competition guarantees competence	Negotiations lead to agreements
6	Markets are decentrally co ordinated through prices	Decisions in representative organs provide control co-ordination	Centrally made rules are decentrally implemented	Central co-ordination through bargaining
7	Constitutional foundation: – freedom of ownership – freedom of profession – freedom to conduct business – freedom of contract	Constitutional foundation: – freedom of speech – freedom of information – freedom of meeting – freedom to demonstrate – freedom of association – freedom of religion	Constitutional foundation: – freedom of appeal – equal treatment – impartiality	Constitutional foundation: – freedom of negotiation and of contract

Figure 2.1 Four theoretical models for decision-making in society

treated in the political sphere.

Certain characteristic features are thus common to all the four spheres: they build on individuals and on pluralism, that is, many small independent units; they build on perfect information and rational action. The four systems of guidance in society are independent of one another; the only common denominator is the individual in his capacity of consumer – voter – member of an organisation.

But even leaving aside for a brief moment the interconnections between the four spheres there are many reasons why reality does not attain the ideal that is posited here. Every system lacks some of the necessary ingredients that are required for the ideal system to develop. Hernes calls these aberrations 'internal perversions'. (See Figure 2.2.)

The market	The democracy	The bureaucracy	Interest organisations
Monopoly or oligopoly	One-party state Instability Oppressive majority	Unruly bureaucracy	Monopoly of membership Forced membership
Market imperfections	Non-representative Parliaments Excessive promises	Own goals dominate	Free riders Non-members are not represented
Unused resources and inoptimal allocation	Political apathy Low electoral participation	'Not-my-table' mentality	Passivist members
Producers decide	Political inequality	Lack of adjustment to differing circumstances	The bigwigs decide

Figure 2.2 **Internal perversions**

On account of lack of information, sticky prices, sticky factors of production, economies of scale, etc., oligopolies and monopolies arise instead of the perfect market. The effect is lower production volumes and higher prices than would have existed under perfect competition. Producers become stronger than consumers and attempt to direct their preferences through advertising. The sovereignty of the consumer disappears.

The preconditions for the perfect democracy must also be questioned. Certain individuals have more political power than others on account of wealth, positions in society, or simply on account of the lack of interest of the majority in most questions. The absence of an active articulation of interests makes it difficult for the politicians to know what the citizens really want. Voters take for granted the fact that communal services will be supplied even though they themselves do not take an active part in the process ('the free-rider problem'). The apathy of the voters give rise to power-hungry politicians and to distortions in decisions, when organised minority interests can defeat an apathetic majority.

A more fundamental reason for political instability is however not taken up by Hernes, namely the impossibility of aggregating individual preferences into consistent societal solutions. Even if all voters had stable and consistent preferences this does not necessarily lead to stable political decisions, since individual preferences cannot be aggregated into a communal preference function in a meaningful manner. Under the majority principle, problems of aggregation create possibilities of variable majorities in different questions ('cycling') and to political instability. This problem will be returned to in Chapter 7, where the majority principle as a rule of decision is discussed.

The perfect bureaucracy must also be questioned. Since the administration has the expertise in a certain question it may dominate its superior politicians. Bureaucrats no longer stand free of own interests separated from those of society but may attempt to maximise their own utility, perhaps in the sense of maximising their power or number of subordinates.

Finally, one can also question the perfect interest organisations. If members are passive the result is most probably a rule of the few. This risk is aggravated if members are forcibly connected to certain organisations (labour unions) that do not compete for members among each other. The individual member believes himself to have so little influence that he prefers to act as a free rider.

But interactions between the four spheres can improve the individual systems of guidance. The market principle could for instance improve upon democracy. Private ownership can lead to a greater interest for the owned dwelling. Profit-sharing systems can lead to a better democracy in the working place. Competition for members and for customers leads to more representative interest organisations and to a more efficient administration.

The political system can also be used to improve the other systems. Political decisions may ensure that there exists goods and services that the market cannot produce because individual interests are not strong enough (collective goods). Political decisions can also counteract oligopoly, improve upon the flow of information in society (employment agencies) and maintain the effective level of demand. Political decisions can make administrations more representative and create systems of control that lead to efficiency and impartiality. By supporting interest organisations and forbidding forced membership, politicians can also improve the efficiency and representativeness in organisations. (See Figure 2.3.)

Improving sphere	Improved sphere			
	Market	Democracy	Bureaucracy	Interest organisations
Market	–	Private ownership	Competition Internal pricing	Competition for members
Democracy	Democracy at the workplace Distribution policy	–	Representative bureaucracy 'Ombudsman'	Support to associations Public mediation in wage negotiations
Bureaucracy	Standards Authorisation Anti-trust legislation and supervision	Supply of expertise Implementation of political decisions	–	Public service to organisations
Interest organisations	Organisations as market participants	Organisations articulate interest Bring up questions between elections	Organisations participate in administrations	–

Figure 2.3 Improvements through interactions

But interactions between the four spheres can also lead to distortions in the systems of guidance, what Hernes calls 'external perversions'. Free market competition may lead to an inferior level of information if newspapers that cannot handle competition go bankrupt. The economic inequalities created by perfectly free competition may lead to political inequalities. Political decisions can also distort the efficiency of the market, as when the state consciously destroys price mechanisms (wage and price freezes) or does not allow inefficient firms to go bankrupt. The situation is made even worse by a collusion of interests between politicians, business leaders and union leaders. (See Figure 2.4.)

The 'power' investigation has thus created an interesting framework for analysis. It has, however, its deficiencies. Perhaps the main deficiency is that it does not treat the international dependency at all. Several supernational organisations such as the International Monetary Fund or the Common Market can directly affect the activities of a country but they cannot be directly referred to the political sphere as specified here. Even in other ways the international interdependencies must be taken into account. The international exchange of trade and capital creates clear boundaries for what it is possible to accomplish in a small open economy. None of the small open economies in Europe has contracted to have a level of unemployment exceeding 10 per cent. They have not promised to conduct the same economic policy as the rest of the world. Still they have great difficulties to depart from what the rest of the world imposes on them in terms of inflation and unemployment. In a situation of conflict or war it is of course even more apparent that the domestic systems of guidance are not the ones of exclusive interest.

Perverting sphere	Perverted sphere			
	Market	**Democracy**	**Bureaucracy**	**Interest organisations**
Market	–	Monetised politics Newspaper deaths	Corruption	Commercialism kills organisations that are non-profit making
Democracy	Industrial subsidies Costs of co-ordination	–	Politiced administrations Slow decision-making	Politicians involved in negotiations
Bureaucracy	Excessive regulation	Politicians dominated by experts	–	Bureaucracy dominates important areas
Interest organisations	Guild system	Lobbying Corporativism	Coalitions between organisations and bureaucracy	–

Figure 2.4 Distortions through interactions ('external perversions')

Another question-mark refers to the role of the press. It can hardly be placed under any of the four included spheres and yet it has a considerable influence on each of them.

The conclusion in the power report as well as here is that one cannot analyse the public sector by studying exclusively the relationship between the government and Parliament, even though this is perhaps the central point of the analysis. The relationship between these two on the one hand and the administration on the other must be included in the analysis, as must be their relationship to various organisations. How the developing strong organisations in co-operation with political and economic interests have created external perversions has recently been discussed (for example, Gylfason and Lindbeck 1982, and Olson 1982).

The Norwegian power investigation, however, failed to employ their own framework for the ensuing analysis. In determining the relative power of such bodies as trans-national companies, urban versus regional politicians, etc., they reverted to the type of analysis they set out to criticise, namely such as 'who has power in this town'. This is all the more surprising since the four spheres of decision-making and their inter-relationships lead naturally to a model for determining the growth of the public sector. It includes the voters and the interest organisations as demand components; it includes the government, Parliament and the administration as suppliers of public goods and services. Furthermore, it specifies many of the inter-linkages that must be considered in the analysis. These are questions that will be taken up later in Chapter 5. But, perhaps most importantly, included in each of the four spheres of interest are the constitutional requirements necessary for a good functioning of decision-making in that sphere. This will be discussed further in Chapter 8. What is the reason, for instance, that in democratic countries the constitutional foundation for the political sphere is always considered in a bill of rights, whereas much less attention is focused on possible constitutional arrangements to make the economy work better?

The figures allow us to focus on many of the factors that have been named as the causes behind the excessive growth of government. Several internal perversions could enter here. Lack of information is one possibility. It is frequently argued that voters are uninformed about the 'tax price' of the supply of collective goods and services. Another possibility is that goods and services are heavily subsidised, leading automatically to excessive demand for public supplies. Lack of political control over administrations and the ensuing 'growth-maximising bureau' is another case. A third breakdown in the ideal state in Figure 2.1 occurs whenever an organisation has a monopoly on its members and hence becomes excessively strong. But external perversions can also be referred to as causes of excessive government growth. Collusions between politicians and bureaucrats is one instance, collusions between politicians and representatives of interest groups another. In these cases representatives of the bureaucracy and/or interest organisations make up a large number of parliamentarians and hence some interests are better articulated than others. Over-representation in Parliament of groups demanding a greater public sector is in turn perhaps a necessary prerequisite for excessive growth of government to occur.

But wherein lies the problem with a larger and larger public sector? I think three separate ingredients can be distinguished in the explanation. The first one centres on harmful variations in the public sector over the business cycle, the second on the budget deficit and the third on the size and influence of the public sector as such.

According to the first explanation, the economies of the industrialised world are rather stable in themselves. Variations in such variables as unemployment and inflation would be relatively small in the absence of governmental interference and the economies would tend to be self-correcting, returning to an equilibrium position of relatively low unemployment and inflation. Politicians that strive to be re-elected seek however to stimulate the economy in various ways to bring unemployment down before an election. The effect of such stimulation may be a higher rate of growth of the economy and lower unemployment for a year or two, but the stimulus cannot go on for ever. The rise in the rate of inflation requires a period of more contractionary economic policy between elections, when politicians must brake the economies in order to get the rate of inflation down. The result is both a greater variability in the rate of growth than the economies would have shown in the absence of interference, and a lower average rate of growth than would otherwise have taken place. The conclusion is that politicians should be subject to constitutional limitations that prevent or impede their possibilities to play the game of the political business cycle. A constitutional demand for budget balance every year could for instance prevent the underbalancing of the budget by excessive expenditures in the period preceding an election (see Wagner 1977).

The question is fundamentally empirical. Firstly, have politicians really sought to influence various macroeconomic variables for the purpose of winning an election? Secondly, even if this is the case, has this had the effect that the average rate of growth has been lowered and stability decreased? To take the second question first, there have been very few investigations of whether an active stabilisation policy really has stabilised the economies. The investigations have almost exclusively centred on American monetary policy and the question of whether a constant rate of growth of money supply according to the prescription advanced by Milton Friedman really would lead to enhanced stability in the economy. Without clear evidence to support them, most economists would probably claim that fiscal policy actions of governments had a stabilising effect on the economies, at least for the period until about 1970. They would support this claim for instance with Erik Lundberg's famous investigation *Instability and Economic Growth*. However, what evidence there is for the 1970s would rather point to the fact that economic policies of developed countries have led to instabilities rather than to increased stability. OECD calculates for instance that something like four-fifths of the total increase in unemployment in the OECD area results from the restrictive policies undertaken by these countries as a result of the oil price increases rather than from the oil price hikes themselves.

The first question, that is, the existence of a politico–economic cycle, is treated further in Chapter 4 where it is found that the influence of economic factors on voters is a very fickle phenomenon. Furthermore, it is very difficult to pinpoint specific instances where governments have reacted with their taxing and expenditure powers to influence the outcome of elections. The conclusion must therefore be, at least until more detailed investigations produce another result, that constitutional limitations can hardly be necessary to restrict politicians' freedom of action in the short-term perspective.

The characteristic feature for most OECD countries is that the increase in the public sector has gone hand-in-hand with a larger deficit in the public budgets. In 1984 only one country, Norway, had a surplus in its general government financial balance. On average the OECD area encountered deficits amounting to 3.6 per cent of GDP. The smaller countries' average was even larger – 4.7 per cent. What problems are caused by the persistent deficits? And is not the deficit in itself a sign that public expenditures have been expanded too fast, that the taxpayers have not wanted to pay for the various reforms the Parliaments have enacted?

This is not the place to take up the economic aspects of the consequences of budgetary deficits. What is of interest however is how the public views the budget deficit. In the United States a survey has found that no less than 66 per cent of the population support a constitutional amendment making federal budgetary deficits impossible. Several reasons are given. Firstly, it is considered that the state as the individual must live within its means. Secondly, people believe that inflation will be limited in this manner. Thirdly, increased efficiency in government is given as a likely result (Blinder and Holtz-Eakin 1983). To my knowledge there does not exist any comparable survey for a European country.

This brings us to the third and more long-run perspective. In my opinion it is by far the most important. Even if the public sector reached budgetary balance again, the government sector would have a decisive influence on society simply as a result of its relative size. A large-share public employment makes an expansion in the private sector difficult. The ensuing high tax ratio makes an even larger marginal tax rate necessary if there is to be any progressivity whatsoever in taxation. Many government expenditures are such that private initiatives are suffocated and people more and more rely on the helping hand of 'Big Brother'. The expenditure side and the income side both create problems that interact in a vicious circle and make problems ever more difficult (see Lindbeck 1983).

I have indicated only some of the problems connected with a powerful state. Many more investigations are necessary about what positive and negative effects a large public sector has on the economy and of how the population views various public activities. One indication may be that voters' attitude towards the Swedish welfare system has changed drastically since the days of growth. In the 1968 Swedish election only 42 per cent of voters wanted to diminish rather than increase welfare payments in society. In the 1979 election this figure had risen to 67 per cent and the increase was found in all parties except the Communist Party (Holmberg 1981). In the 1982 election survey a new question was asked, namely concerning attitudes towards the public sector as such. It was found that 38 per cent of the voters wanted to see a smaller public sector.

These long- and short-run problems will be taken up in more detail in the ensuing chapters. What they lead up to concerning the need for constitutional arrangements is the following: What restrictions can be posited that prevent a further increase in the public sector and its influence on the society without curtailing the possibility of government to interfere in the short-run stabilisation policy? These are the questions to be treated in the normative part of this book.

Notes

1 Buchanan (1954) and Dahl and Lindblom (1953) showed much earlier that this economic argument could be fruitfully applied to the political decision-making process.

2 In Hernes's treatment, interest organisations are placed within the polity. They can however be easily broken out.

References

Blinder, A.A. and Holtz-Eakin, D. (1983), 'Public Opinion and the Balanced Budget', Mimeo.

Buchanan, J.M. (1954), 'Social Choice, Democracy and Free Markets', *Journal of Political Economy* (January).

Dahl, R.A. and Lindblom, C.E. (1953), *Politics, Economics and Welfare* (New York: Harper & Brothers).

Gylfason, T. and Lindbeck, A. (1982), 'Endogenous Politicians and Labor Leaders', Mimeo, Institute for International Economic Studies.

Hernes, G., ed. (1978), *Førhandlingsøkonomi of blandnings-administrasjon*, A Report from the Norwegian 'Power' investigation

(Oslo: Universitetsförlaget).
Holmberg, S. (1981), *Svenska väljare* (Stockholm: Liber).
Lindbeck, A. (1983), 'Budget Expansion and Cost Inflation', *American Economic Review*, 73 (May).
Lundberg, E. (1968), *Instability and Economic Growth* (New Haven: Yale University Press).
Olson, M. (1982), *The Rise and Decline of Nations: Economic Growth, Stagflation and Social Rigidities* (New Haven: Yale University Press).
Wagner, R.E. (1977), 'Economic Manipulation for Political Profit: Macroeconomic Consequences and Constitutional Implications', *Kyklos* (no. 3).

3 The growth of government*

What exactly is the public sector?

The problem in defining the public sector starts firstly with the word 'public'. A public meeting is not necessarily a meeting of state or municipal officials but rather a meeting to which the public is admitted. The same confusion of words occurs also in Germanic languages (cf. *Öffentlichkeit*).

But even leaving this linguistic problem aside, there are still a host of other problems when tentatively defining the public sector as the activities of the state, local authorities and social insurance institutions of public character.[1] Strictly speaking, public services are those that are produced for the benefit of all citizens in a society and where you cannot separate persons utilising the facility from those who do not. Such so-called purely collective goods are traditionally exemplified by defence, courts, police, etc. Private services would then be defined as those that are produced and sold on a private market where each individual user of the service or good can be identified.

But this division between private and the public presupposes that the same sector produces and consumes the good or service in question. But there are many examples of goods and services that are produced

---

* This is a heavily abridged version of my book *Hur stor är den offentliga sektorn?* (LIBER 1984). I am grateful to LIBER for the right to reprint the figures, tables and some text material.

in the private sector but used in the public. Purchases by the defence forces of war material from private enterprises at home or abroad is one example. Similarly, there are many cases where a good or service is produced in a public authority or by a publicly-owned corporation but where the individual user can be identified. Production of electricity and other utilities are good examples, but nationalisation throughout the post-war period has extended this sector. Schools and hospitals are frequently publicly-run throughout Europe, but so is the banking and mining industry. Purely collective goods, where the public sector both produces and consumes the good or service, are therefore very rare. Not even defence is a pure collective good. Air-raid shelters or gas masks cannot be used by one person without another being excluded from use.

This discussion shows how important it is to separate production of good and service from the use of it when it comes to defining whether it is private or public. A third dimension is financing. Traditionally the name tax is used for such public revenues that are used to finance collective goods and services, while the word fee should be used when the user of a certain service produced under public auspices can be identified. Gradually this distinction has come to be eroded and the more neutral term fee is used for revenues that are really taxes. Hence it is now more proper to study total state revenues rather than just tax revenues.

But the public sector does not only produce goods and services. With the help of taxes and transfers it also redistributes income between economic agents in the private sphere: between individuals, local authorities and companies and among these groups. An important question is whether these transfers should also be included in the measure of the size of the public sector. As is seen later this question has a dominant influence on how large the public sector is defined to be.

But there are aspects of public influence in society that cannot easily be measured by any statistical measurement of the size of the public sector. Public decisions interfere in private lives in ways that cannot be measured simply by the number of public employees or the share of public demand in gross national product or the share of tax revenues of national income. The public sector can affect many of the actions that take place in society by regulations that are not included under either taxes or expenditures: price freezes on certain goods, quotas on emissions of gases and liquids that pose environmental hazards, import quotas on certain products, and much more. Since resource allocation is affected so is efficiency in the economy and thereby the rate of growth may be influenced in a positive or a negative direction. Many evaluators of a conservative persuasion are also afraid that the public influence has started to seep into not only private economic decisions but also into what Jürgen Habermas has called the intimate sphere, that is the family. Many people are concerned that the public sector has too much influence when public authorities are allowed to operate extensive data files on the citizens or when some individuals are forced by the state to give information on the income of other individuals.

But these thoughts bring us from the positive and objective to the normative and subjective. It is important to be constantly aware that the various statistical measures that are presented regarding the size of the public sector do not measure the total influence of the public sector on society. Yet these various measurements must still be adhered to, and the measurement that is used must be the most appropriate one for the particular type of problem that is being analysed.

Public expenditures are frequently discussed. However it has already been noted that there are large differences between such expenditures that state and local authorities have for their own use for goods and services and such expenditures that in the form of transfers re-enter the private sector. Public expenditures consumption versus investment must also be separated. But it is frequently difficult to distinguish what is consumption and what is investment. For instance, all investments in war materials are considered consumption, irrespective of actual length of life.

Separation of public versus private use is also more difficult for investment than for consumption. Public consumption is largely (about two-thirds) wages for public employees, while one-third consists of goods and services purchased from private enterprises. Most public investments, however, have a direct positive influence on efficiency and productivity in the private sector. This applies in the short-run to such investments as roads, harbours, airfields, etc., but obviously also in the long-run to educational investments and health care. The latter two would however not be included as investments but as consumption, further contributing to the confusion.

A separate issue is whether public lending should be included in public expenditures. One could maintain that if the state lends money on purely commercial terms and simultaneously borrows a corresponding amount on the private capital market these expenditures should be excluded from public budgets (see Break 1982). This is also the case when one calculates the so-called financial saving in the public sector. Public lending is however still partially included in public expenditures and hence in the measure of the public budget deficit.[2]

It has also been maintained that interest on the public debt should be excluded from state expenditures proper, since it has a different influence on the private sector than have other expenditures. This notion is difficult to put into practice. If one tries to distinguish the effects on the receivers of various types of public expenditures, lending and payment of interest, the same should really be done for all types of expenditures and revenues. It must then be known which multiplier is connected with each type of tax, public purchase of goods and services, public wages, public investments, etc. Hence to break out interest payments only is inconsistent.

Other people have maintained that certain public revenues and expenditures have been left out, particularly those that depend on inflation. The State for instance makes great capital gains from the fact that currency and bonds in circulation are redeemed at the original price, irrespective of the level of inflation since the time of issue. But such gains are not included in public sector income. Similarly, capital gains on publicly-owned property or companies are excluded (see Buiter 1983).

The problems that have concerned us so far are to do with defining the public sector. Another problem is caused by the fact that the production of the public sector is valued in a different manner than that of privately-produced goods and services. In the production of private goods a market price helps to distinguish the value of the product from the value of the resources that have gone in to the good in question. Even for many private services sold in the marketplace the value of the production from its cost can be distinguished. But public services are mostly not sold on a market for a market-determined price. Frequently the service in question is free of charge (for example, roads, police, schools and hospitals in most European countries) or heavily subsidised (daycare centres is one example). Public production cannot then be evaluated from the user side but must be measured from the cost side. Instead of trying to find the value of the fact that a certain number of pupils have been educated in school one measures public production as the wages of the teachers and other staff, depreciation on the school-building and purchases of goods and services from outside.

Hence by definition it is assumed that quality in public service is always unchanged and that there is a strict relationship between quantity produced and cost. A teacher or a doctor or a bureaucrat can by definition never become more productive. This is certainly an exaggerated assumption. Computerisation has for instance led to considerable advances in efficiency in private services such as banking and insurance. Even if the public sector is not the same as these sectors subjected to competition, a certain increase in efficiency and quality must certainly have taken place. In many areas of public production, however, where the possibility of rationalisation is not as large, for instance in hospitals, there are many indications that efficiency has instead declined.

The fact that it is difficult or impossible to measure correctly the development of productivity in the public sector leads to the fact that the growth of the public sector as well as its share of GDP becomes quite different if it is measured in constant or current prices. If it is assumed, for simplicity, that the growth of wages is the same in all parts of society, price increases in the various sectors will depend on the difference between the growth of wages and the growth of labour productivity. The sectors where productivity grows the slowest will have the fastest growth of prices. Measured in current prices these sectors will then increase their share of the total economy, even if their increase in quantitative terms is the same as that of other sectors.

Measured in constant prices when only taking the volume increase into account this effect disappears so long as the base year is held constant. But since the different parts of an economy grow at different rates and their shares of the economy are changed, the base year must be changed in the national accounts. The weights of the base year must reflect actual relationships and these can change drastically if the structure of the economy is affected by such factors as energy price rises. The Swedish national accounts, for instance, have thus had to change the base year more rapidly in later years. Recent base years have been 1959, 1968 and 1975. A transition to base 1980 took place in 1983. With each successive new base year the share of the public sector measured in the constant prices of the new base year approaches the share measured in current prices. Some examples will be given in the next section.

The public sector must however also relate to something. The most common is the GNP or GDP. But the problem encountered may then be that the measure is inconsistent to the extent that the numerator is not a part of the denominator. When, for instance, total public expenditures are defined, including transfers or taxes as a share of GDP, the share of the public sector in the total economy can easily exceed 100 per cent. The only consistent measurements with GDP in the denominator are those where the public sector is measured either from the user's side in the national accounts as consumption plus investment or from the production side as value added in public authorities.[3]

Different measures of the size of the public sector

This section will describe and discuss the content and relevancy of different measurements of the size of the public sector. Sweden is used as an example. A great number of measurements will be shown but it will turn out that they can be adhered to five or six different groups of measurement with different contexts and uses. Initially the different measurements will be described, saving the discussion of their respective uses until the end of the section.

Figure 3.1 contains 13 different measurements of the size of the public sector in Sweden in 1970 and 1981. In the following, each and everyone of these measurements will be discussed, together with others.

Measurement no. 1 refers to total public expenditures in relationship to the GDP. By total expenditures is meant expenditures by the state, by all local authorities and by social insurance institution for their consumption and investment as well as for their transfers. Transfers between the three public sectors, for instance state transfers to local authorities, have been eliminated. Measured in this way the public sector has grown the fastest, from about 40 per cent in 1970 to almost 70 per cent in 1983. As will be seen later it is largely the rapid rise in transfers that is the cause behind this.

Even if this measurement is very often discussed and shown it should not be used too often. In the numerator is found not only public sector expenditures for consumption and investment but also such expenditures as in the form of transfers return to the private sector for final use. Nothing prevents this measure exceeding 100 per cent. It is, as said earlier, an inconsistent measurement.

Different systems of transferring income between individuals make the all-encompassing measurement, total public expenditures, a less than perfect mirror of the intervention of the public sector in the economy. Despite the fact that its support to the households may be the same, the public sector becomes relatively smaller if one has deductions for children in taxation (as is the case in, for instance, Norway, France and Canada) instead of childrens' support as in Sweden. The 'merry-go-round' becomes larger in the latter case and with it the size of the public sector. In the same way the existence of taxed transfers (like all pensions, medical expenses and unemployment benefits in Sweden) make the size of the public sector larger in relationship to countries that prefer untaxed transfers.

Measurements 2–7 in Figure 3.1 are consistent to the extent that they cannot exceed 100 per cent. Measurements 2, 3 and 4 are collected from the uses side of the GDP while measurements 5, 6 and 7 are from or can be derived from the production side in the calculation of the GDP.

Measurement no. 2 indicates the total use of resources in the public sector as a share of GDP. In the use of resources has been included not only the consumption and investment of public authorities but also investment in publicly-owned companies. In Sweden, this measurement has risen from 32 per cent of GDP in 1970 to 38 per cent in 1981, thus with 'only' 6 percentage points to be compared with an increase of 22 percentage points for total public expenditures including transfers

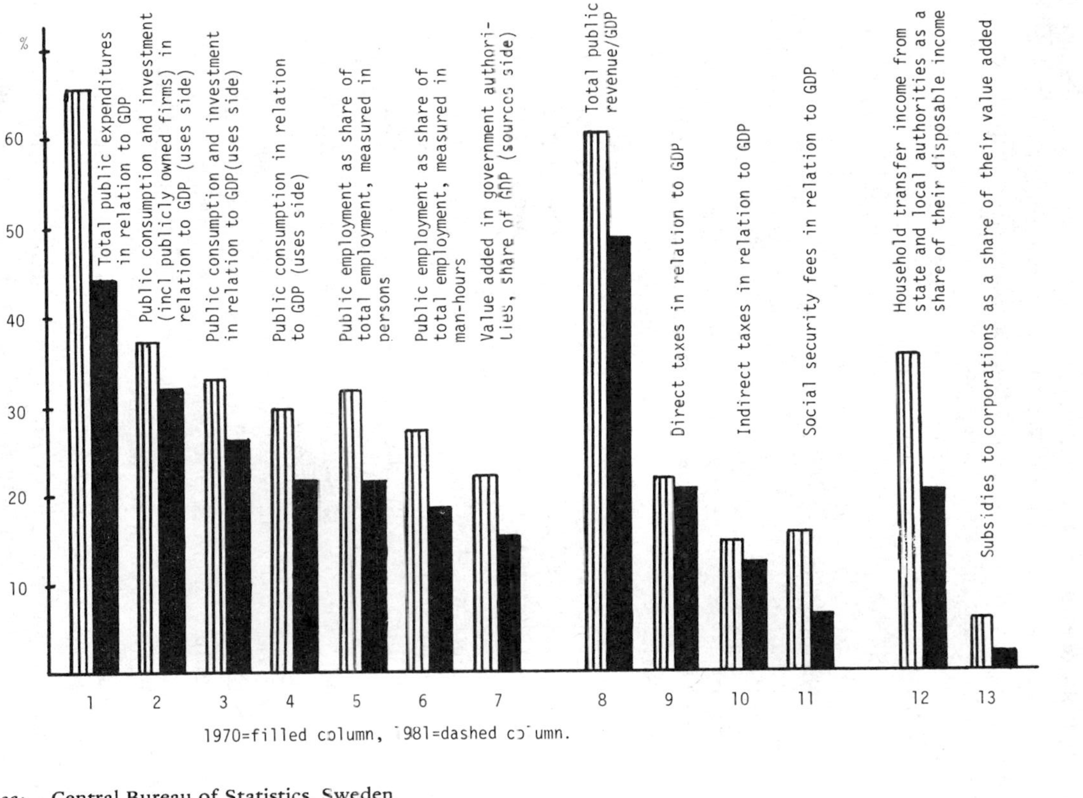

Source: Central Bureau of Statistics, Sweden

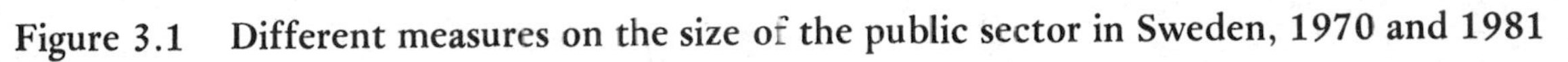

Figure 3.1 Different measures on the size of the public sector in Sweden, 1970 and 1981

during the same period of time.

A similar picture but on a lower level is shown by measurement no. 3, where investment in publicly-owned companies has been excluded. In measurement no. 4 only public consumption as a share of GDP is shown. Even if this measurement in no way measures the total uses size of the public sector, this measure still has the advantage of being an easily accessible measure of the size of the public sector. It is also the measure that is most free of objections as concerns comparison between countries and between different periods in time.

Measures including public investments suffer from many disadvantages. Firstly, investments vary over the business cycle and this applies also to public investments, even if the latter should vary against the business cycle to counteract the tendency of private investments to swing procyclically. The variability of investments over the business cycle makes comparability between countries at different stages of the business cycle difficult. The measurements are also made more complicated if countries use public investments to stimulate the economy or if one prefers to stimulate private investments by means of, for instance, tax credits.

Secondly, the different measures mix inconsistently the different functions of the state. In particular, the measurements that include publicly-owned companies' investments mix up the resource allocating function of the public sector with its function as concerns stabilisation policy. This discussion will be returned to at the end of this section.

Even measurement no. 4, which contains only public sector consumption, suffers from certain disadvantages. It is for instance difficult to compare the public sector in a major power with large defence expenditures with the same measurement in a small economy with small military expenditures. This aspect is discussed later, where the breakdown of expenditures in various countries will be shown.

Measurements 5, 6 and 7 show the share of the public sector in the economy from the production side. The largest of these measures is had if one measures employment in public authorities as a share of total employment. In Sweden, public employment has risen from 21 to 31 per cent of total employment during the 11 years shown in the figure. But compared to the private sector a relatively larger number of people are employed part-time. This means that employment in persons somewhat overstates the share of public employment compared to a measurement in man-hours, measurement no. 6. The difference is not only in levels, but also the increase in public employment becomes somewhat different since part-time has been introduced faster in the public than in the private sector. Measurement no. 7 finally measures the share of production (value added) that takes place in public authorities. This measurement can be compared to GDP and is consistent, since the numerator is a part of the denominator.

It was pointed out earlier how difficult it is to measure efficiency (production per man-hour) in producing public services. Since the production in the public sector is measured from the input side, productivity change, negative or positive, is assumed away. This implies that employment, even measured in man-hours, in the public sector compared to the value added that this employment gives rise to becomes erroneously measured as compared to that in the private economy. In 1981, for instance, 27.4 per cent of the total number of man-hours in the economy only produced 22.3 per cent of total production in society. But this is partly dependent on the labour-intensive production in the public sector as compared to the private and partly a consequence of the method of calculating public sector production.

It was pointed out earlier that the gradual shift in relative prices between the private and the public sector is of major importance for the relative growth of the public sector. This is shown in Table 3.1. Since by definition the labour productivity does not change in the public sector, price development in the public sector becomes faster than in the private, if wages develop at a common rate. This implies that the share of the public sector in total production in society at current prices will increase. In calculating the volume rate of growth of various expenditure categories one attempts to correct for this fact. It can be seen that in all the measures shown in Table 3.1, the increase in percentage points between 1970 and 1981 is approximately twice as fast when measured in current prices as compared to fixed prices.

Table 3.1 Increase in percentage points of the public sector in Sweden on different measures, 1970–81, in constant and current prices

	Constant 1975 prices	Current prices
Production in public authorities	4.0	7.8
Public consumption	4.2	8.1
Public consumption and investment in public authorities	3.0	6.6
Public consumption and investment in authorities and in publicly-owned corporations	3.6	5.7

Table 3.2 shows the effect of the relative price change in a different manner. The table shows public consumption expenditures as a share of GDP in 1975 with the different measures. The lower row shows that even measured at current prices the share may vary between various editions of the statistics. The reason is a revision of the national accounts which has led to a revision upwards of the level of the GDP and a consequent revision downwards of the share of public consumption.

Table 3.2 Public consumption as a share of GDP in Sweden in 1975 with differing base years (per cent)

	1968 = base	1975 = base	1980 = base
Fixed prices	22.0	24.1	26.1
Current prices	25.0	24.1	24.1

The first row shows how changing base year also changes evaluation of the public sector. As can be seen, the change of the base from 1968 to 1975 and then on to 1980 means that the share of public consumption even at constant prices increases. The share of the public sector in constant prices becomes relatively larger when the base year is later than the year analysed (base = 1980). The share of public sector at constant prices becomes relatively smaller when the base year is earlier than the studied year (base = 1968).

The next four measures (8–11) in Figure 3.1 show public revenues in relation to GDP. These measurements are also inconsistent and can well exceed 100 per cent. Measurement 8 shows total public sector revenues as a share of GDP. These revenues have risen from 48 per cent of GDP in 1970 to 61 per cent in 1981. The difference between total revenues, 61 per cent of GDP, and total expenditures this year, 66 per cent, corresponds to the public sector deficit, that is financial saving in the public sector which this year amounted to -5 per cent of GDP.

The next columns (9–11) show how total public revenues are made up. Of total revenues corresponding to 61 per cent of GDP 1981, 21 percentage points were made up of direct taxes, mainly household taxes. This share hardly increased at all during the 1970s. Indirect taxes (value added taxes, customs duties, excise taxes, etc.) corresponded to 15 per cent of GDP and also rose only slightly during the 1970s. Social insurance fees however increased sharply between 1970 and 1981. Other public revenues corresponding to 10 per cent of GDP are made up partly of various fees for public sector services, partly of depreciation on public sector capital. This item on the revenue side corresponds to reinvestment of depreciated capital on the uses side of the national accounts.

Measurements 12 and 13 in Figure 3.1 show how two sectors in society are dependent upon the public sector in 1970 and 1981. One possible measurement of dependency on the public sector on the part of households could be the share of total disposable income that households receive from the government in the form of transfers. It is shown that this share increased from 20 to almost 35 per cent in only 10 years. The disposable income of the average household thus results in two-thirds from its own labour and one-third from various public transfers.

Measurement 13 finally shows a similar measurement of dependency for enterprises, namely subsidies as a share of private value added. The share of subsidies in 1981 is still 'only' 6 per cent but it should be noted that this share has trebled in 10 years.

If desired, measurements 12 and 13 can be called measures of socialisation of society. An even better measurement is arrived at by using the traditional definition of socialism as public ownership. In this case the share of employees in publicly-owned enterprises may be taken as a measurement of socialisation. This measurement is not included in Figure 3.1, since it is only available at one point in time. As will be shown later in the chapter, at the end of the 1970s about 8 per cent of the total number of employees were employed in publicly-owned enterprises in Sweden. This figure should thus be added to the 30 per cent of employees that at the same time were employed by public authorities. Thus in this year in Sweden almost 40 per cent of total employment was to be found in various parts of the government sector.

The various measurements that have been taken up so far have concerned flow magnitudes, that is, revenues or uses or production in a certain year. One could conceivably also study the stock position (wealth) of government. In these wealth measures one could include only real capital (buildings, land, machinery, etc.) or both monetary and real assets.

In Table 3.3 an attempt has been made to compare the net wealth position of the public and the private sector. Public sector in this table includes state and local governments, public insurance institutions and the central banks, and the private sector is defined to include households and non-financial companies. With regard to monetary assets, publicly-held assets cannot be compared with the net financial wealth of the country as a whole. Most items cancel out so that the only thing that remains is Sweden's net claims on foreigners, which, furthermore, was negative (-$82 billion) at the end of 1981.

Table 3.3 Monetary and real assets and liabilities in the public and private sector, Sweden, on 31 December 1981 (SEK Bill)[a]

	Public sector			Private sector		
	Assets	Liabilities	Net	Assets	Liabilities	Net
Financial assets						
Notes, coin deposits, gold, SDR	41.1	37.1	4.0	309.7	–	309.7
Certificates of deposit	1.0	–	1.0	5.7	–	5.7
Treasury bills	40.2	33.2	7.0	–	–	–
Bonds and debentures	154.4	238.5	-84.1	50.3	33.2	17.1
Public enterprises	26.8	–	26.8	–	26.8	-26.8
Shares	16.2	–	16.2	(123.5)	N/A	N/A
Loans	124.3	79.2	45.1	269.6	848.8	-579.2
Investment funds	–	4.2	-4.2	4.2	–	4.2
Claims on financial enterprises	34.4	4.6	29.8	38.5[b]	–	38.5
Taxes accrued	28.6	–	28.6	–	–	–[c]
Other monetary assets	17.2	15.4	1.8	74.7	109.1	-34.4
Discrepancy	-0.2	1.3	-1.5	–	–	–
Total monetary assets	484.0	413.5	70.5	752.7	1017.9	-265.2
Real capital at current prices			543.2			2058.1
Total assets			613.7			1729.9

Notes:

(a) The public sector includes central and local governments, social insurance institutions and the central bank. The private sector comprises households (inc. non-profit organisations) and non-financial enterprises.
(b) Insurance saving.
(c) Should correspond to the asset of the government, but this is not the way the flow-of-funds accounts are set up.

Source: Financial accounts, SM:N 1982:11, preliminary wealth statistics of the Central Bureau of Statistics and the General Accounts Office

The figure that makes most sense concerns real capital at the end of Table 3.3. The publicly-held share of total capital is about 20 per cent, thus somewhat lower than the public share of total production (22 per cent).

It is much more difficult to make sense of the various monetary figures. If only the asset side is taken the total gross wealth held by the public sector is seen to be almost as large as the total gross wealth of the private sector. How the two are divided into various assets and liabilities is shown in Table 3.3.

Turning next to the net figures a comparison is almost meaningless. The public sector has a positive net monetary wealth, while households and non-financial companies together have a net liability of 265 billion. This is naturally caused by borrowing on buildings and other real assets. The sensible figure is obtained only as monetary and real capital are added. The publicly-held share is then 26 per cent.

It is, however, far more difficult to make sense of the various stock figures for the share of government in total society than for the flow figures. Are bank deposits, for instance, an asset of households, taking into account that the same assets are liabilities for banks owned by the private sector? Or are government bonds really net wealth, when one considers that at least part of the public debt some time in the future must be paid off by higher taxes? The problem becomes insurmountable as the evaluation of foreign assets and liabilities are considered. What is the value today of a liability in Swiss francs to be repaid in ten years? And what is the real value of the central bank's gold holdings, which are still valued at the official rate at the beginning of the 1970s, US$ 38 per ounce fine gold, while the current value has fluctuated between 300 and 800 US$ per ounce?

To the valuation problems must be added problems of definition. Are for instance the assets of the national pension insurance fund really an asset to be included in the public wealth or is the fund to be regarded as a collateral for future payments of pensions to be included in the wealth of private households in the same manner as private insurance saving? In the first case the considerable assets of the national pension insurance fund should be included in the public wealth figures, in the second case in those of households.

How should these different measures on the size of the public sector now be used? What is their relevance in various connections? Are there occasions when a certain measurement is not to be used?

Some of the disadvantages of the various measures have already been mentioned. The main warning concerns the difference between consistent and inconsistent measurements. It is popular, for instance, among journalists to consider total public expenditures in relation to GDP, drawing out the trend rate of growth and finding that in a certain year one reaches the figure of 100 per cent. A comment is usually made that this is an impossibility and must cause a reaction in the economy far earlier. However, it is theoretically fully possible for total expenditures or total income of government to exceed GDP and hence for the share to exceed 100 per cent. Both measurements are inconsistent. That the gradual increase of the share of the public sector will indeed create reactions that tend to diminish the rate of growth is quite another matter.

In discussing the relevancy of the various measurements there is reason to remind the reader of the traditional division *à la* Musgrave for the various tasks of the public sector into the allocative function of government, the distributional function and the stabilisational function.

The various measures that have been discussed can be subdivided into five different groups. The first group comprises total public expenditures or total public income set in relation to GDP. This measure is inconsistent. It also means different things when comparing between countries and between different periods of time owing to different methods of supporting households and companies. Countries relying on taxed transfers to households and subsidies to companies (like Sweden) will obviously have a larger government sector than countries relying on deductions for households and firms. But the measure is still of great interest. However deficient it still reflects the total influence on society of governments, the degree of interventionism. It could be assumed that the role of public bureaucracy can be measured by the share of consumption in GDP and other influences of the public sector on the private by the size of transfers.

The growth of total public expenditures in relation to GDP is dominated by the rapid growth of transfers in recent years. Hence this measure is of main interest as concerns the distributional aspect of government. But certain allocative effects may also arise. In many countries governments have consciously slowed down the rate of adaptation to higher energy prices in the 1970s by supporting failing industries (e.g. shipyards, steel, textile). To some part the increase in government expenditures also result from the drawn-out recession since 1973 and hence the measurement is of interest also from a stabilisational point of view.

The second group of measurements includes public use of resources as a share of GDP. This measurement is mainly of stabilisational interest. It shows how public demand directly contributes to effective demand in society and hence to GDP. Increased public demand can substitute for private expenditures, keeping unemployment down in a recession but also add to inflation in an upturn when total demand may exceed total resources.

The third group of measures includes public production as a share of GDP and public employment as a share of total employment. This measure also has a certain stabilisational meaning since increased public employment may be one way of holding unemployment down, at least in the short-run. Another negative stabilisational effect of the increased public employment of the 1970s is that many private firms have had difficulty in attracting non-skilled labour, since these persons have preferred to work in the public sector at existing relative wage structures. Since the dispersion between the higher and lower income groups is much smaller in the government sector than in the private sector, non-skilled labour would generally prefer to work in the public sector. In this way public demand for labour may have contributed to the overly fast growth of wages.

But the measurement also has implications for allocation policy. The size of the public sector measured from the production side should in some way be related to who is best at getting a certain job done, the public authority or a private firm.

The fourth group of measurements encompasses various taxes and fees in relationship to GDP. Even if these measurements are inconsistent, in that they may exceed 100 per cent, they are still of considerable interest. From a stabilisational point of view, (marginal) income taxes influence the supply of labour. But also in allocation policy the measures may be used, for instance if higher taxes lead to an inoptimal allocation of capital: 'investments' in art and stamps instead of real capital, or to a large non-market economy. In both cases it is however probably marginal rather than average taxes which are of interest.

The fifth and final group of measurements reflects the degree of socialisation of individual decisions in society, which primarily has an allocational effect in that it affects the efficiency of society. Obviously the measures of ownership (share of employment in publicly-owned companies) belong in this group, but also the dependence of household-income and private-sector value-added on transfers and subsidies.

Growth of the Swedish public sector in a historical perspective

It is not only the lack of national accounts that makes it difficult or impossible to calculate the share of the public sector in society before, say, the mid-19th century. Changes in the structure of the society, mainly increases in the share of production going through markets, make such comparisons doubtful anyway. It has however been estimated that in Sweden the share of total population employed in the public sector was relatively constant at 2 to 4 per cent from the 17th century up to the First World War. From that time onwards public employment has risen fast and today encompasses about 20 per cent of the total population and 40 per cent of the total number of employees. A similar picture is shown in Figure 3.2 for the period for which Swedish national accounts or similar data is available – from 1861 onwards. The earlier statistics show the size of the public sector every second year. The vertical lines show displacements in the data. Between 1912 and 1914 and between 1948 and 1950 the source is changed. The displacement in 1969 is caused by the revision of the national accounts for the 1970s which lowered the share of public consumption in GDP since GDP was revised upwards.

Despite the statistical deficiencies, the graph provides a clear image of the development. In the same way as was the case for employment the share of the public sector in society was relatively constant from the starting point until the First World War. In the inter-war period there was some growth but mainly variations in the share caused by the rapid shifts in GDP. During the Second World War public expenditures naturally rose again but after the war went back almost to the previous level. From the end of the 1940s starts a rapid and continuing expansion that brings public consumption as a share of GDP from about 10 per cent to over 30 per cent in 35 years.

In Figure 3.3 public consumption is divided into state versus local-authority consumption for the period from 1950 onwards. The series have been spliced from volume growth rates so that the development is unaffected by the relative price change and only the volume development in public consumption and in GDP are shown. The figures are expressed as indices with the base 1950 = 100.

It can be seen from Figure 3.3 that central government consumption has followed GDP rather well, that is its share in constant prices has been virtually unchanged. From around 1970 the share has even fallen slightly. From the mid 1960s local authority consumption has however exploded in relation to GDP. While the GNP after 30 years has reached index 250, local authority consumption has almost attained index 500. This means that local authority consumption in volume has increased four times as compared to one-and-a-half times for GDP.[4]

Figure 3.4 breaks down for the period 1970–81 central government consumer expenditures. The data are again in constant prices. Hence changes in prices and wages do not affect the picture. Only consumption expenditures are included; investments and transfers are excluded.

It can be seen that defence expenditures in constant prices have not changed during the period. The share of state consumption has fallen from 40 per cent in 1970 to 33 per cent in 1981 (the shares for 1981 of total state consumption are indicated in brackets for each curve). The most rapid increase is shown by the category entitled other expen-

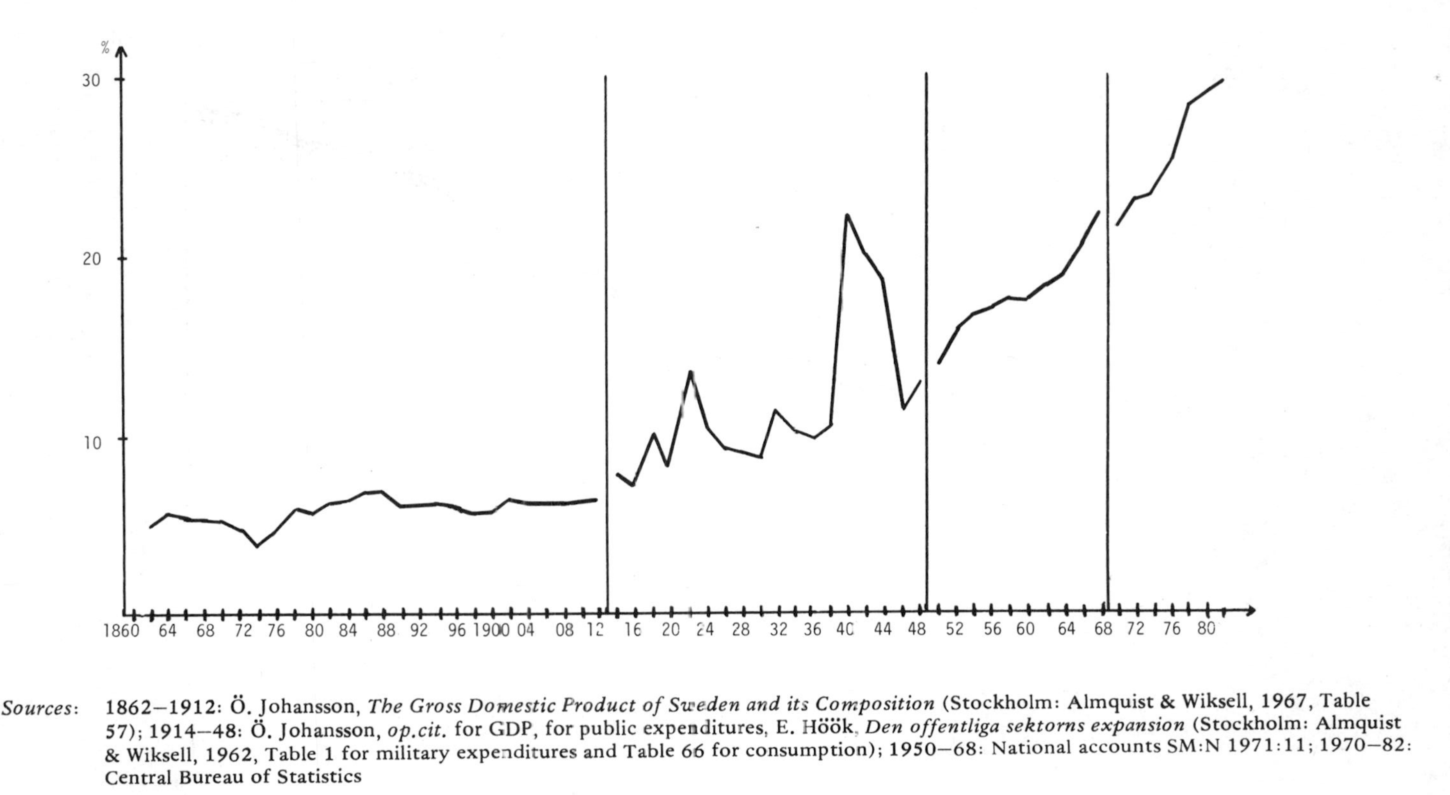

Sources: 1862–1912: Ö. Johansson, *The Gross Domestic Product of Sweden and its Composition* (Stockholm: Almquist & Wiksell, 1967, Table 57); 1914–48: Ö. Johansson, *op.cit.* for GDP, for public expenditures, E. Höök, *Den offentliga sektorns expansion* (Stockholm: Almquist & Wiksell, 1962, Table 1 for military expenditures and Table 66 for consumption); 1950–68: National accounts SM:N 1971:11; 1970–82: Central Bureau of Statistics

Figure 3.2 **Public consumption as a fraction of GDP at current prices, 1862–1982**

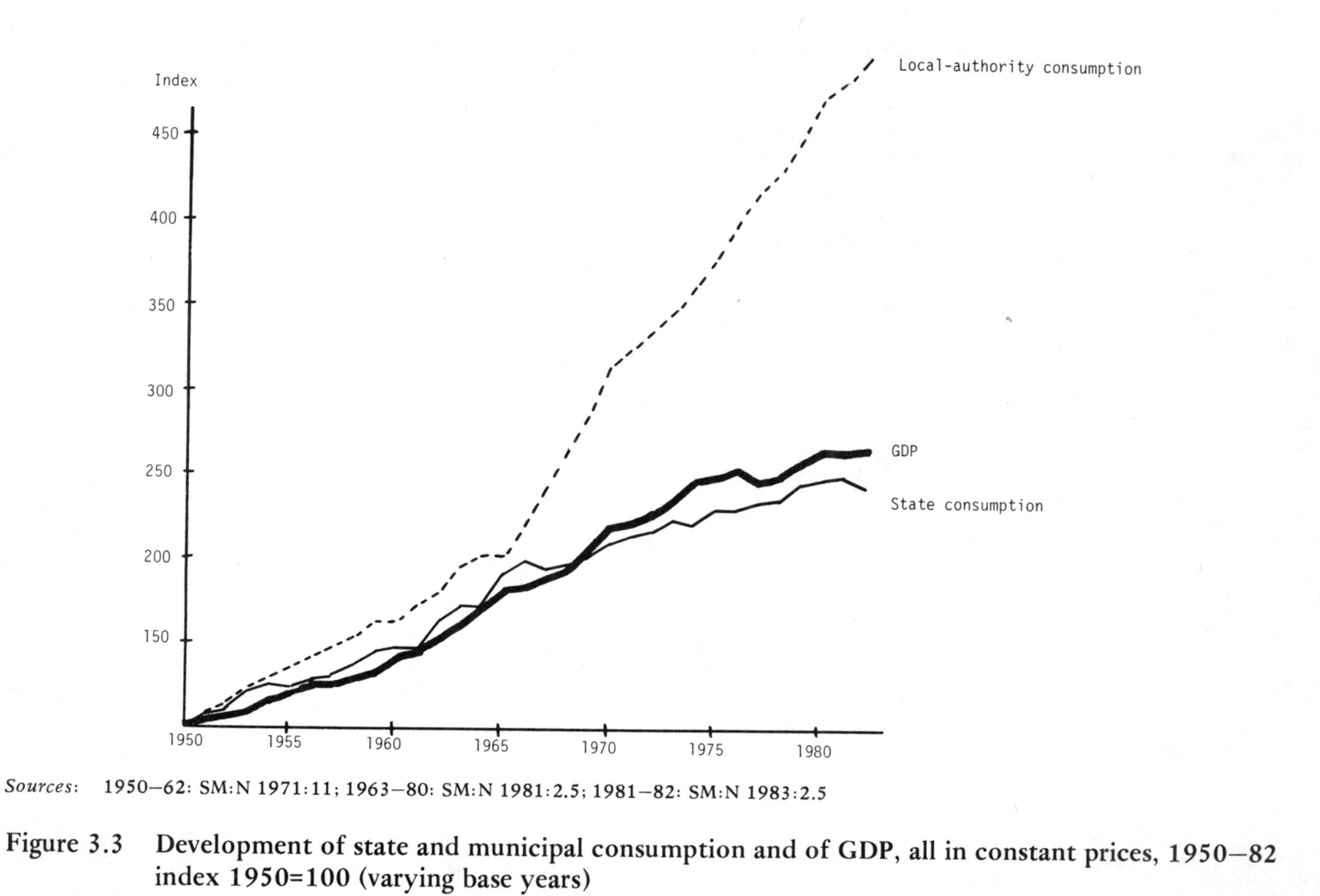

Sources: 1950–62: SM:N 1971:11; 1963–80: SM:N 1981:2.5; 1981–82: SM:N 1983:2.5

Figure 3.3 Development of state and municipal consumption and of GDP, all in constant prices, 1950–82 index 1950=100 (varying base years)

Notes:
Other expenditure includes housing policy, social care, health and medical expenses, culture and business development.

Source: National accounts, SM:N 1983:2.5 Appendix 1

Figure 3.4 Growth of state consumption 1970–81 in constant prices, distributed on various categories, index 1970=100

ditures, in which a major item is for business development (this despite the fact that subsidies do not enter!). Administration, including courts, police, etc. encompass only 25 per cent of consumer expenditures.

Figure 3.5 gives the similar picture for local authorities. The most rapidly growing item is administration, which still accounts for only a small fraction of a total budget. Expenditures for health and medical care and for social care have however risen very fast and now make up over half of total consumer expenditures. They have risen much faster than expenses for education, which is the other heavy local-authority expenditure. In other expenditures it is costs for culture, recreation, etc. that are the largest item.

The public sector in an international perspective[5]

Let us now proceed to look at the growth of the public sector in Sweden compared with other industrialised countries. The exposition is limited to the last 15 or 25 years. This period is however the most interesting, since the development looked at earlier in Figure 3.2 is virtually the same for other industrialised countries, except that the Swedish development has gone further. With the exception of the war years the share of the public sector has held relatively steady until after the Second World War, after which a rapid growth sets in.

Figure 3.6 shows total public expenditures, including transfers, as a ratio to the GDP or GNP for the years 1960 and 1982. The countries have been arranged after diminishing expenditure shares for the latter year.

Let us start by studying the situation in 1960. There are at least two things in the figure worthy of notice. Firstly, it can be seen that the average share for small OECD countries in 1960 was only 20 per cent, lower than for the OECD as a whole. Secondly, Sweden, at about 30 per cent, only marginally exceeded the OECD average. Sweden this year had smaller public expenditures in relationship to GDP than countries such as France, Germany or the UK. But the public sector in Sweden in this year was even larger than in corresponding small OECD economies.

When shifting to 1982 it is found, not unexpectedly, that public expenditures in relation to GDP have increased sharply in all countries on the study. But the increases are drastically different. The average for all OECD countries has increased by 14 percentage points; the average for small OECD economies has however increased by 26 percentage points. The Swedish increase is enormous, no less than 36 percentage points. Only Denmark comes close: an increase of 34 percentage points, but from a lower level.

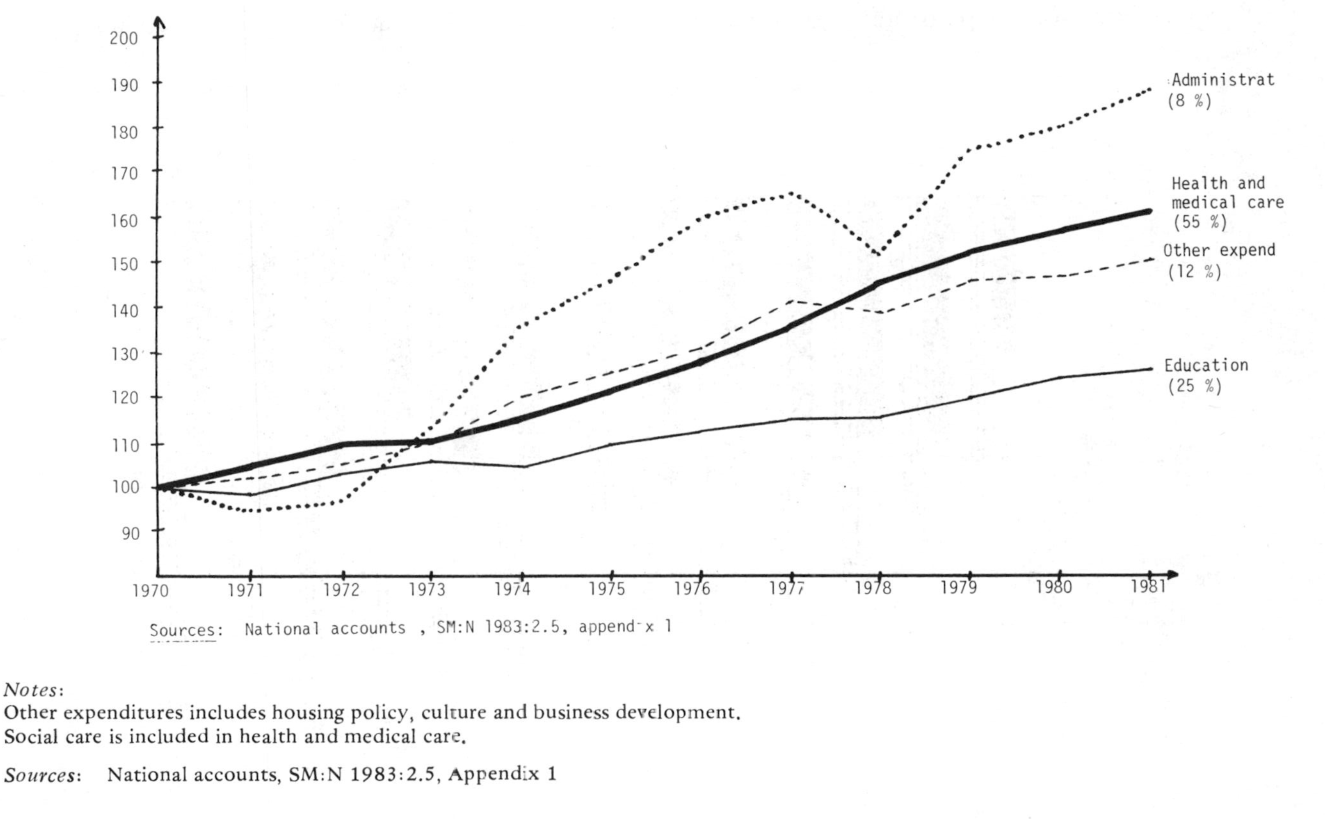

Notes:
Other expenditures includes housing policy, culture and business development.
Social care is included in health and medical care.

Sources: National accounts, SM:N 1983:2.5, Appendix 1

Figure 3.5 **Growth of local-authority consumption distributed on various categories, at constant prices, index 1970=100**

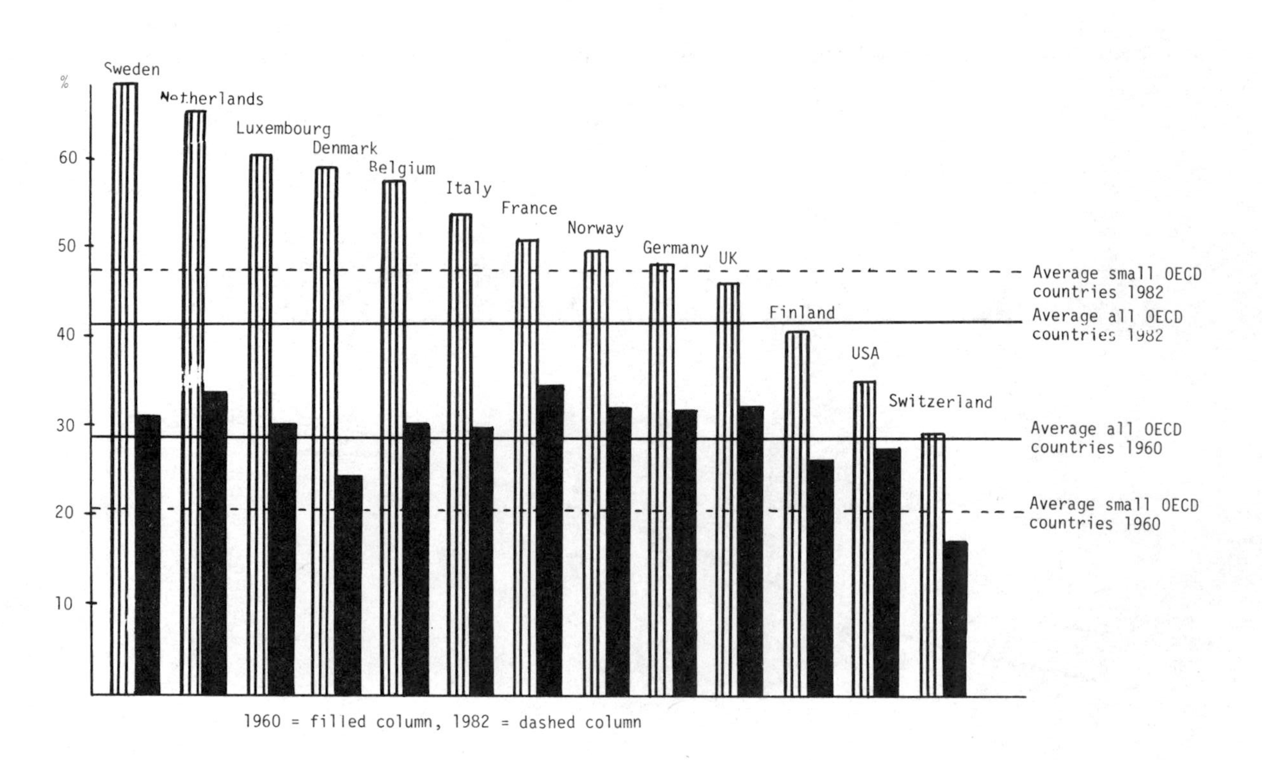

Source: OECD. 'Big Government – How Big is it?', *OECD Observer* (March 1983)

Figure 3.6 Total public expenditures (inc. transfers) in relation to GDP, 1960 and 1982

Also noticeable is that, as of 1960, most OECD countries with the possible exception of Switzerland had expenditure shares of almost equal size. The situation in 1982 was drastically different. The countries are spread out from Sweden at almost 70 per cent down to Switzerland with 30.

Figure 3.7 repeats the same comparison, now with public consumption in the numerator. Note however that the first year is 1970, as a result of lacking data. That the increase is now smaller is thus quite natural. It must also be remembered that this measure is consistent; in contrast to those shown in Figure 3.6 it cannot exceed 100 per cent.

Despite the differences in content a picture is found that resembles that in Figure 3.6. Again the small OECD countries have increased their public expenditure shares much more than the larger countries and thus more than the OECD average. However, the ranking between the countries is changed dramatically. Countries like The Netherlands and France have relatively large public sectors when transfers are included, while they rank among countries with the lowest expenditure shares when only consumption expenditures are included. The United Kingdom moves in the other direction. The UK ranks third among the OECD countries measured by public consumption expenditures, but only tenth when measured by total expenditures including transfers.

It appears to be a common trait among Anglo-Saxon countries (the UK, the USA and Canada) that the public sector proper is relatively large, while the share of transfers is relatively small. Countries like The Netherlands, France and Belgium show the opposite sign, relatively large transfers and relatively small government proper. Sweden and Denmark are singled out from the others since they have a large public sector irrespective of how it is measured.

It could also be pointed out that measured by public consumption the public sector share actually fell in the USA between 1970 and 1982. This is unique for the OECD area but is a consequence of special circumstances, namely the ending of the Vietnam war.[6]

Figure 3.8 shows the third alternative in measuring the size of the public sector, namely value added in public authorities as a fraction of total GDP. The figures are now arranged at a much lower level but again the development is very much the same. Sweden and Denmark are to be found first and also experienced the largest increase between 1970 and 1981. In Canada and the USA changes are small and in the latter the share for public production has even fallen. Again the Vietnam war is probably to blame for the high figure in 1970.

In Figure 3.9 a measure that was previously named a measure of socialisation is introduced, namely employment in the publicly-owned corporations measured as a fraction of total employment. Here Sweden has traditionally been regarded as a relatively little socialised country.

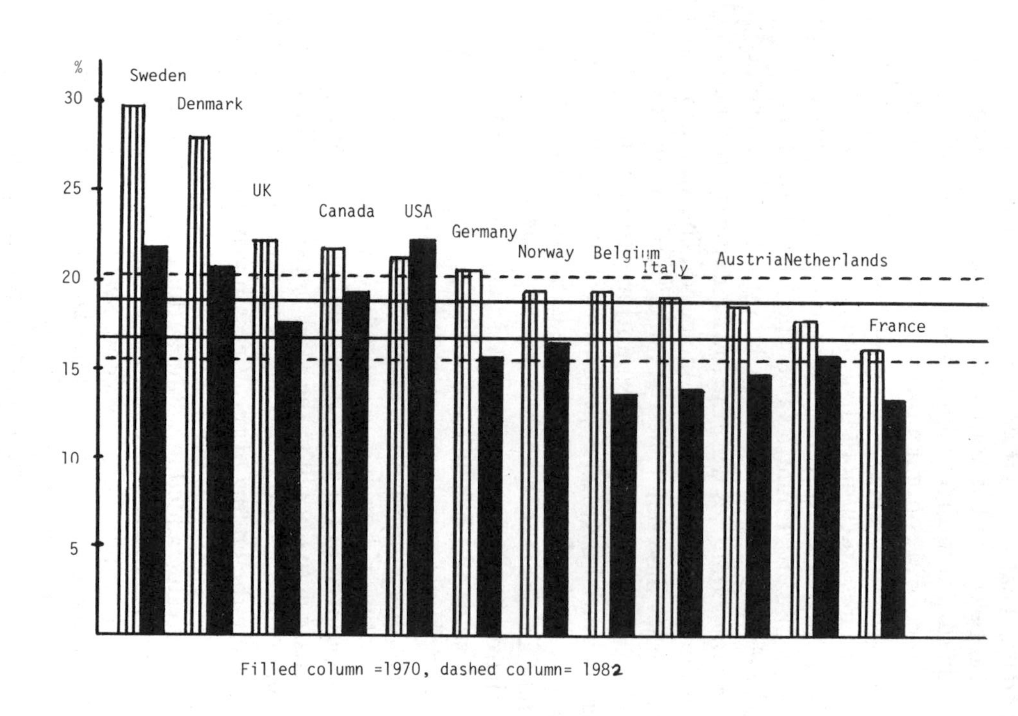

Source: *OECD Observer* (March 1983)

Figure 3.7 Public consumption expenditures as a fraction of GDP, 1970 and 1982

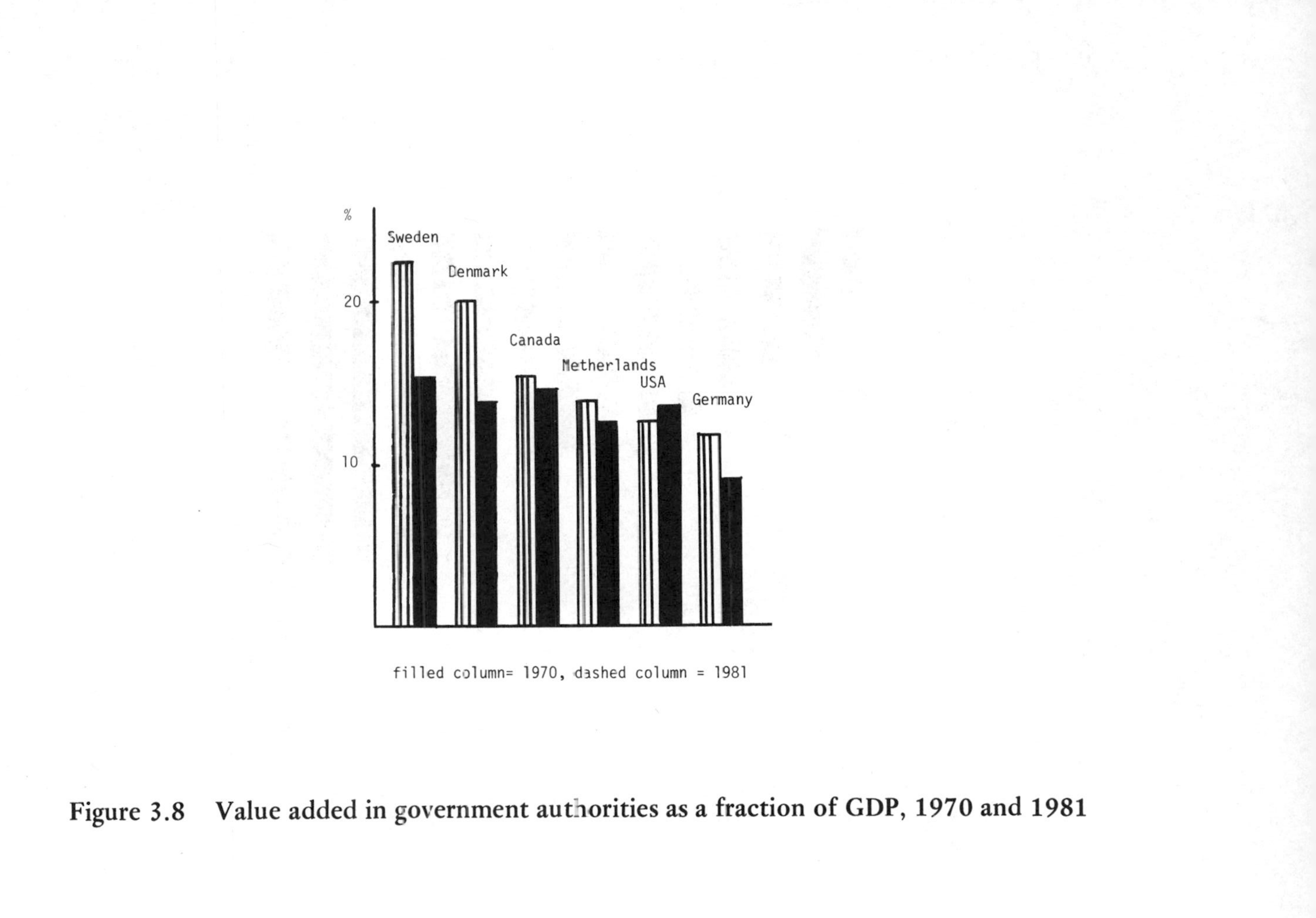

Figure 3.8 Value added in government authorities as a fraction of GDP, 1970 and 1981

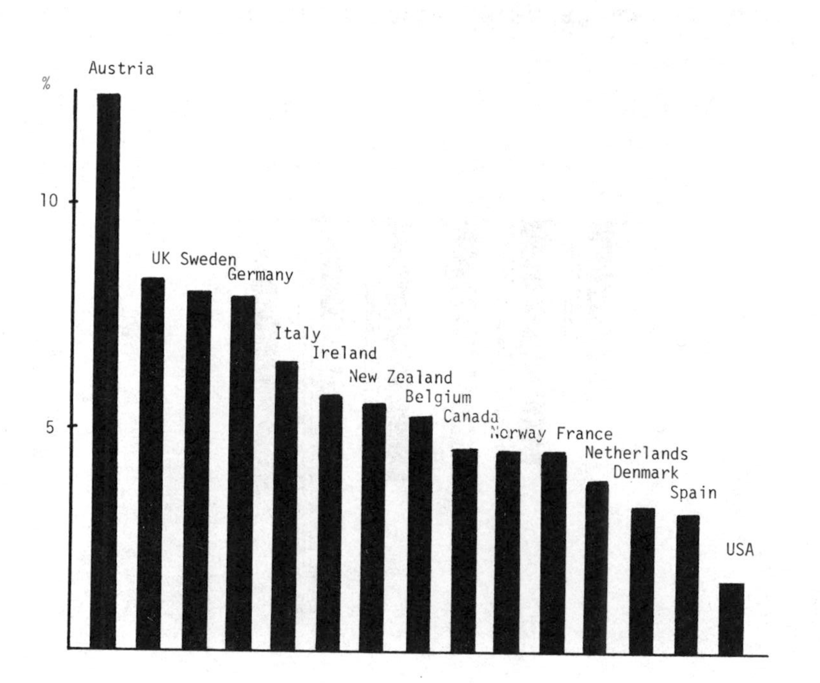

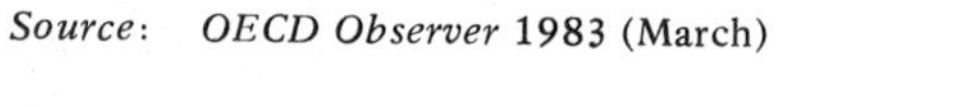

Source: *OECD Observer* 1983 (March)

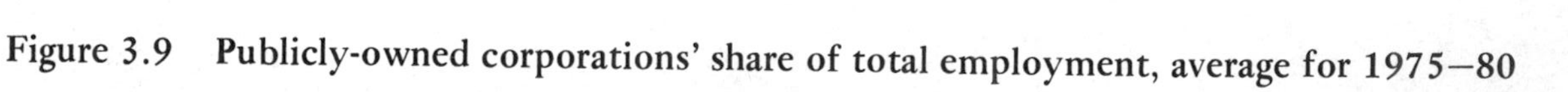

Figure 3.9 Publicly-owned corporations' share of total employment, average for 1975–80

However, it can be seen that at the end of the 1970s even Sweden had come up to second position, dominated only by Austria. The difference between the countries is also much larger than that which concerns the other measures on the size of the public sector. Publicly-owned corporations have 13 per cent of total employment in Austria to be compared with less than 2 per cent in the USA. As so often is the case however, is deficient data partly to blame? With respect to ownership, public utilities in the USA (telephone, electricity, etc.) wind up in the private sector while they are classified as publicly-owned in other countries. Some interesting differences can nevertheless be traced from the figure. It can be seen for instance that Sweden ends up much larger than The Netherlands and Denmark which in the previous figures were comparable with regard to expenditure shares.

It was noticed earlier that the main reason for the fast expansion of Swedish government expenditures is transfers while, in particular, central government consumption and public investments have grown at a relatively slower pace.

In Table 3.4 total public expenditures including transfers are subdivided into various categories for a number of countries for 1980. The eight countries have very similar shares for traditional collective goods. The distribution varies however. The larger countries (and Sweden) devote relatively larger shares to defence, while the smaller countries have relatively larger shares of other collective goods.

Included under welfare state expenditures are firstly goods and services and secondly transfers. That Sweden and The Netherlands lead in total expenditures was not unexpected but the breakdown is interesting. On such items as education, housing, pensions, childrens' benefits and unemployment benefits the share of these two countries is about the same as that of others. The difference is not so much between the various European countries as between the United States on one hand and Europe on the other. Sweden and The Netherlands however rank high on the list as concerns expenditures for medical and health care and medical insurance benefits.

In making these comparisons however two things have to be borne in mind. Firstly, medical and other benefits are taxable in some countries such as Sweden, untaxed in others. This obviously raises the share of public expenditures in such countries. Secondly, the distinction between private and public medical and health care is rather fluid. Take the United States as an example! The two main insurance corporations Blue Cross and Blue Shield are in the private sector, yet the systems are very similar to the compulsory system in most European countries.

Sweden also leads the league in the category mixed economy expenditures, where subsidies to failing industries dominate.

Table 3.4 Breakdown of total public expenditures, in shares of GDP or GNP, 1980 (or 1978 or 1979)

	Sweden	Denmark	France	Germany	Italy	Netherlands	UK	USA
Total expenditure	62.3	48.1	45.2	48.6	45.5	60.3	41.7	32.7
Traditional collective goods	8.0	7.7	7.2	8.5	6.3	10.3	8.5	8.3
Defence	3.4	2.3	3.4	2.9	1.9	3.2	4.7	4.6
Other	4.6	5.4	3.8	5.6	4.4	7.1	3.8	3.7
Welfare state expenditures	42.8	36.2	32.5	32.9	28.2	40.8	25.6	18.7
Mainly goods and services								
Education	7.0	7.6	5.7	5.1	5.5	8.3	5.4	5.6
Medical and health care	8.0	5.6	6.0	6.6	5.9	7.1	4.7	2.5
Housing	2.5	1.6	2.1	1.4	1.1	–	3.3	0.4
Other	1.9	1.7	0.8	0.8	0.3	–	0.5	0.4
Mainly transfers								
Pensions	10.6	7.8	10.5	12.2	11.9	9.8	6.6	6.7
Medical income benefits	4.2	1.3	1.8	0.8	0.7	7.0	0.4	0.1
Childrens' benefits etc.	1.9	1.3	2.1	1.1	1.0	2.3	1.4	0.5
Unemployment benefits	0.4	2.2	1.2	0.0	0.3	0.6	0.7	0.4
Other (largely social care)	6.3	7.1	2.3	4.0	1.5	1.7	2.6	2.1
Mixed economy expenditures	7.4	2.1	4.0	5.3	4.8	4.5	3.0	3.0
Capital outlays	1.8	1.3	1.5	2.2	–	–	1.2	0.7
Subsidies	2.4	0.8	1.7	1.7	–	–	1.0	0.3
Other	3.2	0.0	0.8	1.3	–	–	0.8	2.0
Interest on the public debt	4.1		1.5	1.9	6.2	4.7	4.6	2.7

Sources: Swedish Central Bureau of Statistics, OECD (1983); Chouraqui and Price (1983)

In 1980 Swedish and Dutch interest on the public debt was still relatively small compared to such traditional deficit countries as Italy and Belgium. Already by 1983, however, the total government deficit has risen to 6 per cent of GDP in Sweden and interest on the public debt to 8 per cent of GDP.

Notes

1 Local authorities in Sweden are subdivided into two categories: 24 'landsting' mainly responsible for hospitals and 284 'kommuner', responsible for other tasks.
2 Sweden is currently in the process of lifting part of state lending out of the budget. Thus public expenditures and the state budgetary deficit are diminished overnight by the stroke of a pen. By 1985, the budget deficit had been 'reduced' by 2 per cent of GDP in this way.
3 For more discussions on defining and measuring the public activity see, for example, Beck (1981) and Pathirane and Blades (1982).
4 For a detailed study of the composition of expenditures, see Höök (1962) for the earlier period and Forsman (1977) for later data.
5 For an interesting comparison among industrial countries, see Beck (1981), who also gives extensive references. It should be extended with references for the Nordic countries, namely Bentzon (1984), Hierppe (1982), Petersen (1980) and Sørensen (1984).
6 The difference between Anglo-Saxon and Francophonic countries may perhaps provide some evidence for Wildavsky's theory (1985) on the cultural background to public sector growth and deficits.

References

Beck, M. (1981), *Government Spending: Trends and Issues* (New York: Praeger).
Bentzon, K.-H. (1984), 'Offentligt ansatte i Danmark i et internationalt perspektiv', Institute of Political Studies, University of Copenhagen, Research Report 1984/1.
Break, G.F. (1982), 'Issues in Measuring the Level of Government Economic Activity', *American Economic Review*, 72 (May).
Buchanan, J. and Wagner, R.E. (1977), *Democracy in Deficit* (New York: Academic Press).
Buiter, W.H. (1983), 'Measurement of the Public Sector Deficit and its Implications for Policy Evaluation and Design', *IMF Staff Papers*, 30 (June).

Chouraqui, J.C. and Price, R. (1983), 'Medium Term Financial Strategy', OECD Economics and Statistics Department, *Working Paper*, 9.
Forsman, A. (1977), 'Den offentliga utvecklingen i ett långsiktigt perspektiv – den internationella utvecklingen', in B. Gustafsson, ed., *Den offentliga sektorns expansion* (Uppsala: Almquist & Wiksell).
Hierppe, R.T. (1982), 'Measurement of the Role of the Public Sector in the Finnish Economy', Mimeo.
Höök, E. (1962), *Den offentliga sektorns expansion: en studie av de civila offentliga utgifternas utveckling 1913–58* (Stockholm: Almquist & Wiksell).
OECD (1983), 'Big Government – How Big is it?', *OECD Observer* (March).
Pathirane, L. and Blades, D.W. (1982), 'Defining and Measuring the Public Sector: Some International Comparisons', *Review of Income and Wealth*, 28 (September).
Petersen, J.H. (1980), 'Vaekstern af den offentliga sektor i Danmark 1960–75 i internationalt perspektiv', *Nationaløkonomisk Tidskrift*, 118 (no. 2).
Sørensen, R.J. (1984), 'Veksten i offentlige utgifter i Norge 1949–83', paper presented at the Nordic Political Science Meeting, Lund.
Wildavsky, A. (1984), 'A Cultural Theory of Expenditure Growth and (Un)balanced Budgets', *Journal of Public Economics*, 28 (December).

4 Short-run causes for the growth of government: politico-economic models*

Introduction

Politico–economic models have by now been constructed for many industrialised countries.[1] At least that part of the model which treats voters' behaviour has been estimated for most countries. The purpose of this chapter is to cast some doubt on the stability of such models. A common trait of the authors of the major studies (for instance the several studies by Frey and Schneider and by Hibbs) has been that they place a high degree of confidence on the existence of these models. It is my belief that this confidence is frequently unwarranted.

Figure 4.1 gives the background for two critical comments. It shows that the politico–economic models consist of the interaction of three sets of agents: voters, the government and Parliament, and the traditional agents in the economic sector, households and firms. Voters are believed (Downs 1957) to be rational in their behaviour. Even though most voters may be motivated largely by sluggish ideological factors, there exists a critical group of potential switchers, the median voter or the 'floating voter' (Minford and Peel 1982) or the 'swing voter' (Paldam 1981). These voters hold the incumbent government respon-

---

* This chapter has earlier been published in the *European Journal of Political Research*, 13 (no. 2), 1985. I am grateful to the editor and to North Holland Publishing Company for the right to reprint the article.

sible for events in the last election period, and in particular for such economic factors as unemployment, inflation and the rate of growth of incomes. Since voting only takes place infrequently the behaviour of voters has also been studied by means of popularity functions, where the dependent variable is the popularity of the incumbent government in public opinion polls rather than election results.

The second block in the simultaneous model pertains to the behaviour of governments. As emphasised well by Frey *et al.* (for example, Frey and Lau 1968), to obtain a realistic view of government behaviour utility maximisation rather than simple vote maximisation needs to be assumed. The utility of a government is a function of voter approval and ideological satisfaction. Different governments do however have different preferences regarding full employment versus price stability (Hibbs 1977); they do not behave in a similar way even before elections. On a micro basis, ideological satisfaction may stem from political actor's own preferences as in Lewin (1979) or from parties' necessity to keep a profile in line with that of their core voters.[2]

The third block in Figure 4.1 represents the economic structure, that is the institutions in combination with the behaviour of domestic and foreign households and firms. The ability of the government to manipulate the economy is limited not only by the structure of the economy but also by influences beyond government control such as oil price increases by OPEC or steel quotas by the US government.

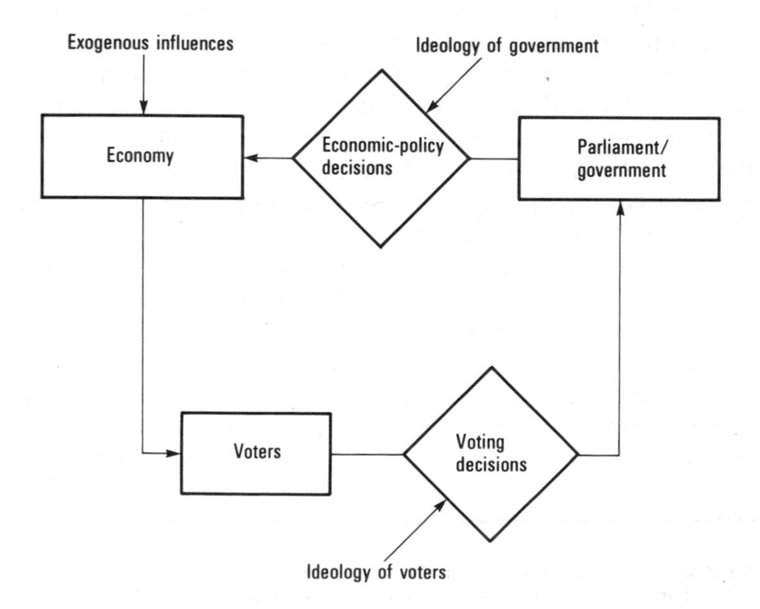

Figure 4.1 Politico–economic interaction

This leads to my first point of criticism, namely that the explicit or implicit structure of the economy in politico–economic models is too simple to be believed. It is traditionally represented as in Figure 4.2 by the expectations-augmented Phillips curve. From a position A the government stimulates the economy in order to win the election at point B. But the stimulus leads to increased inflationary expectations and to a shift in the curve. To come back to point A the government must pursue a contractionary policy with increasing unemployment, moving through positions C and D.[3]

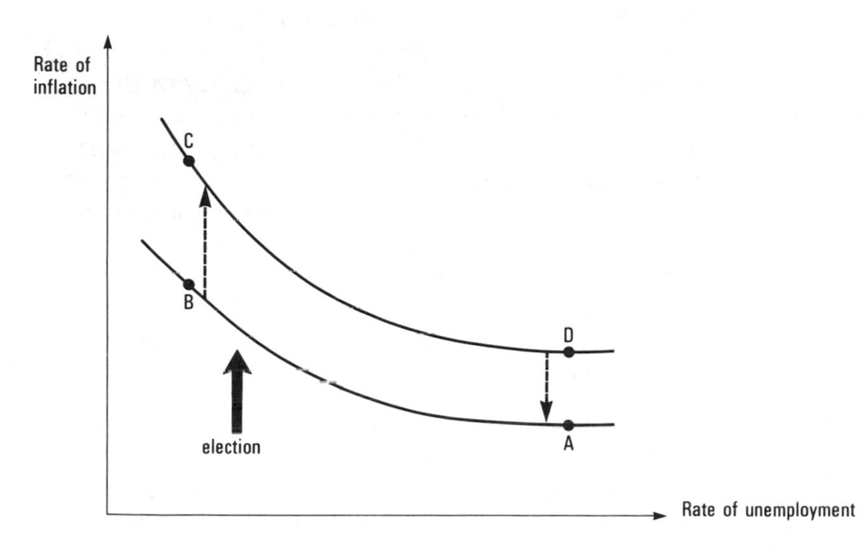

Figure 4.2 The election cycle in Phillips' terms

In a small open economy the Phillips curve is very flat, that is inflation is largely determined from abroad. This does not mean that the government can pick any desired unemployment rate, only that the trade-off is in another dimension than that depicted by the Phillips curve. Other goals which may be affected by keeping the unemployment rate down may be the budget balance, the balance on current account, the tax structure and other distributional goals, etc. It is my contention that one should model the economic structure explicitly rather than adopting the oversimplified view of the Phillips curve.

My second point of criticism is also derived from Figure 4.1, namely that the existing politico–economic models have failed to utilise the information inherent in the fact that the model of politico–economic interaction is a simultaneous system. This point can be subdivided into two points. Firstly, with only a few exceptions, equations relating to voters' behaviour and government's behaviour have been estimated by Ordinary Least Squares (OLS) despite the risk of simultaneity bias.[4] Systems estimators are theoretically motivated. Secondly, analysis of estimated models have generally been confined to a discussion of parameter values and significance test. The interesting thing to do is to run simulations that show how the full system reacts to shocks such as oil price increases. What has been done so far is depicting the reaction of the system to exogenous popularity shocks, coming out of nowhere (Frey 1974) or showing the replicatory or forecasting power of the system by means of historical simulations or *ex post* forecasting (Frey and Schneider 1979, 1982, Schneider and Frey 1983).

The third part of my critique has to do with the stability of the equations. That governments of different political colours will behave in different ways is obvious, as is the fact that the same government will react differently in different circumstances. But my point of contention is that the reaction of voters to economic factors appears to vary substantially between various time periods, as well as between countries and socio–economic groups within countries. This part has been largely hidden in the studies.

For theoretical reasons the lack of stability of the popularity or voting functions may be ascribed to the following:[5]

1 Just as there is no aggregate social welfare function, there cannot be a stable aggregate evaluation function, since voters' preferences cannot be meaningfully aggregated. This is the old Arrow 'impossibility theorem', applied in this context by, for example, Fair (1978).
2 If voters are rational, they will see through the government's behaviour and hence there will be no stable evaluation function (Minford and Peel 1982).
3 Economic events do matter, but they have an asymmetric effect, working only against, never for, a sitting government (Bloom and Price 1975, Miller and Mackie 1973).
4 The correlation between economic factors and government popularity is actually the reverse; there is no causation from economic factors to popularity (Frey and Garbers 1971).
5 The correlation between popularity and economic events is spurious, both factors being caused by a third variable (Miller and Mackie 1973).
6 Voters may be influenced both by their own experiences of inflation and unemployment and of society's macro experiences. The weights between these two shift, leading to unstable

popularity functions (Fischer and Huizinga 1982, Hibbs 1979).
7 If the government is a weak coalition government, voters may not hold it responsible for economic events, as it would a strong majority government (Paldam and Schneider 1980).

In view of these theoretical objections to stability, it is hardly surprising that a bewildering set of results are found when comparing different studies. A summary of results from the major studies is set out in Table 4.1. It is apparent that, with one single exception, no factor has been significant but inflation, unemployment and the growth of real incomes (in varying specifications). But even for the same country one study may find a particular variable significant, while another study may come to the opposite conclusion. Even worse, the coefficients even when significant jump around quite a lot. An increase in unemployment by 1 percentage point will decrease popularity or voting results in various studies by anything from 1 to 6 percentage points. For inflation the results are that even significant coefficients vary by a factor of ten: from -0.4 to -4.

This leads to my fourth critical point, which is that the studies have generally been performed in such a way as to hide such instability. In particular, evaluation and reaction functions are run over several governments, allowing only for constant shifts in the functions.

The purpose of this chapter is to try to study the effects of rectifying these defects regarding Swedish data, 1970–82. Firstly, the methods used will include not only OLS but also Two-Stage and Three-Stage Least Squares of estimation. Secondly, the structure of the economy will occupy a separate building block in the simultaneous model. Thirdly, estimations will be performed for each administration separately. Fourthly, the full model will be subjected to simulations not only of historical character but also of the shocked type.

The model

In this section the model to be estimated will be specified.

The popularity function

$$POP_t = \text{constant} + a_0\, POP_{t-1} + a_1 U + a_2\, PDOT + a_3\, \Delta YD/P + a_4\, TREND + a_5\, STRIKE + u_1$$

The dependent variable is the popularity of the government, POP. It is determined by three economic factors: unemployment (U), inflation (PDOT) and change in real disposable household income (ΔYD/P).

Table 4.1 Economic factors of significance in selected vote or popularity functions

Study	Country	Inflation	Unemployment	Real income growth	Other economic variables
Mueller (1970)	USA	–	Yes	–	–
Kramer (1971)	USA	Yes	No	Yes	–
Stigler (1973)	USA	Yes?	Yes?	Yes?	–
Arcelus and Meltzer (1975)	USA	Yes?	Yes?	Yes?	No
Bloom and Price (1975)	USA	–	–	Yes	–
Fair (1978)	USA	No	Yes[a]	Yes[a]	No
Frey and Schneider (1978a)	USA	Yes	Yes	Yes	–
Chappell (1983)	USA	Yes	–	No	–
Hibbs (1982)	USA	Yes	Yes	Yes	–
Goodhart and Bhansali (1970)	UK	Yes	Yes	No	No
Frey and Garbers (1971)	UK	No	No	–	–
Mosley (1978)	UK	Yes[b]	Yes	–	–
Frey and Schneider (1978b)	UK	Yes	Yes	Yes	–
Hibbs (1982)	UK	Yes	Yes	Yes	Yes (exchange rate)
Minford and Peel (1982)	UK	No	No	Yes[c]	–
Hibbs (1981)	France	Yes	Yes	Yes	–
Frey and Schneider (1981a)	Germany	Yes	Yes	No	–
Hibbs (1982)	Germany	Yes	Yes	Yes	–
Kirchgässner (1976)	Sweden	Yes	Yes	No	–
Jonung and Wadensjö (1979)	Sweden	Yes	Yes	No	–
Hibbs and Madsen (1981)	Sweden	No	Yes	No	No
Paldam and Schneider (1980)	Denmark	Yes	No	Yes	No

Notes: (a) Considered separately.
(b) Only in inflationary crises.
(c) Expected value and variation of real income.

Yes/No means that a variable is significant/insignificant at the 5 per cent level; – that it was not tested.
A question-mark means that a significant coefficient was obtained, but that the authors disbelieve the result.

These variables will be attempted singly and jointly, lagged and unlagged, and exchanged for alternative variables. Thus PDOT will utilise overall consumer prices as well as farm prices; an alternative definition of $\Delta YD/P$ will be increase in real wage income.

The political variable includes a trend term and a political-unrest variable, number of strike days per month. Finally in some formulations a Koyck lag, POP_{t-1}, will be added. u_1 is an error term with conventional properties.

The following signs are hypothesised:

$$a_0 > 0 \quad a_1 \leq 0 \quad a_2 \leq 0 \quad a_3 \geq 0 \quad a_4 \gtrless 0 \quad a_5 \gtrless 0$$

Thus there are priors on the signs of the economic coefficients. The trend effect could however be of either sign, depending on whether the government's political capital appreciates or depreciates. Finally, the strike variable could either strengthen the government ('rally around the flag') or weaken it.

The form of the function is quite conventional. It assumes that the voter will have a certain opinion on the government's handling of the economic situation, irrespective of the previous history of that economic variable. Thus the model does not incorporate the more sophisticated form of the various Hibbs' studies and Chappell (1983) that voters react to unexpected deviations in the economic variables (with expectations being generated in Hibbs' study of Sweden by an AR(2) model). There are two reasons for this treatment. Firstly, the lack of observations. As emphasised earlier, I want to estimate the popularity function over each separate (three-year) election cycle. Hence with only 36 monthly observations, I think it is to ask too much of the data to supply also voters' expectations about the economic development, not to mention the long lags included in the mentioned studies. Also, the separate estimations will automatically take account of different economic histories. Secondly, it appears that the main effect of employing a more sophisticated form of the variables is to increase the level of the estimated parameter, while the significance level is more or less unaffected.

The reaction (or policy) function

In the simplest utility-type policy function, a government responds to economic targets by a constant fraction of the difference between actual popularity and the popularity judged essential for survival (Frey 1974). In later works by Frey (1978, Frey and Schneider 1975, 1978a, 1978b), the policy behaviour is viewed subject to several kinds of constraints:

1 The political constraint, that is the need to be re-elected. In

practice this variable is proxied by entering the 'squared popularity deficit' in Frey and Schneider (1978a) for the USA and the 'lead deficit' in Frey and Schneider (1978b) for the UK.

2 The administrative constraint. This is the 'influence of a bureaucracy's tendency to oppose policy changes. This hinders the government in its attempts to change the direction of or otherwise influence instrument use' (Frey and Schneider 1981a, p.297). The constraint is proxied for by the inclusion of the lagged dependent variable. Lindbeck (1973) has suggested another reason why a government may not have the free use of an instrument, namely that groups negatively affected by the change may be more vocal and aggressive than those who gain. This corresponds clearly to Downs' discussion (1957) of the 'coalition of minorities'.

3 The financial constraint. The possibility to increase expenditures is to some extent limited by the inflow of taxes, or the budget deficit.

4 The economic constraint. This constraint is included in two forms. Firstly, the coefficients in the estimated reaction function reflect the economic structure. Secondly, there may be specific constraints on behaviour in the economy.

Finally, to test for the presence of an election cycle in which expenditures are increased as the election approaches, a time trend for the proximity of election is used.

The policy function in this study will attempt several alternative instruments. The final choice here also affects the equations of the third block of equations, the economic structure. Thus the equation as shown here may be modified.

$$\begin{aligned} \Delta G/P = {} & D\left\{\text{constant} + b_0\, \Delta (G/P)_{t-1} \right.\\ & \left. + b_1 U + b_2\, PDOT + b_3 \frac{DEF}{P} + b_4\, TREND\right\} \\ & + (1-D)\left\{\text{constant} + b_5\, \Delta (G/P)_{t-1} \right.\\ & + b_6 U + b_7\, PDOT + b_8\, DEF/P \\ & \left. + b_9\, TREND\right\} + U_2 \end{aligned}$$

where D = dummy taking the value 0, if the government fulfils its minimum acceptable popularity share, taken to be 49 per cent for socialist governments and 51 per cent for bourgeois.[6]

The policy function will be estimated for each election period separately. In this way levels and changes in ideology will be easily captured. Note also that the government responds to economic factors directly, not to changes in popularity. This allows different governments to adopt different policy mixes in their reactions to certain changes in popularity.[7]

The change in government expenditures on goods and services is respresented by Δ G; expenditures are however limited by the state of government finances, indicated by DEF, the budget deficit. A trend term indicates the presence or absence of a policy cycle.

Four instruments are attempted: change in household real disposable income (Δ YD/P); change in central government real consumption (Δ G/P); change in real transfers to households (Δ TR/P); and changes in household real direct taxes (Δ TAX/P).

Table 4.2 specifies the a priori signs of coefficients in the policy functions. Apart from the lagged instrument, which is believed to carry a positive coefficient on standard assumptions of inertia, there is little that can be said about a socialist uncertain government. How it reacts to economic events (U and PDOT) depends on which is more important: attracting bourgeois voters or stimulating the economy. If it increases expenditures, it may attract voters that react to improvements in the economy but at the same time discourage bourgeois voters who object to increases in government expenditures. Similarly, whether it increases expenditures as the election draws nearer (in which case TREND will have a negative coefficient) depends on the same choice. The economic constraint – the budget deficit (DEF/P) – should however lead to lower expenditures and higher taxes.

An uncertain conservative–liberal government should however increase its expenditures, both to attract socialist voters and to stimulate the economy. In this case expenditures should be increased as unemployment rises, decreased when inflation rises. Expenditures should increase as the election term draws to a close (this holds *mutatis mutandis* for taxes).

As concerns certain governments it is much more difficult to specify a priori the effects of economic variables. What might be expected is that a conservative–liberal government would be more cautious on tax and expenditure increases than a socialist government. However, for the period under study, Sweden 1970–82, the most expansive government was the bourgeois coalition 1976–79. The most restrictive government with regard to government expenditures was the socialist government 1970–73![8]

The structure of the economy

Rather than adopt the simplifying structure of the Phillips curve, the structure of the economy is modelled by a six-equation mini-model, explaining inflation, unemployment, disposable income growth, transfer payments, taxes and the budget deficit as functions of each other and three exogenous variables: government real expenditures, change in real world trade and world inflation.

Table 4.2 Theoretical coefficients in policy functions

Dependent variables	Lagged dep. var.	U_{t-1}	$PDOT_{t-1}$	DEF/P	TREND
		Uncertain socialist government			
$\Delta(\frac{YD}{P})$	+	?	?	-	?
$\Delta(\frac{G}{P})$	+	?	?	-	?
$\Delta(\frac{TR}{P})$	+	?	?	-	?
$\Delta(\frac{TAX}{P})$	+	?	?	+	?
		Uncertain conservative government			
$\Delta(\frac{YD}{P})$	+	+	-	-	-
$\Delta(\frac{G}{P})$	+	+	-	-	-
$\Delta(\frac{TR}{P})$	+	+	-	-	-
$\Delta(\frac{TAX}{P})$	+	-	+	+	+

Results of estimation

In this section will be reported some of the results of estimation by means of OLS. Simultaneous estimations are shown in the next section.

Table 4.3 shows the main results for the popularity function for the four election periods. The following conclusions appear warranted. Firstly, the most important variable is the trend term, which is uniformly significant (except for the 1976–79 period). Addition of the

Table 4.3 Popularity functions in Sweden, 1970–82
(Dependent variable is popularity of socialist and bourgeois bloc, respectively)

Period	Dep. var.	Independent variables				R^2	MSE	DW
		U	PDOT	Δ(Y/P)	TREND			
September 1970–August 1973	Soc	-1.2 (-3.30)	0.1 (1.84)	0.08 (1.49)	0.06 (3.62)	0.60	0.9	1.20
September 1973–August 1976	Soc	-2.2 (-2.39)	0.0 (0.28)	-0.01 (-0.01)	0.14 (3.94)	0.36	2.2	0.83
September 1976–August 1979	Bour	-0.6 (-0.49)	-0.0 (-0.31)	-0.08 (-0.87)	-0.07 (-1.80)	0.14	3.7	0.45
September 1979–August 1982	Bour	3.8 (3.15)	-0.0 (-0.42)	0.05 (1.43)	0.30 (4.55)	0.52	2.8	1.03

Notes:

1 R^2 is the coefficient of multiple correlation.
2 MSE is mean squared error in percentage points.
3 DW is the Durbin–Watson statistic (exchanged for Durbin's h-statistic in equations with lagged dependent variable).
4 t-values in parenthesis.

trend term to a formulation with only economic variables also results in sharply raised explanatory power, for instance from 0.03 to 0.36 in 1973–76 and from 0.08 to 0.52 in 1979–82.

Secondly, the only economic variable of importance is the unemployment rate. But it is only for the 1970–73 period that the coefficient is stable and significant. For 1973–76, only the formulation shown here has a significant and negative coefficient, while the coefficient is either insignificant or positive or both in all other formulations.

Thirdly, the fit of the equation is very bad except for 1970–73. In this period the DW statistic is in the indeterminate range, while for all other periods the hypothesis of no autocorrelation must be rejected. The size of the error also indicates a badly-fitting equation. The total range of variability of socialist popularity for 1973–76 was 7 percentage points, while the estimated confidence interval is 8.8. Hence even in this equation where the rate of unemployment is significant there is a lot left to explain.

These conclusions are further strengthened when the equations are rerun with other definitions of variables, other direct lags, the inclusion of the lagged dependent variable, correction for serial correlation and on individual party data instead of bloc data.[9]

My conclusion from this part of the study is the following. There may be influences from economic factors on government popularity, but the only variable that has attained significance is unemployment. It is, however, apparent that the popularity function is not stable. In particular, it does not appear that the weak bourgeois governments were held responsible for the macroeconomy. The main variance in the series is the result of separate political events rather than of systematic influences.

What these results suggest is that the reason why Hibbs (1981), Jonung and Wadensjö (1979) and Kirchgässner (1976) found significant effects on government popularity from the economy is due to the particular events of 1970–72. During 1969–70 Sweden experienced the strongest boom in the post-war period, largely as a result of excess fiscal stimulus. In early 1971 the government stepped hard on both fiscal and monetary brakes, leading to a sharp contraction, with unemployment rates rising to a record level of 3.5 per cent. It is hardly surprising that this traumatic change should influence voter behaviour. From a technical point of view, almost all variance of the unemployment data for the period covered by the three studies is in this period.

The behaviour of prices is also untypical. From a low of 2 per cent in 1969, inflation 'exploded' to a record 7 per cent in 1970 as a result of the economy hitting the capacity ceiling. In the period preceding the oil price increases such large variability of inflation as well as its level presumably influenced the voters, although this is not captured in my study.

It is however my contention that the sole reason for the significant results in the three mentioned studies is that the events of 1969–72 dominate their data. Rerunning the models for the period from 1973 would lead to much worse results. It should be noted for instance that the impact of unemployment on popularity in my study for 1970–73 has the same level of significance (a t-ratio around 5) as Hibbs (1981) finds for his total period of estimation, 1967–78.

Let us now turn to the policy functions. These have also been estimated for each election period separately, allowing also for different reactions when the popularity level is deemed sufficient for re-election and otherwise. The results are found in Table 4.4.

Firstly, it can be noted that the lagged dependent variable has a positive and mostly significant coefficient. Apart from this term, there are very few significant results at all. Only for the last bourgeois period does combating unemployment appear to be important and the trend term in this period also has a high t-ratio. The sign of the trend effect is however contrary to the expectations in Table 4.2 and hence cannot be judged significant. It should also be observed that Durbin's h for this period indicates severe auto-correlation; hence t-ratios cannot be trusted.[10]

In conclusion the results would bear out the contention that the reaction of an uncertain socialist government to economic events cannot be specified a priori. However, only one coefficient was also found significant for the periods covered by uncertain bourgeois governments and, in general, instability of coefficients is the most noteworthy phenomenon.

The method of separating certain and uncertain governments is of course open to criticism. This criticism applies in particular when one measures the popularity of a coalition government with a minority position in Parliament. It is inherently difficult to measure 'popularity deficits' in periods when the government coalition changes. But this critique would apply to Frey and Schneider's 'squared popularity deficits' as well.

It is also likely that the policy-function approach fails because it is too naive. One of the main studies of the election cycle is Paldam (1979). He looked at the behaviour over the cycle of eight variables in 17 countries. More than half of the individual series were found to move with the reference (election) cycle in a significant manner (for four-year election periods). Yet Paldam finds that the policy functions do not appear to depend on expansive policies in the election year. Instead there is an abnormal expansion of expenditures in the second year!

Table 4.4 Policy functions in Sweden, 1970–82
(Dependent variable is the change in real government expenditures $\Delta(G/P)$)

Period	Independent variables										R^2	MSE	h
	When popularity is deficient					When popularity is adequate							
	Lagged dep. var.	U_{t-1}	$PDOT_{t-1}$	DEF/P	TREND	Lagged dep. var.	U_{t-1}	$PDOT_{t-1}$	DEF/P	TREND			
1970–73 (socialist government)	0.37 (2.43)	32.1 (1.52)	3.81 (1.56)	2.46 (1.34)	1.82 (1.83)	Not enough observations in this period					0.39	3.2	1.28
1973–76 (socialist government)	0.35 (1.71)	36.6 (0.79)	-0.39 (-0.08)	-1.49 (-0.67)	1.01 (0.55)	0.65 (2.21)	98.8 (1.01)	1.66 (0.51)	-3.35 (-0.70)	-4.87 (-0.73)	0.39	5.0	cannot be calculated
1976–79 (bourgeois coalitions)	0.50 (2.77)	16.9 (0.35)	-4.62 (-1.38	-1.73 (-1.20)	2.21 (1.11)	1.01 (2.07	-31.1 (-0.30)	8.01 (0.23)	-3.94 (-1.50)	2.86 (0.61)	0.51	4.1	cannot be calculated
1979–82 (bourgeois coalitions)	0.07 (0.65)	35.7 (2.34)	-0.30 (-0.38)	0.04 (0.96)	3.41 (4.55)	Not enough observations in this period					0.53	0.4	4.1

Note: The shift variable in this table is last month's popularity level. Shifting to current month popularity does not materially affect the conclusions.

Estimation and simulation of the full system

The first step in establishing the properties of the total system is to see whether different methods of estimation yield different results. Thus the system of equations was re-estimated by Ordinary Least Squares (OLS), Two-Stage Least Squares (2SLS) and Three-Stage Least Squares (3SLS). The 'system' in this context consists of the popularity function, the policy function and the economic structure.

To give a sufficiently long simulation period, the estimations were carried out over the full social-democratic reign from October 1970 to September 1976. Results are given in Table 4.5.

Let us first look at the economics. In the popularity function, results are somewhat clearer than in the preceding table. There is now a clear effect of unemployment on popularity, while real-income growth is not significant. The depreciation of the political capital, as represented by the positive coefficient of the negative time trend, is also evident.

In the policy function, only the lagged dependent variable is ever significant. But, with one exception, all other coefficients are at least correctly signed. Higher unemployment increases expenditures; a higher budget deficit lowers expenditures. There is no evidence of increases in expenditures as the election draws closer.

In order to study more closely the effect of various degrees of popularity, the shifting 'minimum popularity to be elected' dummy was set at 48 rather than at 49 per cent. Keeping in mind that the difference between the coefficients is only significant for the lag term, the following may still be noted. At high levels of popularity the speed of reaction appears to be much higher, that is the 'administrative constraint' less binding. This reverses the (insignificant) effects in Table 4.4. Also, the effect of restraint caused by the budget deficit is much smaller at high levels of popularity. This would tend to confirm our tentative hypothesis that a popular social-democratic government is more likely to increase expenditures than a less popular one.

The next line shows the estimates when the full system is estimated simultaneously with effects of cross-equation errors accounted for. It is apparent that there is very little co-variation between the popularity variable SOC and the rest of the model. Parameters are virtually identical to the OLS coefficients. In the policy function there is more change, not surprising since the co-variation of government expenditures with the rest of the economy is more pronounced. Also the low precision of the estimates makes for larger random fluctuations of coefficients. The coefficient most affected by the changes estimation technique is that of the budget deficit, the only current-period endogenous variable in the system.

The next stage is to study the simulation aspects of the model. To

Table 4.5 Simultaneous estimation of model parameters, October 1970–September 1976

(a) Popularity function; dependent variable SOC

Form of estimation	Independent variables				R^2
	Intercept	U_t	$\Delta(Y/P)_t$	TREND	
OLS	48.4 (75.6)	-1.20 (-4.36)	0.03 (0.70)	0.09 (5.98)	0.44
3SLS	48.5 (76.0)	-1.23 (-4.50)	0.05 (1.17)	0.09 (6.00)	–

(b) Policy function; dependent variable $\Delta(G/P)$

Form of estimation	Independent variables									R^2
		When popularity $\leqslant$ 48%				When popularity > 48%				
	Intercept	$\Delta(G/P)_{t-1}$	U_{t-1}	DEF/P	TREND	$\Delta(G/P)_{t-1}$	U_{t-1}	DEF/P	TREND	
OLS	-50.2 (-1.56)	0.69 (4.44)	15.4 (1.02)	-1.78 (-1.06)	1.05 (0.90)	0.32 (1.97)	14.3 (0.71)	-0.12 (-0.06)	1.14 (0.80)	0.35
3SLS	-44.9 (-1.41)	0.77 (5.04)	13.9 (0.93)	-0.74 (-0.45)	0.71 (0.63)	0.34 (2.11)	12.8 (0.65)	1.29 (0.67)	0.96 (0.69)	–

make the model linear the popularity-shift dummy was ignored in the policy function, that is the reaction of the government was assumed to be independent of the popularity level.

The first simulation is to evaluate the tracking ability of the full model. Figure 4.3 shows actual values of the popularity of the social-democratic government 1970–76 (with the communist party included) and the predicted values from a fully dynamic simulation. Remember that the important variables are unemployment and the time trend! It is however obvious that the time trend in the election period is the only factor of importance. The effect of unemployment is minute. The tracking ability of the system regarding the popularity variable is thus hardly impressive. The root-mean-square error is 1.4, which means that a confidence interval (at 95 per cent) would have a width of 5.3 percentage points. The confidence interval would then bracket from 45.4 to 50.6, covering basically all the actual range.

Dynamic shocks of the system are considered next. Since all domestic variables – economic and politic – are endogenous, the only disturbances come from abroad in the form of different rates of international inflation and different rates of growth of world trade in volume.

Since inflation does not appear as an important factor in the model, it is hardly surprising that there is very little impact on a higher rate of international inflation on government popularity. However, a faster rate of growth of world trade leads to higher Swedish exports, lower unemployment and hence to a higher popularity of the government. If the model is to be trusted, a ten-billion US dollar faster increase in world trade (approximately 1 per cent of the 1975 figure) will after 20 months have increased the popularity of the government by about 0.5 per cent.

Summary and conclusions

If there is an interaction between the polity and the economy in the form of voter reactions to economic events and manipulation by the government in order to exploit that interaction (believed or actual) then the usual models of the economy are misspecified. It has been shown for Germany that a model that includes this politico–economic interaction outperforms a conventional econometric model in terms of forecasting ability.

This chapter has attempted to study the simultaneous behaviour of voters and governments in Sweden. To this end, three pieces in the model were presented in theoretical form, discussed and estimated, namely a voter evaluation function of government popularity, a policy

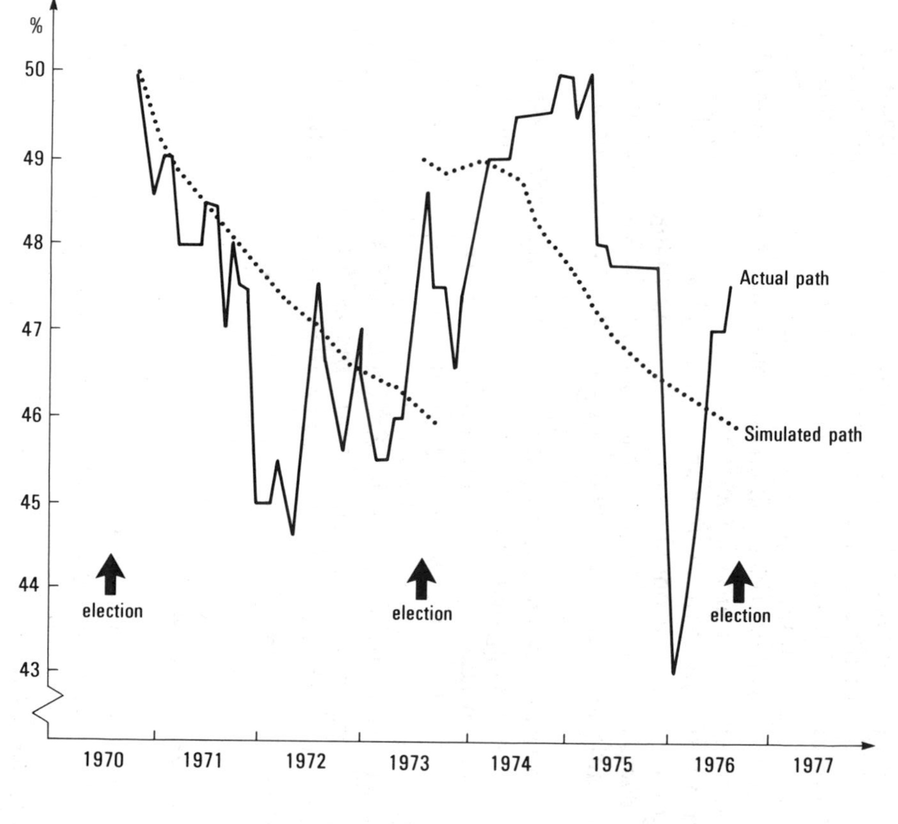

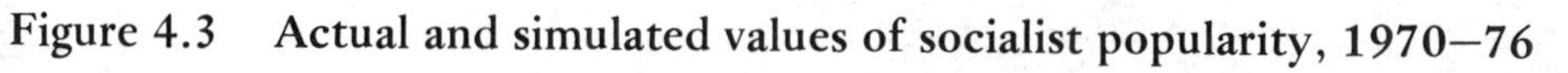
Figure 4.3 Actual and simulated values of socialist popularity, 1970–76

function describing the behaviour of the government, and a set of equations describing the structure of the economy.

The results are rather disappointing to those that believe in the politico–economic models. Firstly, the popularity function is very unstable between time periods. The only economic argument to carry weight is the unemployment rate – and this only in periods of strong governments. Weak governments, like the bourgeois coalitions from 1976 on, have evidently not been held responsible for the deteriorating economy. Moreover, the contribution of the rate of unemployment even in periods when it is significant is minute. Government popularity is determined largely by specific political events, not by any systematic influence from the economy.

Similar negative findings appear for the policy functions. The hypothesised difference in behaviour between socialist and bourgeois governments, or between popular and unpopular governments do not appear. With a few exceptions, no coefficients are significant.

On the other hand, the other elements of the critique appear unwarranted. The amount of simultaneity between the evaluation and the policy function is minute, as is the simultaneity between the political parts of the model and the economic structure. Hence there is little to be gained by more advanced estimation techniques and little to be learned from simulations of the full politico–economic system.

Notes

1 See Frey (1978, 1979), Frey and Schneider (1981b) and Paldam (1981) for surveys.
2 Holmberg (1981) shows taxes, for instance, as the major factor for conservative voters, while employment was the second most important factor for social-democrats (after 'class politics').
3 This simple view is explicit or implicit in Lindbeck (1973, 1975, 1976), Nordhaus (1975), Tufte (1978) and Wagner (1977), to mention just a few well-known works.
4 Crotty (1973) was the first to point out that econometric models that failed to incorporate government behaviour would have biased coefficients; adding the behaviour of voters to economic events would increase the bias further.
5 The references certainly do not mean to imply that respective authors believe in the case in question, only that they have taken up the issue.
6 Non-parliamentary parties get between 1 and 5 per cent in the popularity figures. Since most of these voters are regarded as bourgeois, the requirements for socialist government popularity

should be less stringent than that for bourgeois governments.

7 See also Hibbs (1977) and Schmidt (1982).

8 The clear hypothesis on signs means that t-tests will be one-sided, whereas two-sided t-tests will be employed where the sign is uncertain.

9 Further results of estimation and more information on data used can be obtained from the author on request.

10 Results for the other policy instruments are similar. The only fact worthy of notice is that the minority liberal government in 1978–79 increased transfers to households as the election drew nearer. This coefficient is significant.

References

Arcelus, F. and Meltzer, A.H. (1975), 'The Effect of Aggregate Economic Variables on Congressional Elections', *American Political Science Review*, 69:1232–1239.

Bloom, H.S. and Price, H.D. (1975), 'Voter Response to Short-Run Economic Conditions: The Asymmetric Effect of Prosperity and Depression', *American Political Science Review*, 69:1240–1254.

Chappell, H.W. Jr. (1983), 'Presidential Popularity and Macro-economic Performance: Are Voters Really so Naive?', *Review of Economics and Statistics*, 65:385–392.

Crotty, J.R. (1973), 'Specification Error in Macro-Econometric Models: The Influence of Policy Goals', *American Economic Review*, 63: 1025–1030.

Downs, A. (1957), *An Economic Theory of Democracy* (New York: Harper & Row).

Fair, R.C. (1978), 'The Effect of Economic Events on Votes for President', *Review of Economics and Statistics*, 60:159–173.

Fischer, S. and Huizinga, J. (1982), 'Inflation, Unemployment and Public Opinion Polls', *Journal of Money, Credit and Banking*, 14: 1–19.

Frey, B.S. (1974), 'The Politico–Economic System: A Simulation Model', *Kyklos*, 27:227–254.

Frey, B.S. (1978), 'Politico–Economic Models and Cycles', *Journal of Public Economics*, 9:203–220.

Frey, B.S. (1979), 'Politometrics of Government Behavior in a Democracy', *Scandinavian Journal of Economics*, 81:308–322.

Frey, B.S. and Garbers, H. (1971), 'Politico–Econometrics – On Estimation in Political Economy', *Political Studies*, XIX:316–320.

Frey, B.S. and Lau, L.J. (1968), 'Towards a Mathematical Model of Government Behavior', *Zeitschrift für Nationalökonomie*, 28:

355–380.
Frey, B.S. and Ramser, H.J. (1976), 'The Political Business Cycle: Comment', *Review of Economic Studies*, 43:553–556.
Frey, B.S. and Schneider, F. (1975), 'On the Modelling of Politico–Economic Interdependence', *European Journal of Political Research*, 3:339–360.
Frey, B.S. and Schneider, F. (1978a), 'An Empirical Study of Politico–Economic Interaction in the United States', *Review of Economics and Statistics*, 60:174–183.
Frey, B.S. and Schneider, F. (1978b), 'A Political–Economic Model of the United Kingdom', *Economic Journal*, 88:243–253.
Frey, B.S. and Schneider, F. (1979), 'An Econometric Model with an Endogenous Government Sector', *Public Choice*, 34:29–43.
Frey, B.S. and Schneider, F. (1981a), 'Central Bank Behavior', *Journal of Monetary Economics*, 7:291–315.
Frey, B.S. and Schneider, F. (1981b), 'Recent Research on Empirical Politico–Economic Models', in D.A. Hibbs, Jr. and H. Fassbender, eds, *Contemporary Political Economy* (Amsterdam: North Holland).
Frey, B.S. and Schneider, F. (1982), 'Politico–Economic Models in Competition with Alternative Models: Which Predict Better?', *European Journal of Political Research*, 10:241–254.
Goodhart, C.A.E. and Bhansali, R.J. (1970), 'Political Economy', *Political Studies*, XVIII:43–106.
Hibbs, D.A. (1977), 'Political Parties and Macroeconomic Policy', *American Political Science Review*, 71:467–487.
Hibbs, D.A. (1979), 'The Mass Public and Macroeconomic Performance: The Dynamics of Public Opinion toward Unemployment and Inflation', *American Journal of Political Science*, 23:705–731.
Hibbs, D.A. Jr. (1981), 'Economics and Politics in France', *European Journal of Political Research*, 9:133–145.
Hibbs, D.A. Jr. (1982), 'On the Demand for Economic Outcomes: Macroeconomic Performance and Mass Political Support in the United States, Great Britain, and Germany', *Journal of Politics*, 44: 426–462.
Hibbs, D.A. Jr. and Madsen, H.J. (1981), 'The Impact of Economic Performance on Electoral Support in Sweden, 1967–78', *Scandinavian Political Studies*, 4:33–50.
Holmberg, S. (1981), *Svenska väljare* (Stockholm: LIBER).
Jonung, L. and Wadensjö, E. (1979), 'The Effect of Unemployment, Inflation and Real Income on Government Popularity', *Scandinavian Journal of Economics*, 81:343–353.
Kirchgässner, G. (1976), *Rationales Wählerverhalten und optimales Regierungsverhalten*, doct. diss. University of Konstanz.
Kramer, G.H. (1971), 'Short-Term Fluctuations in US Voting Behavior

1896–1964', *American Political Science Review*, 65:131–143.
Lewin, L. (1979), *Det politiska spelet* (Stockholm: Rabén & Sjögren).
Lindbeck, A. (1973), 'Endogenous Politicians and the Theory of Economic Policy', IIES Seminar Paper (no. 35).
Lindbeck, A. (1975), 'Business Cycles, Politics, and International Economic Dependences', *Skandinaviska Enskilda Banken Quarterly Review*, 53–68.
Lindbeck, A. (1976), 'Stabilization Policy in Open Economies with Endogenous Politicians', *American Economic Review*, 66:1–19.
Miller, W.L. and Mackie, M. (1973), 'The Electoral Cycle and the Asymmetry of Government and Opposition Popularity', *Political Studies*, XXI:263–279.
Minford, P. and Peel, D. (1982), 'The Political Theory of the Business Cycle', *European Economic Review*, 17:253–270.
Mosley, P. (1978), 'Images of the "Floating Water" or the Political Business Cycle Revisited', *Political Studies*, XXVI:375–394.
Mueller, J.E. (1970), 'Presidential Popularity from Truman to Johnson', *American Political Science Review*, 64:18–34.
Nordhaus, W.D. (1975), 'The Political Business Cycle', *Review of Economic Studies*, 42:169–190.
Paldam, M. (1979), 'Is there an Election Cycle?', *Scandinavian Journal of Economics*, 81:323–342.
Paldam, M. (1981), 'A Preliminary Survey of the Theories and Findings on Vote and Popularity Fractions', *European Journal of Political Research*, 9:181–199.
Paldam, M. and Schneider, F. (1980), 'The Macroeconomic Aspects of Government and Opposition Popularity in Denmark 1957–78', *Nationaløkonomisk Tidskrift*, 118:149–170.
Schmidt, M.G. (1982), *Wohlfahrtsstaatliche Politik unter bürgerlichen und sozialdemokratischen Regierungen: Ein internationaler Vergleich* (Frankfurt: Campus Verlag).
Schneider, F. and Frey, B.S. (1983), 'An Empirical Model of Politico–Economic Interaction in the US: A Reply', *Review of Economics and Statistics*, 65:178–182.
Stigler, G.J. (1973), 'General Economic Conditions and National Elections', *American Economic Review*, 63:160–167.
Tufte, E.R. (1978), *Political Control of the Economy* (Princeton: Princeton University Press).
Wagner, R.E. (1977), 'Economic Manipulation for Political Profit: Macroeconomic Consequences and Constitutional Implications', *Kyklos*, 30:395–410.

5 Long-run causes for the growth of government

A survey of empirical studies

Introduction

There is no need to complain about lack of studies on the growth of government. The most complete survey of theories and studies to date, Larkey, Stolp and Winer (1981), lists no fewer than 393 references! There is, however, a dearth of empirical studies that attempt to explain the continued growth of the public sector in developed societies. And scarcity is even more noticeable if empirical studies that use correct methodology and correct data are desired. Lowery and Berry (1983) lament in their paper that 'Tarschys' essay on government expansion identifies nine distinct alternative explanations of government growth ...To date, the various explanations have not been tested or have been tested inappropriately' (p.665).

Unfortunately, Lowery and Berry do not live up to their own critique. Their methodology is also at fault. One of the purposes of this chapter is to explain why most previous empirical studies build on a defective methodology and to propose a better model.

This chapter will not survey existing theories in detail; the reader is referred to some of the other surveys for this purpose.[1] Only empirical studies that report on tests of the hypotheses will be scrutinised. The presentation of Tarschys' (1975) model cannot be avoided however, since it is (or should be) fundamental to all studies in the field. It also provides a convenient means of grouping the various theories (see Table 5.1).[2]

Tarschys separates two groups of deciding agents: those who demand and consume public goods and services[3] and those who produce and supply them. But a third perspective is added, that of finance. It is not necessarily an independent agent of its own but is better viewed as a necessary condition behind the other two perspectives. For example, if taking the extreme demand view, it would be argued that the growth of the public sector is solely due to increases in demand for public goods and services. How these are financed is irrelevant. But the availability of progressive taxes may facilitate the provision of public services. Hence their existence may be a precondition why demand has been satisfied. Or viewed from the supply side: progressive taxes may have been necessary to finance the growth of the public sector that the politicians and the administrators have desired.

Hence in many cases the financial perspective may be merged with either the demand or the supply perspective. It is however crucial to distinguish these two, since the underlying decision units are different.

But Tarschys also separates three horizontal levels. The socio–economic level may be regarded as more technical background, referring to such factors as changes in technological, economic, social and demographic structure. Individuals are more directly visible in the second level, the ideological–cognitive level, where such factors as changes in knowledge, beliefs, desires and attitudes are taken into account. Finally, a change in desired demand or supply must also be articulated and channelled into an actual change in public output. This level then focuses on the institutional set-up in society.

It should be apparent from this brief overview that Lowery and Berry cannot have read Tarschys' article very closely. There is certainly nothing there that limits the number of explanations for public sector growth to nine; rather Tarschys himself distinguished 25 different arguments. The important thing is that the various explanations can be conveniently grouped into categories depending on who decides (consumer/producer) and on what grounds (institutional change/ demographic or other change/value change).

The important distinction is of course between the categories of decision. If the growth of the public sector is to be explained by changes in behaviour, the utility function of deciding agents needs to be derived – explicitly or implicitly. It is therefore surprising that so few of the surveys bother to make this distinction: most just name the various arguments randomly. An important exception to this rule is Peacock (1979), who separates supply and demand factors, and Buchanan (1977), who discusses government as 'responsive' (that is demand oriented) or 'excessive' (from the point of view of consumer

Table 5.1 Different causes of the growth of government disaggregated *à la* Tarschys (1975)

	Consumer perspective	Financial perspective	Producer perspective
SOCIO–ECONOMIC LEVEL	Greater demand for public services as a result of increased geographical mobility, industrial reorganisation, population changes and so forth. Education, medical and elderly care moved from private to public sector.	A relatively larger public sector requires larger taxes, which is possible only in a richer society. Many of the functions of the public sector presuppose a developed economy.	Horizontal differentiation, (specialisation), decreased working hours and increased inefficiency require more public employees even at a given level of communal service.
IDEOLOGICAL–COGNITIVE LEVEL	Greater demand for public services at higher income levels. Public goods are 'luxuries' with an income elasticity in excess of unity.	The larger tax burden is tolerated by the citizens in a relatively rich society. A high tax ratio is also dependent on the legitimacy of the government.	'Bureau maximisation' by administrators and professionalisation lead to a larger public sector on account of status and ideologies.
POLITICAL–INSTITUTIONAL LEVEL	Greater demand for public services on account of strong interest groups, lobbying, and collusion between interest organisations on one hand and Parliament and administration on the other.	Progressive taxes and more taxes also allow for a larger tax yield. Vertical differentiation of public functions increases expenditures.	More parliamentarians and voters are also public employees, which decreases the possibility to restrain internal demands from the public apparatus. Coalitions between various groups in society make matters worse.

and voter sovereignty).

We will proceed by taking up and discussing the factors that can be ascribed to the demand and the supply side, respectively. The focus in these sections is on how to measure the various influences and on the results from previous studies. Then the next section will discuss the testing of theories jointly.

The focus is on testable theories, however. There will be no discussion of recent theories such as that of Wildavsky (1985) who views the different rates of growth of the public sector in different countries as resulting from differences in cultural background. This may be so, but it is hardly obvious. Why in that case has the public sector growth in The Netherlands, Luxembourg and Belgium been among the fastest in the OECD area, while that in France is among the lowest? Why have Sweden and Denmark relied on public supply and Norway on private supply to a much larger extent?

Another easy way out is to explain different growth rates of government expenditures by differing attitudes towards the public sector. In the 1982 election, for instance, 39 per cent of Swedish voters were of the opinion that the public sector was too large and should be shrunk. Similarly, a question asked at every election survey since 1964 indicates that more and more voters would rather see a cut-back in social transfers than an increase (Gilljam and Nilsson 1984). But these are irrelevant findings until the reasons for the changes in attitudes can be found.[4]

Demand factors

Wagner's law: first interpretation (industrial and demographic change)
The most well-known explanation for the increase in public expenditures out of total production is that of Wagner (1883, 1893). He observed the transition from the agricultural, self-contained society into the modern, industrialised and urbanised society and made the prediction that this change would lead to a greater demand for public sector performance as functions previously produced within the family would now have to be supplied by the state. There are several examples: medical and elderly care, education, to name but a few. The increased urbanisation and industrialisation would also require infrastructure investments by the state.

Wagner's thoughts have been carried further by many. Among those less well-known internationally are Höök (1962) and Zenker (1972). They view publicly-produced goods and services as complementary to private ones, that is they are necessary for the private sector to function well.

There are objections to be made to these hypotheses. Firstly, they do not square with the facts. As shown by many students of long-term changes in government-sector shares (e.g. Beck 1981, Forsman 1977, Nutter 1978), the growth of government at a greater speed than that of total production is a post-war phenomenon. Apart from temporary increases associated with war, the share of public expenditures in GDP was only slightly higher in 1950 in most countries than at the turn of the century. The use of resources by the public sector for consumption and investment in Sweden was relatively steady as a per cent of GDP at around 10 per cent from 1860 to the First World War. In 1950 it was around 15 per cent only to rise to some 35 per cent in the early 1980s.

A second objection is theoretical. Why should it necessarily be the public sector that is supposed to furnish the services that the family no longer supplies? Why are private solutions not demanded (or tolerated by politicians)?[5]

Among recent empirical studies on exactly this interpretation of Wagner's law, one finds Lowery and Berry (1983). In their study of US expenditure growth 1948–78 they included variables to account for population growth, change in demographic structure towards more minors and elderly, and changes in urbanisation. None of the variables came close to being significant. In a similar study of Norway 1949–83, however, Sørensen (1984) found urbanisation to have a significant influence on the public income share of GDP. In a cross-section study of Swedish local authorities, Murray (1981) also found population density as well as the degree of urbanisation to lead to significantly higher public expenditures per capita.[6]

Wagner's law: second interpretation (high income elasticity)

A second interpretation of Wagner's law focuses on the character of public goods and services. As concerns consumption, the public sector supplied education, medical care, culture and so forth, all of which were believed to be income-elastic, that is the demand for them would increase faster than GDP. Even the capital investments carried out by the public sector were believed to have a high income elasticity, simply because there were indivisibilities requiring great amounts of capital (railways etc.).

This version of Wagner's law has been tested extensively. I focus here on recent results, those that are interesting on account of their methodology and those that are not known to the international public.

A first way of testing is to regress expenditures on income or per capita income in a time-series analysis in one country. These results have frequently failed. Lowery and Berry (1983) found the share of the public sector not significantly dependent on income, that is an income elasticity not significantly different from unity (USA 1948–78).

The same finding appears in Cameron (1984) for federal expenditures 1900–82. Pelzman (1980) has objected to the use of current income as a regressor and proposes permanent income instead. Yet he finds the income elasticity to be unity, in which case the growth of the share of the public sector is not explained.

Ganti and Kolluri (1979) have however objected to the use of Ordinary Least Squares in this context on account of simultaneous-equation bias.[7] Instead they use a maximum-likelihood estimator and find that Wagner's law is confirmed for the USA.

There are two ways of avoiding simultaneity by structural specification. One is to analyse the demands for components of public expenditures. Several studies have for instance derived and estimated the demand for goods and services provided by local governments. They agree however that most categories are income-*in*elastic. For instance, compare the study of American municipalities by Borcherding and Deacon (1972) with a corresponding Swedish one by Ysander (1979). The income elasticities are found as shown in Table 5.2. Although somewhat different for different categories the studies agree that most expenditure categories have income elasticities well below unity, that is they are consistent with a falling share of public expenditures in income over time. Borcherding and Deacon (1972, 1977b, 1978, 1985), alone or together, conclude that the average income elasticity of demand is 0.75 in the United States, a figure corroborated by Bergström and Goodman (1973) who wind up with 0.64 (not significantly different from 0.75).

Table 5.2 Income elasticities of demand for certain publicly provided goods and services

	Borcherding and Deacon	Ysander
Local education	0.94	1.16 (Local and high-school education combined)
High-school education	0.69	
Roads	0.10*	1.14
Medical care, hospitals	0.15*	0.19
Fire	0.88	negative*
Recreation	2.74	—
Police	0.82	
Social care	—	0.34
Other expenditures	—	0.44

* not significantly different from 0

A second way to avoid simultaneity bias is to employ cross-section data for many countries. OECD (1983) finds however that only 10 per cent of the difference in public expenditure shares in GDP are attributable to differences in GDP per capita.[8] Cameron (1978) also could find no significant effect in his study of 18 developed countries for the period 1960–75. Wagner and Weber (1977) studied 34 developed economies for the period 1950–72 and found 'weak' support for Wagner's hypothesis in that some countries showed a high income responsiveness. Note however that the model employed is very simplistic with government expenditures made a function of income and a time trend to account for all other factors. It is difficult to see that much can be deduced from a formulation like that.

Wagner's law: third interpretation (war-related displacement effects)
Wagner himself explicitly mentioned the increasing cost of defence expenditures over time as one reason for the growing share of government. His hypothesis has been further elaborated by Peacock and Wiseman (1961). They propose a ratchet or 'displacement' effect whereby public expenditures rise in times of war or crisis but do not return to previous levels after the event since the public (i.e. the voters) have got accustomed to and accept higher levels of spending.

While they themselves found some support for the theory with regard to the United Kingdom, other studies (discussed by Borcherding 1977a, p.38) have not found a similar effect in other countries. It can be shown for instance that for Sweden there was only a minimal displacement effect in the Second World War; total public consumption in 1946 was basically back to the level of 1938.

A recent empirical study, Cameron (1984), finds for the United States that war is by far the most important determinant of changes in public expenditure shares. But Cameron decomposes the result into a mobilisation effect (war deaths in the first two years) and a demobilisation effect, finding that they cancel out. Hence federal expenditures were not permanently increased as a result of wars (1900–82).

Fourth explanation: price-elastic demand
As in all demand functions there should also be a price effect in the demand for public goods and services. The only problem is how to measure the cost to the consumer who usually does not pay directly at all (police, defence, streets and highways, education in many countries, etc.) or pays a heavily subsidised price (medical care, day-care centres, etc.).

There are, in principle, two ways of proceeding.[9] One is to focus on the tax price to the consumer, that is the tax burden he carries, particularly for municipal provisions. The tax price, that is the local tax, may depend on the individual's characteristics but is independent of the total volume of public expenditures demanded or consumed by the taxpayer.[10] Bergström and Goodman (1973) take this approach to the demand for US municipal expenditures, finding a price elasticity for general expenditures of -0.23 (significantly different from zero). Similarly, Ysander (1979) uses tax prices in his study of the demand for disaggregated local-authority goods and services. He finds significant price elasticities for some components, namely highways and social care (both around -0.80), whereas other categories are found to be price inelastic (not significantly different from zero).

The other approach is to use some measure of the cost at which public goods and services are produced. Assuming that the consumer knows these costs, and that public goods would have been priced at marginal costs, and that the production function is a Cobb–Douglas with constant returns to scale, and supplies of labour and capital are elastic, then wage rates in public services are proportional to prices and can be used in demand functions instead of these. These not-very-easily-satisfied conditions have been used *inter alia* by Borcherding and Deacon (1972), who find that some items are heavily price-elastic such as local education and hospitals, while most others are not significantly price responsive at all. One wonders why such necessary items as police, hospitals and lower education would be price elastic, while higher education, highways and recreation are not. One would a priori have thought it would be the other way around.

Nevertheless, the studies surveyed by Borcherding (1977b, 1984) have price elasticities of -0.50 on average. The study by Deacon (1978) however is important, since it is, to my knowledge, the only one to deduce compensated price elasticities for the demand for municipal services, finding it to be on average -0.40.[11]

The question of price elasticity on the supply side will be returned to under the heading of 'Baumol's disease', since the relative price shift involved under this heading must enter also the demand side for technical reasons (see p.83).

Fifth explanation: demand for income redistribution

As noted by many observers, the growth of the public sector lies mainly on the transfer side, while supplies of state and municipal goods and services have increased at a lower rate. Indeed, Beck (1981) finds that, after a careful deflation of the nominal growth rates, transfers are the only item to have grown in constant prices in recent years. What this implies is that explanations behind the demand and supply for public goods and services should not be sought but rather try to focus on various categories of transfers and their causes (Lindbeck 1985).

The tradition in the field goes back to Downs' 1957 classic *An*

Economic Theory of Democracy, which in turn builds on Hotelling's 1929 article 'Stability in Competition'. These theories establish the critical role of the median voter, that is the voter who is in the middle of the distribution of values on 'the' critical issue or the voter who is at the centre of the income distribution. Trying the maximise vote returns, political parties will adapt to the will of the median voter. Hence if the mean income of society is much higher than the median income, there is room for a vote-getting redistribution.

The theory has been elaborated in Meltzer and Richard (1981) and tested by them in their 1983 article. Despite the many requirements on the theory (no uncertainty, linear tax system, all government expenditures are lump-sum transfers, the voter also takes account of effects of taxes on other peoples' incentive to work and consume, etc.) it receives but a qualified support from the data. Tullock (1983) also criticises the testing procedure from both methodological and data points of view.

Sixth explanation: redistribution to strong interest groups

While the former argument concerning income redistribution concerned income classes (and particularly redistributions to the median voter), the present argument concerns redistribution to organised groups in society. This is one of the oldest arguments in the public-choice tradition, advanced *inter alia* in Buchanan and Tullock (1962). The point is that each interest organisation – be it Houseowners' Association, Tenants' Union, Car Owners' Club, Goldfishpond Operators' Organisation, as well as traditional labour unions and employer federations – can articulate the demands for lower taxes and higher subsidies for a minority in society. To satisfy this particular group costs relatively little in increased taxes, which are spread amongst everybody, but can yield a high profit at the polls from the particular group satisfied. But adding all groups together will amount to a great deal of new expenditures.

The theory should be tested on, for example, such variables as membership in unions, number of interest organisations, per cent of population involved in at least one interest organisation, etc. To date only very few such tests have been carried out. Schmidt (1982) finds for instance in his cross-section study that union membership is barely significant as a contribution to the level of taxes (a partial correlation coefficient *à la* Spearman of 0.38 as compared to the critical level of 0.37 at 5 per cent significance). Sørensen (1984) however finds the number of interest organisations highly correlated with the growth of the public expenditure share; indeed apart from urbanisation, it is the only significant explanatory variable in Norway.

The theory also appears in some other guises. As noted earlier in

Chapter 3, the fastest growth rate of public expenditures has taken place in the small open economies of Europe: Sweden, The Netherlands, Belgium, Denmark to mention the leaders. There appears to be no intuitive explanation for this fact. Cameron (1978), who is usually credited for the observation on the importance of the open economy, refers to the argument that expenditures may be increased to counter the effects on production and unemployment which in a small open economy are largely set by foreign demand. A side argument is that a high dependency on trade may foster a climate in which strong unions can thrive, in turn having a decisive influence on government.

It is difficult how this theory is to be tested, independently of the former argument on interest groups. Several investigators have confirmed that the degree of openness is indeed important, for example, Schmidt (1982), who finds a Pearson partial correlation coefficient of 0.57 for this argument. Sørensen (1984) however rejects the theory for Norway as do Lowery and Berry (1983) for the United States. Hence the negative time series findings will have to be confronted with the positive cross-section findings and, in any case, there is still basically a finding in search of a theory to explain it.

A third variant of the redistributive argument has been put forward by Pelzman (1980), who claims that it alone explains all of the growth of US spending in the last 50 years! He builds on differences among classes as the main source of redistribution. But the theory in turn requires that there exist political parties that are built up on these class cleavages to carry out the redistributions. Again, the theory is hard to test.[12] Just finding that the colour of the party in power affects the growth rate of government expenditures – something that is discussed later on the supply side – does not mean that Pelzman's theory has been proven correct.

Seventh explanation: 'fiscal illusion' and other information problems

Following the lead of Downs' *An Economic Theory of Democracy*, it has been proposed that the expansion of the public sector has resulted from misinformed consumers. Even if those demanding public goods and services attempt to calculate the tax price of these supplies, there are many reasons why they tend to underestimate the true tax burden (Goetz 1977, Wagner 1976). One reason is reliance on indirect taxes, where the tax is less visible than is the case for direct income taxes. Also presumed is that the number of items subjected to various excise and turnover taxes may contribute to the confusion. It has also been suggested that countries relying on PAYE systems of collection where taxes are withheld at source may more easily fool the taxpayers.

In systems where no indexing of income-tax brackets occurs, a higher rate of inflation will automatically increase the tax bite out of a constant real income without any discussion in Parliament ('bracket creep' or 'fiscal drag'). A third possibility for the government to hide the true cost of government services is of course to underbalance the budget.[13, 14]

There is little to confirm any of these hypotheses. Lowery and Berry (1983) find none of their attempted variables of right sign significant. Cameron's (1978) cross-country study did get a positive but insignificant coefficient for the argument 'reliance on indirect and social-security taxes'. Finally, Sørensen (1984) found that the increase in the public sector was significantly related to the price *level* (*sic*!), hardly unexpected, since both have a positive trend.

Supply factors

Eighth explanation: 'Baumol's disease'

In 1967 Baumol advanced a two-sector model of wage and price determination which is basically identical to the simultaneously and independently developed 'Scandinavian' model of inflation. The basic proposition is that wages are formed in that part of the economy where productivity growth is fastest, e.g. manufacturing industry. Productivity rises faster in this sector, since it is less labour intensive than the rest of the economy. In the other sectors, in particular the service industries, productivity growth is slower but the wage rate of growth the same, implying a shift in relative prices to the disadvantage of the service industries over time.[15]

Some studies have attempted to measure the implications of Baumol's disease by testing the relative productivity gain in the public sector compared to the other sectors of society (e.g. Pelzman 1980 and Spann 1977). But this is beside the point. What is relevant is that the public sector in the national accounts is given a certain productivity growth rate, usually zero or 1 per cent. This figure may be too high or it may be too low. But what it implies is that as measured in the national accounts, the public sector will come to increase in relative terms over time, even though the underlying volume rate of growth may be the same as in other sectors. And, after all, the data in the national accounts are what people use to study the growth of government!

What some people who attempt to 'test' the construction of the national accounts do not seem to realise is that this effect of relative-price change is mixed with the demand effect of the shift in relative prices to the detriment of public-sector goods and services. Hence, as described well in Borcherding (1984), the effect on the increase in the share of the public sector in total production (measured in terms of relative increases) of relative prices is one minus the elasticity of demand for public-sector goods. Hence, if one finds no significant effect of relative prices on the change in the share of the government sector, this does not mean that Baumol's disease does not exist, but that the price elasticity is so close to unity (in absolute value) that the two effects cancel out.

Ninth explanation: budget-maximising bureaucrats

Another of the traditional public-choice arguments for the expanding public sector is that of the self-aggrandising bureaucrat. The argument, whose main proponent is Niskanen (e.g. 1971) is two-pronged. Firstly, public administrators maximise utility functions of their own instead of passively following directives from above. In this utility may be included the status and higher pay associated with more subordinates, as well as the desire to do a good job. Since administrations are not subjected to profit maximisation, they will instead drive employment and production to the point where revenues and costs coincide, which is far to the right of the optimal quantity under profit maximisation (something that Buchanan and Tullock 1977, refer to as 'Wagner squared').

The second part of the argument, which is also necessary if the theory is to be correct, is that bureaucrats possess the power to set their own production levels. In the usual situation where administrators are the ones to have the knowledge advantage over their overseeing parliamentary committee, one may presume that the bureaucrats may dominate the outcome.[16] A special aspect of this theory put forward *inter alia* by Kau and Rubin (1981) is that the size of government revenues depend on the restructuring of society (increased urbanisation etc.). Then the theories of the maximising bureaucrat are used to explain why the largest possible amount of government revenue is always spent.

The theory may be correct and important, but it is essentially untestable, at least in macro terms. Again the construction of the national accounts is the culprit. Since the output of public authorities is not sold on a market for market-determined prices, the value of the output cannot be distinguished from the value of the inputs. Hence the increase in real terms of the public-sector share is basically identical to the increase in the relative employment of the sector. When regressing the change in the public-sector share of production on the change in public employment, one basically has the same variable on both sides. It is thus hardly surprising that Cameron (1984) found that public employment was a highly 'significant' determinant of the relative size of the public sector.

Tenth explanation: public employees as voters
A special variant of the bureaucrat theory focuses on the role of public employees as voters (Bush and Denzau 1977, and Frey and Pommerehne 1982). In a country like Sweden, where 40 per cent of total employment is in the public sector (including publicly-owned corporations), this factor may be quite important. It may be presumed that the attitude of public-sector employees towards growth of the sector is different from the rest of the population. Yet, it is not possible to measure this effect at the macro level, but one must make do with survey data expressing the preferences of various groups in society. Since preferences cannot meaningfully be aggregated, it is not possible to draw any macro conclusions from these, however.

Eleventh explanation: counter-cyclical policy
Some studies such as Cameron (1984) include a target of cyclical policy, e.g. unemployment, in the functions. Since unemployment does not rise trendwise it is difficult to see what it has to do in a long-run study. But even so, it cannot just be thrown in, since it is influenced by public expenditures as well as being an influent factor. Simultaneity bias again!

Twelfth explanation: socialist control of government
Another factor which has been treated extensively in the literature on politico–economic cycles is the possibility that governments of a socialist persuasion tend to increase taxes and public expenditures at a faster rate than bourgeois governments. It is not entirely clear why this would necessarily be the case; one possible answer is of course the greater income redistributions that a socialist government may feel are both possible and necessary. Van Arnhem and Schotsman (1982) find for instance that both the variables – strength of labour unions and strength of leftist parties – are accompanied in a cross-country study by less income inequality.

As pointed out well by Castles (1982) there are several problems connected with linking public-sector growth and colour of party in power. One is that different results may be obtained depending on how left-right in the party structure is defined.[17] A second is that the attitude towards public expenditures by different parties may depend on what kind of expenditure is involved. Thus parties of the right may be favourable to an increase in expenditures on defence or education, while parties of the left may favour expenditures for medical care or social transfers. The correlograms given in Castles (1982) provide some support for this view.

Hence it is not surprising that there is no clear evidence in favour of the hypothesis that socialist parties tend to increase public expenditures more than bourgeois do. Schmidt (1982) rejects the relationship (measured by socialist seats in Parliaments), while Cameron (1978) gives it a barely significant effect. As concerns individual countries, it is rejected for Norway in Sørensen (1984) but supported in the cross-section study of Swedish local authorities by Murray (1981).

Thirteenth explanation: centralisation of power

There exists but one additional cause for the growth of government, which should perhaps have been referred to an institutional aspect rather than to the supply side. It concerns the power of the ruling party *vis-à-vis* other bodies in government/Parliament or in relation to regional authorities.

The first question then is whether a coalition government will have a greater tendency to increase expenditures than will a one-party government. Some evidence would suggest that this is indeed the case. The small open economies which have increased government expenditures the fastest are traditionally ruled by broad coalitions: The Netherlands, Belgium, Italy. Finnish political scientists claim that expenditures have been increased when broad coalitions have ruled. In Sweden, there is no doubt that the explosion of public expenditures occurred under the 'lottery Parliament' of 1973–76 (when the two blocs held equal number of seats in Parliament) and under the ensuing weak bourgeois coalitions. But on the other hand there is the case of Switzerland, where the public sector is small and has grown at a slow rate, while there is a permanent coalition government.

This theory has yet to be tested. The only evidence I know of is Schmidt (1982), who finds that cohesion of the bourgeois parties may have contributed to less increase, while no similar effect occurred for cohesion among leftist parties.

The other part of the theory has to do with the power of the central government and of states/local authorities, respectively. The idea is that a strong central government may have greater ease to agree and to squeeze more taxes out of the citizens. A strongly decentralised system of government – like the Swiss one – would be consistent with relatively lower expenditures and taxes.

As for the United States, there appears to be something to say for the theory. Both Cameron (1984) and Lowery and Berry (1983) find that a greater share for the federal government increases expenditures. On the other hand, there is the risk that what they capture is really only the effect of war, when total expenditures and federal expenditures rise hand in hand. This risk is particularly evident in Lowery and Berry who insist on 'testing' one factor at a time. It is also unclear whether Cameron (1984) with the variables/war deaths in first two years/ demobilisation captures all the spending increase. Be this as it may, there is however no tendency in the cross-country study of Cameron (1978) to yield higher taxes and expenditures in more federalised states.

Testing the theories together

It can of course always be debated what is a sensible way to test a theory. As I have tried to indicate in the discussion above, I feel that some of the tests performed have been terribly naïve, such as when one regresses the growth of government expenditures on the growth of public employees. But there is a far more fundamental objection that can be made. As is well known from any elementary course in econometrics, the estimated coefficients are biased unless all relevant variables have been included in the regression equation.

This means that in testing the 13 different explanations of government-sector growth individually, it would have to be believed that they are mutually exclusive explanations for the growth of the public sector. Now this is clearly not the case; it is theoretically fully possible for all the stated explanations to be true at the same time. Whether they are is an empirical question.

It can therefore unequivocally be stated that the 'tests' performed *inter alia* by Cameron (1978), Lowery and Berry (1983), Schmidt (1982) and Sørensen (1984) cannot be taken as more than weak indications of what the evidence is. Certainly the use of t-ratios is erroneous, when one knows the estimating equation to be mis-specified.

Again, Lowery and Berry (1983) have placed the emphasis where it belongs, though without coming up with an answer. They write: 'It is tempting to complete this paper by calling for a simple combination of the separate models. Unfortunately, it is not at all clear how they should be combined. Therefore, we have resisted attempting to integrate the models by simply taking the variables from each that "work" and combining them. While such an "integrated model" would no doubt receive some empirical support, it would hardly be conceptually satisfying inasmuch as simply adding them together at this point would be an entirely *ad hoc* exercise'.

They are, of course, entirely right. One simply cannot and should not simply add factors that come from the demand side and the supply side, respectively. Yet this is exactly what people like Cameron (1978, 1984) have done! Cameron (1978), for instance, relates the increase in government revenue's share of GDP between 1960 to 1975 to the following factors: the dependent variable in 1960, increase in real GDP (Wagner's law), per cent of revenues obtained from indirect taxation and social security fees (fiscal illusion), per cent of electoral base composed of Labour parties (supply factor), per cent of revenues obtained at the federal level (supply factor or institutional factor), and the degree of openness of the economy (representing the demand factor interest groups in society). What on earth is a mongrel like that supposed to mean?

There are two ways to proceed. One is to assume that demand adjusts completely and fully to supply or vice versa. Thus the demand studies by *inter alia* Borcherding and Deacon (1972), Bergström and Goodman (1973) and Deacon (1978) are consistent, since they analyse demand factors under the assumption that the supply of government goods and services is passive. Similarly, the studies on local-authority behaviour by Murray (1981) and Ysander (1979) are consistent since they assume that the municipalities can get the public to accept what they care to supply.

The other solution is to propose a consistent model that integrates both the supply side and the demand side. This is the purpose of the next section.

The model

There are at least three separate issues that have been mishandled in most earlier studies. One is the derivation of functions. In very few studies is there a clear link between a theory and the tested form. A second is the definition of variables. A third is the aggregation of the separate variables.

This chapter makes no pretension to being a contribution in any of the first two aspects. However, it hopes to show the importance of testing theories in a combined fashion and showing one conceivable way to do it.

The demand side

One of the few studies to provide a clear theory is Borcherding and Deacon (1972). They show that the rate of growth of the share of publicly-supplied services in income is related to the rates of growth of prices, income, population and the ratio of mean to median income. The theory however has several drawbacks. For instance, how does one account for the role of separate interest groups in aggregate demand? Is the effect of interest groups direct on demand for publicly-supplied services or do the organisations work through 'normal' private demand? Is it possible at all to aggregate demand for separate categories of government goods and services, not to mention many kinds of transfers? Are Borcherding and Deacon's individuals fully informed and, if not, how is lack of information about true prices incorporated into the theory?

Rather than attempting to derive an explicit theory but one that cannot be aggregated over individuals and categories, I will simply postulate that the demand side can be written as follows. Table 5.3 shows what the variables are and how they are to be defined.

$$\frac{G}{Y} = f\,(\overset{+}{\text{IND}},\ \overset{+}{\text{URBAN}},\ \overset{-}{\text{DPOP}},\ \overset{?}{\text{Y}},\ \overset{+}{\text{DUMWAR}},\ \overset{+}{\text{PC/PGDP}},$$

$$\overset{-}{\text{YMED/YBAR}},\ \overset{+}{\text{XM}},\ \overset{+}{\text{ORG}},\ \overset{+}{\text{NOORG}},\ \overset{+}{\text{INFL}},\ \overset{+}{\text{NOTAX}},$$

$$\overset{-}{\text{DIRTAX}},\ \overset{-}{\text{DEFICIT}})$$

where we have definite ideas on how most of the terms will influence the development in the share of GDP devoted to government, G/Y. These signs should be obvious from the earlier discussion, perhaps with the exception of the income-redistribution term, YMED/YBAR. The idea behind this argument is that the smaller the ratio of the median income to the mean income, the more unequal is the distribution of income and the more scope is there to gain votes by a redistribution towards the median voter and income-earner.

For the variables DPOP, Y, PC/PGDP, YMED/YBAR we also have definite ideas as to magnitudes. These can be used when estimated to get at the underlying parameters.

The supply side

The first step in estimating the supply side is to get an instrument for the simultaneous variables that relate government expenditures to public employment and to unemployment. As regressors in this first stage are used all explanatory variables on the demand and the supply side.

The theoretical derivation of the supply-side determinants is even less satisfactory than the corresponding demand-side equation. One reason is that the supply side really involves three sets of agents: parliamentarians, government officials and administrators. The division could go on, if we also want to include separate utility functions of the state-level officials and administrators and their counterparts in all the municipalities.

Instead of repeating arguments that in politico–economic models constitute the reaction function of the government, let it suffice here to state the arguments of the supply function:

$$\frac{G}{Y} = g\,(\overset{+}{\text{PC/PGDP}},\ \overset{+}{\widehat{\text{PUBP}}},\ \overset{+}{\widehat{\text{UNEMPL}}},\ \overset{+}{\text{DUMSOC}},\ \overset{?}{\text{DUMCOAL}},$$

$$\overset{?}{\text{DUMFED}},\ \overset{?}{\text{STAX}})$$

Table 5.3 Dependent and independent variables in explaining government growth

Dependent variables	
G+TR/Y	Share in GDP of total government expenditures including transfers
G/Y	Share in GDP of government expenditures excluding transfers
TAX/Y	Share in GDP of total tax revenues
Independent variables	
First explanation: industrial and demographic change	
IND	Share of total employment in manufacturing
URBAN	Share of total population in urban areas
DPOP	Total population, percentage change
Second explanation: high income elasticity of demand	
Y	Real per capita disposable income, percentage change
Third explanation: war-related displacement effects	
DUMWAR	Dummy variable taking on the value of 0.5 or 1 depending on intensity of war
Fourth explanation: price-elastic demand	
PC/PGDP	Ratio of the price on government expenditures to the GDP deflator
Fifth explanation: demand for income redistribution	
YMED/YBAR	Ratio of median to mean income
Sixth explanation: redistribution to strong interest groups	
XM	Ratio of the sum of exports and imports to GDP
ORG	Share of the labour force belonging to a union
NOORG	Number of interest organisations in society (proxied for by their share of employment)
Seventh explanation: fiscal illusion and other information problems	
INFL	Percentage change in consumer prices
NOTAX	Number of taxes, percentage change
DIRTAX	Share of total taxes collected by direct taxation
DEFICIT	Share in GDP of total government budget deficit
Eighth explanation: Baumol's disease	
PC/PGDP	Ratio of the price on government expenditures to the GDP deflator
Ninth explanation: budget-maximising bureaucrats	
PUBP	Share of government employees in total employment
NB: This relationship must be estimated by a consistent estimator, e.g. TSLS	
Tenth explanation: public employees as voters	
This relationship cannot be estimated independently from the previous one, since adding it would lead to almost perfect multi-collinearity.	
Eleventh explanation: counter-cyclical policy	
UNEMPL	Share of labour force unemployed
NB: This relationship must be estimated by a consistent estimator, e.g. TSLS	
Twelfth explanation: socialist control of government	
DUMSOC	Dummy variable taking the value 1 if prime minister is a social-democrat, labourite or equivalent
Thirteenth explanation: centralisation of power	
DUMCOAL	Dummy variable taking the value 1 if government is a coalition and 2 if it is a coalition across blocs, 0 elsewhere
DUMFED	Dummy variable taking the value 1 in the cross-country study if the country is a federal state
STAX	Percentage change in the share of total taxes collected by the federal level or state level for non-federal states

where $\wedge$ indicates an instrument and where the believed signs have been indicated. With regard to magnitudes, it is believed that the elasticity of the relative price term should be unity.

Putting the model together

So far the model has been very conventional; not one of the arguments is new in itself. The novelty lies in testing the theories of demand and supply together in a coherent model.

Two lines of research will now be pursued. Firstly, it is not assumed here as with previous authors that demand adjusts to supply or vice versa. Instead, initially the complete models of the demand and the supply side will be estimated. This procedure will facilitate a discarding of erroneously included arguments. It can also be used to see which side fits the data best. This approach will be used first for Sweden, then for a sample of other OECD countries and finally on a pooled data set of all the included countries together.

Secondly, however, a new disequilibrium approach to the growth of government will be tried. In ordinary models of supply and demand, the price level will adjust to equilibrate the two. But even though the relative price of government expenditures appears in both the demand and the supply equation in the model posited here, there is no belief that the relative price will move in such a way as to make demand equal to supply. The actual price faced by consumers is either zero or very low; it bears little relation to the national-accounts price which consists of the production cost of government goods and services.

Instead, it is assumed that when the demand side exceeds the supply side, demand rules. Politicians and bureaucrats will adapt to a surge in demand, irrespective of the consequences for the government deficit. Similarly, when the supply side exceeds the demand side, supply determines the actual quantity. Since the politicians are the actual decision-makers, this assumption should be easier to swallow. Note that this assumption goes contrary to the standard argument in economics that the short side always rules. In mathematical terms the model stated is then

$$G/Y = MAX\ (DEMAND,\ SUPPLY)$$

In each period the model is told to search for the part of the model demand or supply – that leads to the largest increase in the public sector. How this is accomplished in practice will be discussed in the next section.

Results of estimation: Sweden

In this section the Swedish model will be estimated for the period 1950–82, with a minimum of 19 degrees of freedom. The interaction between supply and demand will be concentrated on for total government expenditures. In the next section estimates for Sweden and other countries for all the three definitions of the size of the public sector will be discussed.

The demand side for total government expenditures including transfers 1950–82 gives the following result in OLS estimation (with t-ratios in brackets):

$$
\begin{aligned}
G+TR/Y = \; & \underset{(1.11)}{15.1} \; \underset{(-3.04)}{- 0.82} \; IND \; \underset{(0.42)}{+ 0.07} \; URBAN \; \underset{(0.09)}{+ 0.08} \; DPOP \\
& \underset{(-2.36)}{- 0.21} \; Y \; \underset{(5.22)}{+ 26.4} \; PCPGDP \; \underset{(-0.13)}{- 1.44} \; YMED/YBAR \; \underset{(0.61)}{+ 0.03} \; XM \\
& \underset{(0.78)}{+ 0.12} \; ORG \; \underset{(2.35)}{+ 2.54} \; NOORG \; \underset{(-0.08)}{- 0.01} \; INFL \; \underset{(-0.74)}{- 0.02} \; NOTAX \\
& \underset{(-1.01)}{- 0.09} \; DIRTAX \; \underset{(-1.61)}{- 0.22} \; DEFICIT
\end{aligned}
$$

Coefficient of determination: 0.9986
F-ratio: 1019
Mean squared error: 0.44
Durbin–Watson d statistic: 2.29

The total explanatory power of the equation is quite impressive and there is little indication of autocorrelation of residuals. However, there are only two variables that are significant and of correct sign, namely the relative price ratio and the number of employees in interest organisations. The elasticity of demand that is implied in the coefficient of the relative price term is very small, not significantly different from zero.

The supply model for total Swedish government expenditures including transfers 1950–82 gives the following results (TSLS estimation):

$$
\begin{aligned}
G+TR/Y = \; & \underset{(0.46)}{8.30} \; \underset{(1.94)}{+ 18.74} \; PCPGDP \; \underset{(3.38)}{+ 1.05} \; PUBP \; \underset{(0.35)}{+ 0.32} \; UNEMPL \\
& \underset{(-1.68)}{- 2.56} \; DUMSOC \; \underset{(-2.24)}{- 1.55} \; DUMCOAL \; \underset{(-1.08)}{- 0.15} \; STAX
\end{aligned}
$$

Coefficient of determination: 0.983
F-ratio: 248
Mean squared error: 3.84
Durbin–Watson d statistic: 0.53

The supply model fits the data much worse. Not only are the summary statistics worse but there is also indication of severe autocorrelation of residuals leading to overstated t-ratios.

As for individual coefficients, the relative price term is important. But the share of public employees is even more important and has an effect that is independent of the pure definitional effect of the cost term. The coalition argument is seen to hold down expenditures in this version in contrast to the short-run model of the previous chapter. The two models agree however that unemployment and the colour of the government are not important determinants of government expenditures.

In the equation for expenditures proper however, unemployment received the expected positive and significant coefficient.

The procedure is now to eliminate the uninteresting variables. Those that remain are then used to estimate a demand and a supply side for each period. The model then takes that data point that is indicated by the model, that is demand is estimated in the next step only on those observations that have been indicated to belong to the demand-determined regime and similarly for supply. With the data points belonging to the demand and the supply regime given exogenously from the previous step, summary statistics for the total model can now be calculated. For step 2 the model gives the following results:

$$G{+}TR/Y = \underset{(-1.25)}{-32.3} - \underset{(-0.37)}{0.07}\,Y + \underset{(7.69)}{32.7}\,PCPGDP + \underset{(0.72)}{22.7}\,YMED/YBAR$$

$$+ \underset{(4.11)}{4.14}\,NOORG \text{ (demand side)}$$

$$\underset{(-3.83)}{-21.8} + \underset{(5.28)}{44.2}\,PCPGDP + \underset{(0.32)}{0.11}\,PUBP - \underset{(-0.34)}{0.28}\,UNEMPL$$

$$+ \underset{(0.33)}{0.17}\,DUMCOAL \text{ (supply side)}$$

Coefficient of determination: 0.995
Mean squared error: 1.28

The model indicates the following division of data points into regimes (by the principle of maximum share of the government sector):

1950	S
1951	S
1952	S
1953	S
1954	D
1955	S
1956	D
1957	D
1958	D
1959	D
1960	D
1961	D
1962	D
1963	D
1964	D
1965	D
1966	D
1967	D
1968	S
1969	D
1970	D
1971	D
1972	D
1973	D
1974	D
1975	D
1976	D
1977	D
1978	D
1979	D
1980	D
1981	D
1982	D

The model then takes this new distribution into demand and supply regimes and re-estimates the parameters, which gives rise to a new regime division again. Successively the model converges.

After around five iterations the model parameters and regime division settle down. What is interesting is that the final important variables on the demand side include not only the relative price term but also real disposable income (with a strongly significant negative coefficient) and the number of employees in interest organisations. On the supply side only the relative price term remains.

As for regimes, some of the Ds above turn into Ss. But in all iterations the years from 1975, that is the years of extreme growth in the size of the public sector, are placed in the demand regime! The remaining periods of supply determination are also quite weak to the extent that predictions from the supply and the demand side are very close.

Hence there are several indications that much if not all of the growth of the Swedish public sector has actually been demanded, namely:

1 the better performance of the demand equation than the supply equation;
2 evidence that the pure supply equation is misspecified, whereas the pure demand equation is correctly specified;
3 evidence from the disequilibrium formulation that the demand side dominates most of the years when the growth of the public sector has been at its strongest.

The following are the final parameters from iteration no. 7:

$$G+TR/Y = \underset{(-1.08)}{-6.30} - \underset{(-3.80)}{0.68}\,Y + \underset{(12.4)}{30.7}\,PCPGDP - \underset{(-0.57)}{4.9}\,YMED/YBAR$$

$$+ \underset{(11.2)}{4.7}\,NOORG \quad (R^2 \text{ for the demand part } 0.999)$$

$$\underset{(-5.21)}{-19.3} + \underset{(9.31)}{47.2}\,PCPGDP - \underset{(-0.79)}{0.17}\,PUBP - \underset{(-1.14)}{0.90}\,UNEMPL$$

$$\underset{(-1.08)}{-0.48}\,DUMCOAL \quad (R^2 \text{ for the supply part } 0.991)$$

The brunt of my argument above has concerned the need to take an integrated view of demand for and supply of the public sector. Of that I hope the reader has become convinced. However, while I personally would regard the MAX criterion as more convincing than a MIN argument, the main thing to keep in mind is that there must be a disequilibrium framework.

Hence to satisfy the unconvinced reader I have also re-estimated the equations following instead a MIN criterion, where the observations are allocated to regime according to which provides for the lowest share of the public sector in that period, i.e. fitting:

$$G/Y = MIN\,(DEMAND, SUPPLY)$$

This rule gives the following result for total public expenditures in iteration no. 7, i.e. fully comparable to the results above:

$$G{+}TR/Y = \underset{(1.18)}{13.3} - \underset{(-1.36)}{0.20}\, Y + \underset{(8.18)}{39.6}\, PCPGDP - \underset{(-2.95)}{38.9}\, YMED/YBAR$$

$$+ \underset{(2.31)}{4.15}\, NOORG \quad (R^2 \text{ for the demand part } 0.997)$$

$$- \underset{(-2.54)}{11.9} + \underset{(3.67)}{22.5}\, PCPGDP + \underset{(5.35)}{0.96}\, PUBP + \underset{(1.21)}{0.65}\, UNEMPL$$

$$- \underset{(-4.26)}{1.55}\, DUMCOAL \quad (R^2 \text{ for the supply part } 0.995)$$

On the whole the results show the same picture. Most observations after 1969 are still allocated to the demand regime; only the very last years change from being demand to being supply-determined. The coefficients also appear to be better determined. In particular it can be noted that the ratio of median to mean income on the demand side is now highly significant. Similarly, on the supply side, both the share of public employees and the coalition dummy now becomes significant.

On the negative side however, the MIN criterion appears to lead to a higher serial correlation, indicative of mis-specification. The estimated serial correlation coefficient rises from zero to 0.4 on the supply side when switching from MAX to MIN and from -0.40 to -0.75 on the demand side. The t-ratios shown are still valid since correction has been performed, but nevertheless such high levels of serial correlation are worrying, leading to the suspicion that maybe the MAX formulation is better.

Results of estimation: a cross-country study

For 12 OECD countries most of the required data for the period 1960–82 were easily available. I had to abandon real disposable income, the ratio of median to mean income, number of taxes and number of interest organisations. Detailed results are found in the Appendix. Note that the demand part was estimated by OLS, the supply part by TSLS throughout.

United States

The demand models work badly with no significant coefficient of right sign. While the supply models have lower degrees of explanatory power, they are much more attractive in that several coefficients are significant and rightly signed.

If the total expenditure definition is focused on, it is also found that most of the observations are dominated by supply. In particular, the whole period from the Nixon re-election in 1972 through Ford and Carter is placed in the situation that the public sector expanded more than the public wanted.

Canada

The results for Canada also point clearly in the direction of supply domination. For total expenditures none of the demand coefficients are correct and significant, for the other definitions the urbanisation variable comes through but nothing else. The supply model works well, on the other hand. For total expenditures all coefficients are highly significant. The Durbin–Watson statistic is always very close to 2, giving no inkling of mis-specification.

Australia

Perhaps surprising for a region of recent settlement, the Wagner variables do not work for Australia either. Only the degree of labour unionisation works for the broadest concept of expenditures. As for the supply model all coefficients are correctly signed and mostly significant. In terms of summary statistics it is difficult to make any clear-cut discrimination.

United Kingdom

The different expenditure categories give rather different results for the UK. For total expenditures, including transfers, there is some indication that the supply model is better, since not only the relative-price variable but also the dummies for Labour and for coalitions come through. For expenditures proper however the demand model is superior with several significant coefficients (URBAN, PCPGDP, INFL) and the summary statistics are much better. The same holds true for the definition with taxes as the dependent variable.

Germany

For Germany it may perhaps be said that the supply model receives somewhat more support than the demand model, though inferior in terms of the summary statistics. Public employment is seen as a clear determinant of expenditures inclusive of transfers. It can also be noted that the existence of coalitions has held down expenditures on all three categories. On the demand side the degree of organisation has some effect.

France

None of the models receives particularly clear support. As for the demand model nothing works. On the supply side it may be noted that the unemployment variable is always important, indicative of an active stabilisation policy absent in the countries studied so far.

Italy

On the demand side no variable works with the exception of the unionisation variable for the broadest definition of expenditures. The supply side is better though not impressive. Apart from the relative-price term, both the unemployment measure and the share of state taxes appear to determine the share of the public sector. The low Durbin–Watson statistic warrants caution however.

The Netherlands

No interesting conclusions can be gained from these estimations. The only variable to carry any weight is relative prices. The unemployment variable also turns out to be important for transfers. An indication of the Dutch welfare system? In terms of overall fit, the demand side is as always somewhat superior.

Belgium

The Belgian model contains several interesting features both on the demand and the supply side. As for demand, the urbanisation variable comes through as does population on two of the three definitions. The money-illusion variable inflation is also significant. On the supply side public employment is highly significant. The Durbin–Watson statistic is however a warning regarding total expenditures for the supply side.

Austria

The most noticeable feature for Austria is the extremely close fit, especially for expenditures proper. On the demand side this is related to the significance of the urbanisation variable as well as population. On the supply side, the best explanatory power is for total expenditures where relative prices and the socialist dummy are important. Unemployment also increases expenditures proper.

Norway

An odd feature with the Norwegian estimates is that expenditures proper are estimated with a very good fit, while the other two categories – total expenditures and taxes – perform much worse. For G, both the demand and the supply model also have acceptable Durbin–Watson ratios, while the other models, and in particular the supply models, fare much worse.

For individual coefficients, it is found, as by Sørensen (1984), that urbanisation is indeed an important variable for Norway. Money illusion and relative prices are also significant on the demand side. The supply equations are carried not only by relative prices and the number of employees in the public sector but also by the dummies for socialist and coalition government, both of which are seen to hold down expenditures proper.

Sweden

The results for Sweden confirm those obtained earlier in this chapter for data for the period 1950–82 as well as the short-term results in the previous chapter. Relative prices is always important. On the demand side, the degree of labour organisation also turns out to be significant. On the supply side, public employment has an influence quite separate from that of relative prices. Short-term variables such as unemployment or the colour of the government have no effect.

For the expenditure categories the demand side is estimated with much more precision than the supply side. The supply side is beset by autocorrelation problems. Thus as earlier it appears that most of the growth of the Swedish public sector is indeed to be referred to demand.

Summary and conclusions

Several hypotheses have been summarised and tested in this chapter. One way of reviewing the results is to study how many of the individual coefficients were found to be significant and of correct sign. This is shown in Table 5.4.

Most of the theories receive at least partial support. However, taking into account that the theory has been tested for 12 countries and for three different definitions, there is a maximum of 36 agreements. The maximum in Table 5.4 is 21.

Of the 'Wagner variables' both the degree of urbanisation and the level of population receive some support from the data. The relative price variable is not surprisingly the most important one. However, money and tax illusion as indicated by the variables INFL and DEFICIT are also in evidence. The degree of labour unionisation has also some role to play. The share of direct taxes has not.

Table 5.4 Number of significant coefficients

Variable name	Hypothesised sign	Number of significant coefficients
Demand side		
IND	+	0
URBAN	+	11
DPOP	-	9
PCPGDP	+	16
XM	+	1
ORG	+	6
INFL	+	4
DIRTAX	-	0
DEFICIT	-	16
Supply side		
PCPGDP	+	21
PUBP	+	18
UNEMPL	+	11
DUMSOC	+	1
DUMCOAL	?	3
DUMFED[a]	?	
STAX	?	15

Notes:

[a] Used only for pooled data.

On the supply side, the two political variables DUMCOAL and DUMSOC are the ones to carry least weight. The relative price term is ubiquitous, but note also the frequent and independent role of the number of government employees as indicated by PUBP. The need to combat unemployment also appears more important in many countries than in Sweden, rather surprisingly.

With regard to the relative predictive power of the demand-related and the supply-related theories, there are two countries – Sweden and the United Kingdom – where the demand model clearly dominates. In the United States, Canada and France, on the other hand, the supply model is clearly better. For the other seven countries it is difficult to make any clear-cut decisions.

However, there is obviously a much stricter test available, namely to pool the data from all the 12 countries and estimate a joint equation. The variables URBAN and STAX were not available for all countries and were dropped. Tests on ten countries indicated that they were insignificant anyway. The remaining variables estimated on 12 countries for 23 years gives us no less than 244 degrees of freedom on the demand side and 246 on the supply side!

Three further technical notes. Firstly, on the supply side the estimation technique is Two-Stage Least Squares as for individual countries. Secondly, the model is estimated with separate intercepts for each country. It turned out that the estimated coefficients were rather unaffected by the separation of intercepts or the use of a common intercept, but the coefficient of determination and the Durbin–Watson statistic were much worse with a common intercept. Thirdly, there was a quite severe autocorrelation even with separate intercepts. This was counteracted by correction by the Cochrane–Orcutt procedure with separate autocorrelation coefficients being estimated for each country.

Tables 5.5–5.8 give the final pooled results for the two expenditure variables. If total government expenditures inclusive of transfers are studied first, it is found that the degree of explanatory power is somewhat higher for the supply model than the demand model. On the demand side the major variables are relative prices and the deficit. Population gives some further help in explanation. No other variable is significant, not even the degree of unionisation ORG which was important in many of the country estimates.

On the supply side, relative prices is also the main variable. Public employment is not significant here. Unemployment comes through very strongly, which is remarkable since its role in the country studies was much more limited. Finally, federal states are found to have a lower level of expenditures, *ceteris paribus*.

Similar conclusions can be drawn for expenditures proper. Here however ORG (i.e. unionisation) is also significant on the demand side. On the supply side, there is a clear tendency for socialist countries to have lower expenditures rather than higher. Federal states are found to have higher expenditures rather than lower.

All in all, it may be stated that with the exception of the role played by relative prices, both as in 'Baumol's disease' and as a price *per se*, there are very few variables that are always significant. It does indeed appear that there is a clear correlation between government expenditures and unemployment, but this does not necessarily signify that the politico–economic cycles are correct.

As for the role played by interest groups, it receives a qualified

Table 5.5 The growth of government, 1960–82

Country: Pooled data for 12 industrial countries

Definition of government: G+TR/Y

Explanatory variable	Coefficient	t-ratio
For demand model		
Intercept	varies between countries	
IND	–0.46	–8.53
URBAN	does not exist for all 12 countries	
DPOP	–0.84	–2.49
PCPGDP	17.84	10.56
XM	–0.04	–3.44
ORG	0.06	1.28
INFL	0.05	1.26
DIRTAX	0.33	5.93
DEFICIT	–0.61	–9.55
For supply model		
Intercept		
PCPGDP		
PUBP		
UNEMPL		
DUMSOC		
DUMCOAL		
DUMFED		
STAX		

Coefficient of determination: 0.965

F-ratio: 369.4

Mean squared error: 1.75

Durbin–Watson d statistic: 1.52

Estimated coefficient of serial correlation: varies between countries

Table 5.6 The growth of government, 1960–82

Country: Pooled data for 12 OECD countries

Definition of government: G+TR/Y

Explanatory variable	Coefficient	t-ratio
For demand model		
Intercept		
IND		
URBAN		
DPOP		
PCPGDP		
XM		
ORG		
INFL		
DIRTAX		
DEFICIT		
For supply model		
Intercept	varies between countries	
PCPGDP	28.18	20.85
PUBP	0.17	1.74
UNEMPL	1.18	10.94
DUMSOC	–0.29	–0.89
DUMCOAL	0.23	1.04
DUMFED	–12.65	–7.30
STAX	not available for all countries	

Coefficient of determination: 0.966

F-ratio: 429.4

Mean squared error: 1.94

Durbin–Watson d statistic: 1.60

Estimated coefficient of serial correlation: varies between countries

Table 5.7 The growth of government, 1960–82

Country: Pooled data for 12 industrial countries

Definition of government: G/Y

Explanatory variable	Coefficient	t-ratio
For demand model		
Intercept	varies between countries	
IND	–0.02	–1.12
URBAN	not available for all 12 countries	
DPOP	–0.29	–2.46
PCPGDP	8.29	12.54
XM	–0.01	–2.10
ORG	0.06	3.30
INFL	0.01	0.61
DIRTAX	0.08	4.44
DEFICIT	–0.17	–7.48
For supply model		
Intercept		
PCPGDP		
PUBP		
UNEMPL		
DUMSOC		
DUMCOAL		
DUMFED		
STAX		

Coefficient of determination: 0.980

F-ratio: 666.9

Mean squared error: 0.20

Durbin–Watson d statistic: 1.53

Estimated coefficient of serial correlation: varies between countries

Table 5.8 The growth of government, 1960–82

Country: Pooled data for 12 OECD countries

Definition of government: G/Y

Explanatory variable	Coefficient	t-ratio
For demand model		
Intercept		
IND		
URBAN		
DPOP		
PCPGDP		
XM		
ORG		
INFL		
DIRTAX		
DEFICIT		
For supply model		
Intercept	varies between countries	
PCPGDP	9.40	19.40
PUBP	0.04	1.36
UNEMPL	0.38	11.02
DUMSOC	–0.25	–2.21
DUMCOAL	0.07	0.95
DUMFED	3.29	7.17
STAX	not available for all 12 countries	

Coefficient of determination: 0.979

F-ratio: 717.3

Mean squared error: 0.23

Durbin–Watson d statistic: 1.62

Estimated coefficient of serial correlation: varies between countries

support from the data. As a demand component there is some evidence of a positive relationship between the degree of unionisation and government expenditures. On the supply side the share of public employment frequently exerts an influence separate from that of relative prices. The latter effect does not however carry over to the pooled data.

All in all, the explanatory power of the equations is rather high, considering the fact that only a few variables enter. In particular, I am surprised and pleased that it is possible to achieve a coefficient of determination of 0.96–0.98 on pooled data with some 250 degrees of freedom. One should however take note of the fact that serial correlation is a much more severe problem for the pooled data than it was found to be in any of the 12 component countries. This is a clear indication that the model may be correctly specified for each of the individual countries and yet the same model is not applicable to the aggregate of countries.

Apart from the obvious perfection of the component models, an important task for future research must be to study further the aggregation problems, if there is ever to be a 'world model' explaining government growth.

Notes

1 As mentioned, Larkey, Stolp and Winer (1981) is the most detailed. Other good surveys are Peacock (1979) and Pelzman (1980). Brief surveys are found in Borcherding (1977a, 1985), Buchanan (1977), Cameron (1978), Forsman (1977), Gustafsson (1977), Lowery and Berry (1983), Myhrman (1980), Sørensen (1984) and Tarschys (1977).

2 It should be noted that this table is not taken directly from Tarschys (1975) but is my interpretation of his arguments, subject to error and misinterpretations.

3 'Goods and services' must be interpreted to include also the supply of redistributive transfers, which in most countries grow the fastest of all components of public expenditures.

4 On the other hand, 'attitude' may be a better left-hand variable than public-sector growth itself, if we want to focus solely on factors on the demand side.

5 This point is further elaborated by Gustafsson (1977) and Myhrman (1980).

6 The latter finding does not however say anything about expenditures in relation to an aggregate measure of production or income.

7 Government expenditures depend on income (or GDP) but are also

a major component and determinant of GDP. Since the variability in the ratio of government expenditures to GDP is often caused by war-related expenditures raising GDP, care must be taken.

8 Note that this finding refers to developed countries only. No one denies that the effect may be larger if countries at substantially different levels of development are compared.

9 There is a third way not taken up here, because it deals with the demand for individual goods and services, namely to conduct experiments with individuals to establish their willingness to pay for public goods and services.

10 These stand in contrast to so-called Lindahl prices, where the individual is charged his marginal utility for the public good in question.

11 By compensated price elasticities is meant the pure substitution effect that is caused by a price change after the effect on income of the price change has been compensated for and taken away.

12 As pointed out by Lybeck (1985a) it is really quite impossible to test the old Lipset–Rokkan theory that the present party system is a function of cleavages existing at the time when the modern party systems were formed.

13 It is interesting to note that Downs is the father of the argument that the public sector is too large, because citizens are uninformed about the true cost of public goods. Simultaneously he is also father of the argument that the public sector is too small, since governments also suffer from lack of information and tend to underestimate the true needs and willingness to pay of the population. (See Downs 1960!)

14 Recent surveys of Swedish taxpayers, however, appear to show that they tend to overestimate the share of income paid in taxes in various brackets.

15 Further technical descriptions of this relative-price shift can be found in Höök (1962) and Tengblad (1977).

16 Findlay and Wilson (1984) in an interesting paper derive the implications for the excess size of government that follow from different assumptions concerning collusion between bureaucrats and Parliament.

17 This problem is treated further on p.101 as a classification in the cross-country study is attempted.

References

Baumol, W.J. (1967), 'Macroeconomics of Unbalanced Growth', *American Economic Review*, 57 (June).

Beck, M. (1981), *Government Spending* (New York: Praeger).
Bergström, T.C. and Goodman, R.P. (1973), 'Private Demands for Public Goods', *American Economic Review*, 63 (June).
Berry, W.O. and Lowery, D. (1984), 'The Growing Cost of Government: A Test of Two Explanations', *Social Science Quarterly*, 65 (September).
Bogdanor, V., ed. (1983), *Coalition Governments in Western Europe* (London: Heinemann).
Borcherding, T.E., ed. (1977), *Budgets and Bureaucrats: The Sources of Government Growth* (Durham: Duke University Press).
Borcherding, T.E. (1977a), 'One Hundred Years of Public Spending 1870–1970', in Borcherding, ed. (see above, Ch. 2).
Borcherding, T.E. (1977b), 'The Sources of Growth of Public Expenditures in the United States, 1902–70', in Borcherding, ed. (see above, Ch. 3).
Borcherding, T.E. (1985), 'The Causes of Government Expenditure Growth: A Survey of the US Experience', *Journal of Public Economics*, 28 (December).
Borcherding, T.E. and Deacon, R.T. (1972), 'The Demand for Services of Non-Federal Governments', *American Economic Review*, 62 (December).
Buchanan, J.M. (1977), 'Why Does Government Grow?' in Borcherding, ed. (see above, Ch. 1).
Buchanan, J.M. and Tullock, G. (1962), *The Calculus of Consent* (Ann Arbor: University of Michigan Press).
Buchanan, J.M. and Tullock, G. (1977), 'The Expanding Public Sector: Wagner Squared', *Public Choice*, 31 (Fall).
Bush, W.C. and Denzau, A. (1977), 'The Voting Behavior of Bureaucrats and Public Sector Growth', in Borcherding, ed. (see above, Ch. 5).
Cameron, D.R. (1978), 'The Expansion of the Public Economy: A Comparative Analysis', *American Political Science Review*, 72 (December).
Cameron, D.R. (1984), 'Impact of Political Institutions on Public Sector Expansion', paper presented at the Nobel Symposium on the growth of government, Stockholm.
Castles, F.G. (1982), 'The Impact of Parties on Public Expenditure', in his *The Impact of Parties* (Beverly Hills: Sage Publications).
Deacon, R. (1978), 'A Demand Model for the Local Public Sector', *Review of Economics and Statistics*, 60 (May).
Downs, A. (1957), *An Economic Theory of Democracy* (New York, Harper and Row).
Downs, A. (1960), 'Why the Government Budget is Too Small in a Democracy', *World Politics*, 12 (June).

Findlay, R. and Wilson, J.E. (1984), 'The Political Economy of Leviathan', Institute of International Economic Studies, Stockholm, Mimeo.
Forsman, A. (1977), 'Den offentliga sektorn i långsiktigt perspektiv: den internationella utvecklingen', in B. Gustafsson, ed., *Den offentliga sektorns expansion* (Uppsala: Almquist & Wiksell).
Frey, B.S. and Pommerehne, W.W. (1982), 'How Powerful are Public Bureaucrats as Voters?', *Public Choice*, 38 (no. 2).
Ganti, S. and Kolluri, B.R. (1979), 'Wagner's Law of Public Expenditures: Some Efficient Results for the United States', *Public Finance/Finance Publiques*, 34 (no. 2).
Gilljam, M. and Nilsson, L. (1984), 'Svenska folket och den offentliga sektorn', paper presented at the Swedish Political Science Association Annual Meeting, Umeå.
Goetz, C.J. (1977), 'Fiscal Illusion in State and Local Finance', in Borcherding, ed., (see above, Ch. 10).
Gustafsson, B. (1977), 'Inledning', in his *Den offentliga sektorns expansion* (Uppsala: Almquist & Wiksell).
Höök, E. (1962), *Den offentliga sektorns expansion* (Stockholm: Almquist & Wiksell).
Hotelling, H. (1929), 'Stability in Competition', *Economic Journal*, 34 (February).
Kau, J.B. and Rubin, P.H. (1981), 'The Size of Government', *Public Choice*, 37 (no. 2).
Larkey, P.D., Stolp, C. and Winer, M. (1981), 'Theorizing About the Growth of Government: A Research Assessment', *Journal of Public Policy*, 1 (May).
Lindbeck, A. (1984), 'Redistribution Policy and the Expansion of the Public Sector', *Journal of Public Economics*, 28 (December).
Lowery, D. and Berry, W.D. (1983), 'The Growth of Government in the United States: An Empirical Assessment of Competing Explanations', *American Journal of Political Science*, 27 (November).
Lybeck, J.A. (1985a), Is the Lipset–Rokkan Hypothesis Testable?', *Scandinavian Political Studies*, 20 (no. 1).
Lybeck, J.A. (1985b), 'A Simultaneous Model of Politico–Economic Interaction in Sweden 1970–82', *European Journal of Political Research*, 13 (no. 2) (Chapter 4 of this book).
Mackie, T.T. and Rose, R. (1982), *The International Almanac of Electoral History* (London: Macmillan).
Meltzer, A.H. and Richard, S.F. (1981), 'A Rational Theory of the Size of Government', *Journal of Political Economy*, 89 (October).
Meltzer, A.H. and Richard, S.F. (1983), 'Tests of a Rational Theory of

the Size of Government', *Public Choice*, 41 (no. 3).
Murray, R. (1981), *Kommunernas roll i den offentliga sektorn*, dissertation, University of Stockholm, Department of Economics.
Musgrave, R.A. (1985), 'Excess Bias and the Nature of Budget Growth', *Journal of Public Economics*, 28 (December).
Myhrman, J. (1980), 'Varför växer den offentliga sektorn så snabbt?', *Ekonomisk Debatt*, 8 (no. 5).
Niskanen, W.A. (1971), *Bureaucracy and Representative Government* (Chicago: Aldine).
Nutter, G.W. (1978), *Growth of Government in the West* (Washington, DC: American Enterprise Institute).
OECD (1983), 'Big Government – How Big is it?', *OECD Observer* (March).
Peacock, A.T. (1979), *The Economic Analysis of Government and Related Theories* (New York: St Martin's Press).
Peacock, A.T. and Wiseman, J. (1961), *The Growth of Public Expenditures in the United Kingdom*, NBER General Series no. 72 (Princeton: Princeton University Press).
Pelzman, S. (1980), 'The Growth of Government', *Journal of Law and Economics*, 23 (October).
Schmidt, M.G. (1982), *Wohlfaartsstaatliche Politik unter bürgerlichen und sozialdemokratischen Regierungen: ein internationaler Vergleich* (Frankfurt: Campus Verlag). A summary of the book is contained in F.G. Castles, ed. (1982), *The Impact of Parties* (Beverly Hills: Sage Publications).
Sørensen, R.J. (1984), 'Veksten i offentlige utgifter i Norge 1949–83: en empirisk prøvning av syv teorier', paper presented at the Meeting of the Nordic Political Science Association, Lund.
Spann, R.M. (1977), 'Rates of Productivity Change and the Growth of State and Local Governmental Expenditures', in Borcherding, ed., (see above, Ch. 6).
Tarschys, D. (1975), 'The Growth of Public Expenditures – Nine Modes of Explanation', *Scandinavian Political Studies*, 10 (no. 1).
Tarschys, D. (1977), 'Forskning om den offentliga sektorns expansion', in B. Gustafsson, ed., *Den offentliga sektorns expansion* (Uppsala: Almquist & Wiksell).
Tengblad, A. (1977), 'Principer och riktlinjer för fastprisberäkningar av offentlig verksamhet', in B. Gustafsson, ed., *Den offentliga sektorns expansion* (Uppsala: Almquist & Wiksell).
Tullock, G. (1983), 'Further Tests of a Rational Theory of the Size of Governments', *Public Choice*, 41 (no. 3).
Van Arnhem, C.M. and Schotsman, G.J. (1982), 'Do Parties Affect the Distribution of Incomes?', in F.G. Castles, ed., *The Impact of*

Parties (Beverly Hills: Sage Publications).
Wagner, A. (1883), *Finanzwissenschaft*, partly reprinted in R.A. Musgrave and A.T. Peacock, *Classics in the Theory of Public Finance* (London: Macmillan, 1958).
Wagner, A. (1893), *Grundlegung der politischen ökonomie* (Leipzig: C.F. Winter).
Wagner, R.E. (1976), 'Revenue Structure, Fiscal Illusion and Budgetary Choice', *Public Choice*, 25 (no. 1).
Wagner, R.E. and Weber, W.E. (1977), 'Wagner's Law, Fiscal Institutions and the Growth of Government', *National Tax Journal*, 30 (January).
Wildavsky, A. (1985), 'A Cultural Theory of Expenditure Growth and (un-)Balanced Budgets', *Journal of Public Economics*, 28 (December).
Ysander, B.C. (1979), 'Offentlig ekonomi i tillväxt', in G. Eliasson *et al.*, *Att välja 80-tal* (Stockholm: IUI, Almquist & Wiksell).
Zenker, R. (1972), 'Den offentliga sektorns tillväxt', in E. Lundberg, ed., *Svensk finanspolitik i teori och praktik* (Stockholm: EFI).

Appendix

List of sources

G+TR/Y	OECD *National Accounts.*
G/Y	OECD *National Accounts.*
TAX/Y	OECD *National Accounts.*
IND	1950: *Yearbook of Labor Statistics.* 1960–82: OECD; the intervening years have been interpolated.
URBAN	*Demographic Yearbook* every five years, other years being interpolated.
DPOP	OECD *Labor Force Statistics.*
Y	Swedish national accounts.
PC/PGDP	1948–80: Madsen and Paldam, 'Economic and Political Data for the Main OECD Countries 1948–80'; 1981–82 OECD *National Accounts.*
YMED/YBAR	Unpublished data, Swedish Central Statistical Bureau.
XM	*International Financial Statistics.*
ORG	Anders Kjellberg, *Facklig organisering i tolv länder* (Lund: Arkiv 1983).
NOORG	Swedish national accounts. (Note: This variable is defined as the number of employees in interest organisations.)
INFL	OECD *National Accounts.*
NOTAX	Swedish Association of Tax Payers, Accounting Office.
DIRTAX	OECD *National Accounts.*
DEFICIT	1950–61 OECD *Statistics of National Accounts.* 1962–82 OECD *Economic Outlook*, December 1984.
PUBP	Unpublished information received directly from OECD for 1960–69; *Historical Statistics* 1970 onwards.
UNEMPL	1962–82 OECD *Economic Outlook*, December 1984. Earlier Swedish data from *Arbetsmarknadsstatistisk Årsbok* 1974.
DUMSOC	Created from T.T. Mackie and R. Rose, *The International Almanac of Electoral History*, 2nd ed (London: Macmillan, 1982).
DUMCOAL	Derived from V. Bogdanor, ed., *Coalition Governments in Western Europe* (London: Heinemann Educational Books, 1983).

DUMFED	Own knowledge.
STAX	OECD *National Accounts*. (Note: defined to include central government taxes and social security contributions as a share of all tax collections.)
DUMWAR	Dummy taking the value 0, 0.5 or 1. Used only for the US, UK and France. Own knowledge.

SAS 12:59 WEDNESDAY, APRIL 24, 1985

OBS	COUNTRY	YEAR	GTP	G	TAX	IND	URBAN	DUMWAR	PC	PGDP	POP	XM	ORG	INFL	DIFTAX	DEFICIT	PUB	DUMPL	DUMSCL	DUMCOAL	DUMFED	STAX
1	AUS	1960	23.0	9.6	20.5	30.7	81.1	0	3.68	3.07	10275	31.8	58	4.2	46.9	0.0	22.3	4.1	0	1	1	84.2
2	AUS	1961	23.7	10.2	21.1	30.5	81.5	0	2.34	1.28	10508	32.4	57	0.6	47.5	-0.3	22.4	4.0	0	1	1	84.5
3	AUS	1962	23.5	10.0	20.8	30.4	81.9	0	1.76	1.20	10705	31.4	57	1.0	48.2	-0.7	22.3	3.0	0	1	1	84.7
4	AUS	1963	23.3	9.7	20.9	30.3	82.2	0	5.08	3.79	10907	32.2	57	1.7	49.9	-1.1	22.4	1.4	0	1	1	85.4
5	AUS	1964	23.7	10.3	22.2	30.2	82.6	0	4.92	2.55	11116	33.5	56	3.2	52.3	-2.1	22.4	1.5	0	1	1	85.7
6	AUS	1965	25.6	11.0	23.4	30.3	83.0	0	3.00	3.05	11333	33.3	56	3.3	52.6	-1.4	22.3	1.3	0	1	1	85.1
7	AUS	1966	25.6	11.6	22.7	27.5	83.3	0	5.42	3.28	11599	31.0	53	3.1	52.6	-0.6	22.7	1.5	0	1	1	86.5
8	AUS	1967	26.3	12.3	23.5	27.6	83.8	0	4.87	2.74	11809	31.6	52	3.2	53.0	-0.7	23.0	1.6	0	1	1	84.8
9	AUS	1968	25.1	12.5	23.3	27.1	84.2	0	4.86	3.35	12061	30.7	51	2.7	53.4	-1.7	23.1	1.8	0	1	1	84.8
10	AUS	1969	25.1	12.1	24.1	27.1	84.7	0	7.26	4.47	12296	30.3	50	2.9	55.1	-2.5	23.1	1.8	0	1	1	85.2
11	AUS	1970	25.5	12.2	24.4	26.4	85.1	0	10.51	5.15	12507	30.7	50	3.9	56.1	-2.3	22.9	1.6	0	1	1	86.1
12	AUS	1971	26.2	12.5	25.0	26.6	85.6	0	12.08	6.89	12937	29.6	52	6.1	56.3	-2.2	22.9	1.9	0	1	1	83.2
13	AUS	1972	26.3	12.6	24.0	25.5	86.0	0	10.86	9.92	13177	28.2	53	5.8	55.5	-0.9	23.3	2.6	1	0	1	81.1
14	AUS	1973	26.7	13.0	25.7	25.7	86.0	0	16.83	14.17	13380	28.9	54	9.5	56.8	-1.8	23.2	2.3	1	0	1	81.8
15	AUS	1974	30.4	13.9	27.7	25.1	86.0	0	24.24	18.40	13599	32.9	55	15.1	59.2	-0.4	23.7	2.6	1	0	1	82.1
16	AUS	1975	32.4	15.5	28.5	23.3	86.0	0	15.07	14.79	13771	30.4	56	15.1	57.1	-1.4	25.5	4.8	0	1	1	81.5
17	AUS	1976	32.8	16.0	28.9	23.3	86.0	0	11.02	10.95	13915	31.0	55	13.5	58.0	-1.0	25.1	4.7	0	1	1	81.6
18	AUS	1977	34.2	16.3	29.0	23.0	86.0	0	7.88	8.15	14074	32.8	55	12.3	58.5	-2.0	25.3	5.6	0	1	1	81.6
19	AUS	1978	33.6	16.8	28.3	21.8	86.0	0	6.27	7.83	14249	32.1	56	7.9	55.6	-2.5	25.9	6.2	0	1	1	81.6
20	AUS	1979	33.2	16.0	29.4	22.1	86.0	0	9.62	10.43	14514	35.3	56	9.1	55.4	-0.7	25.9	6.2	0	1	1	82.0
21	AUS	1980	33.6	16.6	29.9	21.8	86.0	0	12.84	10.46	14695	36.5	55	10.2	56.6	-0.2	25.4	6.0	0	1	1	82.5
22	AUS	1981	34.4	17.1	30.7	21.3	86.0	0	11.23	9.01	14923	34.3	56	9.7	57.5	0.0	25.2	5.7	0	1	1	82.4
23	AUS	1982	34.7	17.4	30.7	20.7	86.0	0	14.08	11.72	15178	33.9	55	11.2	55.7	-2.1	25.4	7.1	0	1	1	81.3
24	SWE	1960	29.4	15.8	32.0	31.5	72.8	0	5.73	4.96	7499	46.5	68	3.9	64.1	2.5	12.3	1.8	1	0	0	87.5
25	SWE	1961	29.4	15.9	33.5	30.0	73.7	0	4.70	3.12	7542	44.0	69	2.4	65.0	2.2	13.1	1.3	1	0	0	83.7
26	SWE	1962	32.4	16.7	31.6	28.6	74.6	0	7.13	4.54	7581	43.3	69	4.6	64.4	3.1	13.4	1.5	1	0	0	76.7
27	SWE	1963	34.7	17.3	32.2	28.5	75.5	0	5.49	3.43	7627	44.0	70	3.1	64.9	1.9	14.3	1.7	1	0	0	75.8
28	SWE	1964	35.0	17.2	32.6	28.5	76.5	0	7.68	4.42	7695	44.8	70	3.6	66.0	1.9	14.9	1.6	1	0	0	75.3
29	SWE	1965	36.1	17.8	35.0	28.4	77.4	0	8.44	5.98	7773	45.0	71	5.3	66.8	3.5	15.3	1.2	1	0	0	76.2
30	SWE	1966	38.3	18.9	36.5	28.0	78.2	0	9.67	6.55	7843	43.8	71	6.3	66.5	3.0	16.0	1.6	1	0	0	73.9
31	SWE	1967	40.1	19.6	37.7	27.4	79.0	0	11.95	5.00	7893	42.6	71	4.3	67.3	2.6	17.2	2.1	1	0	0	72.3
32	SWE	1968	42.8	20.6	39.9	26.6	79.8	0	4.55	2.39	7935	43.7	71	1.9	66.4	2.9	18.3	2.2	1	0	0	72.1
33	SWE	1969	43.1	20.8	40.3	26.6	80.6	0	4.26	3.42	8004	46.4	72	2.7	67.9	3.6	19.3	1.9	1	0	0	72.4
34	SWE	1970	43.7	21.4	41.0	27.6	81.4	0	7.41	5.18	8081	48.8	73	7.0	68.9	3.3	20.6	1.5	1	0	0	74.0
35	SWE	1971	45.9	22.5	43.4	27.3	81.7	0	10.85	7.69	8115	47.5	75	7.4	65.5	4.1	22.0	2.5	1	0	0	73.8
36	SWE	1972	46.5	22.7	43.2	27.1	81.9	0	8.12	7.14	8120	46.9	76	6.0	66.8	3.3	23.1	2.7	1	0	0	70.6
37	SWE	1973	45.1	22.7	41.5	27.5	82.2	0	8.09	7.16	8144	52.0	77	6.7	67.6	3.0	23.8	2.5	1	0	0	71.4
38	SWE	1974	48.5	23.2	42.5	28.3	82.4	0	12.21	8.37	8177	65.2	79	9.9	68.4	0.7	24.8	2.0	1	0	0	72.5
39	SWE	1975	49.4	23.8	44.0	28.0	82.7	0	14.70	14.85	8208	56.5	82	9.8	68.3	1.5	25.5	1.6	1	0	0	74.2
40	SWE	1976	52.2	24.9	48.5	26.9	82.6	0	14.14	11.62	8236	57.0	81	10.3	70.1	3.4	26.6	1.6	0	1	0	75.4
41	SWE	1977	58.0	27.5	51.3	25.9	82.9	0	15.61	10.66	8267	56.4	84	11.4	70.1	0.4	27.8	1.8	0	1	0	72.4
42	SWE	1978	59.7	27.9	50.8	24.9	82.9	0	9.88	9.97	8284	55.4	85	10.0	72.5	-1.7	29.0	2.2	0	1	0	68.9
43	SWE	1979	61.2	28.3	50.2	24.5	83.0	0	8.40	7.43	8303	61.8	85	7.2	73.0	-4.3	29.9	2.1	0	0	0	69.2
44	SWE	1980	62.1	28.8	49.5	24.2	83.1	0	13.76	11.97	8318	61.5	85	13.7	72.6	-5.0	30.7	2.0	0	1	0	70.1
45	SWE	1981	65.3	29.3	51.0	23.3	83.1	0	8.41	9.42	8323	61.1	86	12.1	71.3	-6.3	31.5	2.5	0	1	0	70.2
46	SWE	1982	67.3	29.3	50.6	22.4	83.2	0	8.27	8.56	8327	65.9	86	8.6	71.0	-7.6	31.8	3.1	1	0	0	69.1
47	NOR	1960	31.8	12.9	31.8	28.7	37.0	0	4.57	2.62	3585	76.0	64	0.8	54.8	2.9	12.3	1.7	1	0	0	72.4
48	NOR	1961	31.6	12.8	32.6	28.8	37.2	0	2.59	2.43	3615	76.9	64	1.2	54.8	3.9	12.6	1.2	1	0	0	72.3
49	NOR	1962	31.5	14.0	34.0	28.8	37.4	0	7.66	2.92	3639	79.5	64	5.4	56.9	4.0	12.9	1.4	1	0	0	70.6
50	NOR	1963	33.1	14.3	33.9	28.9	37.9	0	4.89	2.42	3667	80.7	64	2.7	57.4	2.4	13.2	1.7	1	0	0	73.7

OBS	COUNTRY	YEAR	GTR	G	TAX	IND	URBAN	DUMWAR	PC	PGEE	POP	XM	ORG	INFL	DIRTAX	DEFICIT	PUB	DUMPL	DUMSOC	DUMCOAL	DUMFED	STAX
51	NOR	1964	33.1	14.5	33.7	29.2	38.3	0.0	5.21	5.48	3694	82.2	64	5.3	56.8	2.9	13.6	1.5	1	0	0	74.6
52	NOR	1965	34.2	15.0	34.6	29.7	40.9	0.0	5.68	4.79	3723	82.3	64	4.0	56.9	2.6	13.8	1.3	0	1	0	74.8
53	NOR	1966	34.8	15.5	35.8	30.1	40.3	0.0	7.59	3.98	3753	83.1	64	3.5	57.4	3.5	14.1	1.2	0	1	0	74.5
54	NOR	1967	36.4	16.1	37.3	30.1	41.3	0.0	4.19	2.96	3785	85.7	64	4.4	59.3	3.9	14.6	1.1	0	1	0	75.6
55	NOR	1968	37.9	16.6	37.6	30.3	42.3	0.0	5.42	4.42	3819	84.2	64	3.5	60.2	3.2	15.2	2.1	0	1	0	75.5
56	NOR	1969	39.9	16.8	41.1	30.4	42.7	0.0	5.45	4.19	3851	82.4	64	3.1	60.8	3.4	15.9	2.0	0	1	0	76.1
57	NOR	1970	41.0	16.9	41.2	31.0	42.6	0.0	9.08	12.81	3879	94.9	64	10.6	55.7	2.5	16.4	1.6	0	1	0	78.3
58	NOR	1971	43.0	17.9	44.6	31.1	43.8	0.0	11.36	6.67	3903	83.7	62	6.2	58.3	3.6	17.0	1.5	1	0	0	79.2
59	NOR	1972	44.6	18.2	46.2	31.3	44.9	0.0	6.93	5.00	3933	80.6	59	7.2	60.1	3.8	17.7	1.7	0	1	0	79.0
60	NOR	1973	44.6	18.2	47.4	31.1	44.7	0.0	8.26	9.18	3961	87.6	57	7.5	61.7	5.0	18.4	1.5	1	0	0	79.3
61	NOR	1974	44.6	19.3	46.1	31.6	44.8	0.0	11.97	11.71	3985	95.4	56	9.4	61.9	3.9	18.7	1.5	1	0	0	78.5
62	NOR	1975	46.6	19.3	47.1	32.2	44.6	0.0	13.56	8.59	4007	90.3	55	11.7	62.3	3.0	19.2	2.3	1	0	0	78.7
63	NOR	1976	49.5	20.0	48.2	31.8	44.5	0.0	10.61	7.48	4026	91.7	55	9.1	62.3	2.4	19.7	1.8	1	0	0	78.2
64	NOR	1977	50.1	20.2	48.4	28.1	44.2	0.0	7.99	8.32	4043	90.3	56	9.1	60.8	0.9	20.1	1.5	1	0	0	77.6
65	NOR	1978	52.3	20.4	48.6	27.0	43.9	0.0	7.01	6.42	4059	82.8	56	8.1	63.4	-0.3	20.8	1.8	1	0	0	78.1
66	NOR	1979	50.9	19.5	48.5	26.0	43.7	0.0	3.32	6.61	4073	85.7	58	4.8	64.4	1.0	21.2	2.0	1	0	0	79.7
67	NOR	1980	48.9	18.8	50.7	26.1	43.6	0.0	9.54	14.31	4086	88.5	58	10.9	66.1	5.3	21.9	1.7	1	0	0	82.5
68	NOR	1981	48.5	19.1	48.8	26.0	43.5	0.0	11.40	14.95	4100	87.5	58	13.6	65.2	4.3	22.4	2.0	0	0	0	81.6
69	NOR	1982	48.8	19.4	48.4	25.5	43.4	0.0	11.10	10.99	4115	85.3	58	11.3	65.1	4.0	22.9	2.6	0	0	0	81.4
70	BEL	1960	28.8	12.4	25.1	34.8	86.3	0.0	1.20	0.89	9154	66.7	57	-0.4	54.5	-2.2	12.2	5.4	0	1	0	95.4
71	BEL	1961	28.9	11.9	26.4	35.4	86.4	0.0	0.19	1.07	9184	68.5	56	2.3	53.9	-0.9	12.2	4.2	0	2	0	95.3
72	BEL	1962	30.5	12.3	28.2	35.4	86.4	0.0	1.27	1.64	9221	68.4	54	1.0	56.5	-1.3	12.5	3.3	0	2	0	95.4
73	BEL	1963	31.5	13.0	28.6	35.2	86.5	0.0	1.98	3.02	9290	70.5	56	3.7	57.3	-2.1	12.7	2.7	0	2	0	95.3
74	BEL	1964	30.9	12.5	29.1	35.4	86.5	0.0	3.45	4.62	9378	72.6	55	4.2	58.1	-0.8	12.9	2.2	0	2	0	95.7
75	BEL	1965	32.7	12.8	30.0	35.3	85.6	0.0	5.37	5.02	9464	72.6	55	4.5	59.7	-1.5	13.2	2.4	0	2	0	95.7
76	BEL	1966	33.5	13.1	31.8	35.0	85.7	0.0	5.26	4.16	9528	73.4	60	4.1	58.5	-1.1	13.5	2.7	0	1	0	95.5
77	BEL	1967	34.5	13.5	32.2	34.1	85.8	0.0	3.99	3.17	9581	72.5	61	2.9	58.2	-1.3	13.9	3.7	0	1	0	95.6
78	BEL	1968	36.7	13.6	32.9	33.6	85.8	0.0	4.24	2.72	9619	77.3	62	2.7	59.4	-2.5	14.0	3.1	0	2	0	94.9
79	BEL	1969	36.1	13.6	33.5	33.9	86.7	0.0	4.60	4.23	9646	83.1	63	3.8	60.3	-1.8	14.0	2.3	0	2	0	95.1
80	BEL	1970	36.5	13.4	34.2	32.7	86.6	0.0	6.28	4.62	9651	85.5	61	3.9	62.3	-1.3	13.9	2.1	0	2	0	95.2
81	BEL	1971	38.0	14.1	35.0	32.3	86.8	0.0	8.79	5.36	9673	84.9	63	4.3	63.9	-2.3	14.0	2.2	0	2	0	95.3
82	BEL	1972	35.2	14.5	35.2	31.9	87.0	0.0	8.64	6.23	9711	83.9	64	5.5	65.4	-3.3	14.4	2.7	1	2	0	95.0
83	BEL	1973	39.1	14.5	36.3	31.8	87.1	0.0	8.05	6.90	9739	93.0	65	7.0	68.0	-2.7	14.6	2.8	1	2	0	95.4
84	BEL	1974	39.4	14.7	37.4	31.5	87.1	0.0	14.61	12.23	9783	106.4	65	12.7	69.2	-1.7	14.7	3.1	0	1	0	95.3
85	BEL	1975	44.5	16.4	40.0	30.1	87.2	0.0	17.75	12.68	9795	91.9	66	12.8	71.8	-4.1	15.8	5.1	0	1	0	95.5
86	BEL	1976	45.0	16.5	40.1	29.1	87.2	0.0	9.07	7.68	9811	97.1	67	9.2	70.7	-4.8	16.4	6.6	0	1	0	95.7
87	BEL	1977	46.6	16.8	41.5	28.1	87.3	0.0	7.87	7.30	9822	105.4	67	7.1	71.6	-4.9	16.8	7.5	0	2	0	95.7
88	BEL	1978	47.9	17.4	42.4	27.0	87.3	0.0	4.83	4.10	9830	102.8	68	4.5	71.8	-5.4	17.6	8.1	0	2	0	95.4
89	BEL	1979	49.4	17.6	42.8	25.9	87.4	0.0	5.34	4.25	9837	114.0	68	4.5	72.5	-6.2	18.3	9.4	0	2	0	95.4
90	BEL	1980	51.1	17.9	42.3	25.4	87.4	0.0	7.71	4.34	9847	121.9	69	6.6	72.2	-8.1	18.7	9.0	0	2	0	96.0
91	BEL	1981	55.6	18.8	42.7	24.7	87.4	0.0	7.84	5.07	9853	132.2	69	7.6	72.0	-11.9	19.1	11.1	0	1	0	95.9
92	BEL	1982	56.6	19.3	44.2	24.1	87.5	0.0	7.27	7.02	9856	140.0	70	8.7	72.8	-11.2	19.5	13.1	0	1	0	95.4
93	FRA	1960	34.4	13.8	33.8	28.2	61.5	0.5	2.92	3.27	45684	25.2	23	3.4	51.6	0.3	12.9	1.2	0	1	0	89.8
94	FRA	1961	35.9	13.0	35.0	28.0	62.5	0.5	5.08	4.46	46163	24.5	23	3.1	52.1	0.1	12.9	1.0	0	1	0	89.8
95	FRA	1962	37.0	13.3	33.0	28.2	63.4	0.0	7.61	4.74	46998	23.3	22	4.3	49.9	-0.7	13.0	1.1	0	1	0	90.3
96	FRA	1963	37.8	13.4	33.8	28.4	64.5	0.0	10.36	6.10	47816	23.6	22	5.0	50.3	-0.7	13.0	1.4	0	1	0	90.4
97	FRA	1964	38.0	13.3	34.8	28.7	65.6	0.0	5.33	4.00	48310	24.3	22	3.4	51.1	0.0	13.1	1.1	0	1	0	90.6
98	FRA	1965	38.4	13.1	35.0	28.8	66.7	0.0	3.00	2.47	48758	24.1	21	2.6	51.8	0.0	13.1	1.3	0	1	0	90.6
99	FRA	1966	39.5	13.0	35.0	28.5	67.8	0.0	4.12	2.95	49164	25.0	21	3.0	51.7	-0.1	13.2	1.4	0	1	0	90.2
100	FRA	1967	39.0	13.0	34.8	28.5	68.9	0.0	3.36	2.84	49549	24.8	22	2.7	52.8	-0.8	13.2	1.8	0	1	0	90.7

OBS	COUNTRY	YEAR	GTR	G	TAX	IND	URBAN	DUMWAR	PC	PGDP	POP	XM	ORG	INFL	DIRTAX	DEFICIT	PUB	DUMPL	DUMSOC	DUMCGAL	DUMFED	STAX
101	FRA	1968	40.3	13.5	35.2	28.3	70.0	0.0	7.59	4.45	49914	25.4	23	4.5	54.5	-1.5	13.3	2.6	0	1	0	90.0
102	FRA	1969	39.6	13.3	36.1	28.0	70.4	0.0	8.13	6.57	50325	27.8	23	6.4	54.9	0.2	13.4	2.3	0	1	0	93.2
103	FRA	1970	38.9	13.4	35.3	27.8	70.9	0.0	7.91	5.63	50772	30.3	23	5.2	56.9	0.1	13.4	2.4	0	1	0	93.7
104	FRA	1971	38.3	13.4	34.7	28.0	71.3	0.0	7.85	5.76	51251	31.1	23	5.5	57.1	0.0	13.8	2.6	0	1	0	94.0
105	FRA	1972	38.3	13.2	34.8	28.1	71.7	0.0	7.18	6.19	51701	31.5	23	6.2	57.3	-0.1	14.0	2.7	0	1	0	93.8
106	FRA	1973	38.5	13.2	35.2	28.3	72.2	0.0	10.14	7.77	52119	33.9	24	7.3	57.9	0.1	14.3	2.6	0	1	0	91.5
107	FRA	1974	39.7	13.6	35.8	28.4	72.6	0.0	17.18	11.14	52461	42.5	24	13.7	59.8	-0.3	14.4	2.8	0	1	0	95.5
108	FRA	1975	43.5	14.4	36.6	27.9	73.0	0.0	14.83	13.39	52705	36.4	25	11.8	61.6	-3.2	14.9	4.1	0	1	0	92.2
109	FRA	1976	44.0	14.6	38.6	27.4	73.4	0.0	10.30	9.86	52893	39.4	25	9.6	62.4	-1.5	15.1	4.4	0	1	0	92.3
110	FRA	1977	44.2	14.7	38.6	27.1	73.8	0.0	11.76	8.99	53079	40.5	25	9.4	64.1	-1.8	15.2	4.7	0	1	0	92.6
111	FRA	1978	45.2	15.0	38.4	26.6	74.2	0.0	10.61	9.53	53278	39.2	25	9.1	63.5	-2.9	15.4	5.2	0	1	0	92.7
112	FRA	1979	45.5	14.9	39.8	26.1	74.6	0.0	11.22	10.14	53480	41.4	25	10.8	63.8	-1.8	15.4	5.9	0	1	0	93.0
113	FRA	1980	46.4	15.2	41.6	25.8	75.0	0.0	13.34	11.64	53714	44.0	25	13.6	64.6	-0.9	15.5	6.3	0	1	0	92.7
114	FRA	1981	49.2	15.8	41.7	25.1	75.4	0.0	14.02	12.03	53963	46.5	25	13.4	65.0	-3.1	15.8	7.3	1	1	0	92.6
115	FRA	1982	50.7	16.2	42.6	24.7	75.8	0.0	14.42	12.50	54219	46.2	25	11.8	65.4	-3.8	16.1	8.0	1	1	0	92.9
116	AUT	1960	32.4	12.7	30.2	32.1	50.4	0.0	5.27	3.90	7048	49.6	63	2.0	53.4	-0.2	10.5	3.7	0	2	1	74.5
117	AUT	1961	32.7	12.4	32.7	32.2	50.6	0.0	7.55	5.11	7074	47.8	63	3.5	54.4	1.9	10.6	2.9	0	2	1	74.5
118	AUT	1962	33.6	12.8	33.5	32.3	50.8	0.0	6.22	3.69	7130	48.2	63	3.9	55.2	0.4	10.9	2.7	0	2	1	74.2
119	AUT	1963	34.7	13.3	33.6	32.4	50.9	0.0	6.97	3.49	7172	49.2	63	3.2	55.6	-1.1	11.1	2.9	0	2	1	74.3
120	AUT	1964	38.2	13.3	34.0	32.4	51.1	0.0	4.51	3.18	7215	50.7	63	2.9	53.4	-0.4	11.4	2.7	0	2	1	75.7
121	AUT	1965	37.9	13.4	34.8	32.5	51.2	0.0	8.45	5.32	7255	51.8	63	4.1	54.2	0.6	11.6	2.7	0	2	1	75.8
122	AUT	1966	38.3	13.7	35.7	32.5	51.4	0.0	6.45	3.10	7290	53.2	63	2.4	54.4	1.0	12.0	2.5	0	0	1	75.4
123	AUT	1967	40.5	14.6	35.4	32.5	51.5	0.0	8.98	3.29	7323	53.0	62	4.0	54.9	-1.4	12.5	2.7	0	0	1	75.6
124	AUT	1968	40.6	14.8	35.4	32.6	51.6	0.0	5.54	2.85	7360	53.8	63	2.8	53.1	-1.7	13.1	2.0	0	0	1	75.4
125	AUT	1969	40.3	15.1	35.9	32.6	51.7	0.0	9.09	2.74	7393	58.0	63	3.1	54.3	-0.8	13.4	2.0	0	0	1	75.0
126	AUT	1970	39.2	14.7	36.0	32.7	51.8	0.0	5.90	4.78	7426	63.9	62	4.4	54.7	0.5	13.7	1.4	1	0	1	74.0
127	AUT	1971	39.7	14.8	36.7	32.6	51.9	0.0	8.69	6.21	7459	63.0	61	4.7	54.8	0.8	14.1	1.3	1	0	1	74.0
128	AUT	1972	39.8	14.6	37.4	32.6	52.0	0.0	8.62	7.60	7495	62.4	60	6.3	55.0	1.3	14.6	1.2	1	0	1	73.7
129	AUT	1973	41.3	15.1	38.6	32.9	52.1	0.0	13.47	8.05	7525	64.4	59	7.6	54.2	0.6	15.0	1.1	1	0	1	73.2
130	AUT	1974	41.9	15.8	38.6	32.3	52.2	0.0	12.54	9.51	7533	70.9	59	9.5	56.2	0.6	15.6	1.4	1	0	1	73.4
131	AUT	1975	46.1	17.2	38.1	31.4	52.3	0.0	11.59	6.55	7520	66.6	59	8.4	55.9	-3.2	16.4	1.7	1	0	1	73.6
132	AUT	1976	46.9	17.6	38.3	31.0	52.4	0.0	8.43	5.53	7513	70.8	59	7.3	55.5	-4.5	16.9	1.8	1	0	1	73.6
133	AUT	1977	46.8	17.4	39.0	31.1	52.5	0.0	4.79	5.27	7518	71.6	58	5.5	56.4	-3.1	17.4	1.6	1	0	1	74.4
134	AUT	1978	49.7	18.3	41.9	30.8	52.6	0.0	7.38	5.31	7508	70.0	58	3.6	60.5	-3.5	17.7	2.1	1	0	1	75.4
135	AUT	1979	48.9	18.1	41.5	30.5	52.7	0.0	4.31	4.42	7503	75.0	58	3.7	60.4	-3.1	18.0	2.1	1	0	1	76.7
136	AUT	1980	48.8	17.9	41.7	30.6	52.8	0.0	5.31	4.64	7505	79.7	58	6.4	60.8	-2.5	18.2	1.9	1	0	1	75.8
137	AUT	1981	50.1	18.4	42.9	30.2	52.9	0.0	7.21	6.39	7508	85.4	58	6.8	61.6	-2.3	18.7	2.5	1	0	1	75.8
138	AUT	1982	50.3	18.6	41.7	29.4	53.0	0.0	7.14	6.59	7510	80.6	58	5.4	61.0	-3.6	19.2	3.5	1	0	1	75.0
139	USA	1960	28.2	16.9	27.9	26.4	68.5	0.0	2.67	1.69	180684	9.2	26	1.5	66.2	0.8	15.7	5.5	0	0	1	70.8
140	USA	1961	29.9	17.8	27.9	26.3	69.0	0.0	2.32	1.19	183756	9.0	26	0.9	65.9	-0.9	16.2	6.7	0	0	1	70.1
141	USA	1962	28.8	18.0	27.8	26.2	69.5	0.0	1.43	1.18	186538	9.0	26	1.0	66.2	-1.8	16.6	5.5	0	0	1	70.0
142	USA	1963	28.8	17.9	28.3	26.6	70.0	0.0	8.22	0.85	189242	9.0	26	1.2	66.6	-1.3	16.6	5.7	0	0	1	70.1
143	USA	1964	28.3	17.5	27.2	26.5	70.5	0.5	3.70	2.18	191889	9.3	26	1.2	65.5	-1.8	16.7	5.2	0	0	1	68.4
144	USA	1965	27.9	17.1	27.3	27.0	71.0	0.5	3.00	1.88	194303	9.3	26	1.4	66.0	-1.4	16.5	4.5	0	0	1	68.3
145	USA	1966	29.1	18.1	28.1	27.8	71.5	0.5	3.31	2.79	196560	9.7	26	2.5	68.3	-1.8	17.1	3.8	0	0	1	69.0
146	USA	1967	31.1	19.4	28.4	27.8	72.0	0.5	3.46	3.09	198712	9.8	27	2.8	68.4	-3.4	17.7	3.8	0	0	1	68.6
147	USA	1968	31.3	19.2	30.2	27.5	72.5	1.0	5.25	4.36	200706	10.2	27	4.2	69.6	-2.0	17.8	3.5	0	0	1	69.2
148	USA	1969	30.9	18.9	30.5	27.3	73.0	1.0	5.84	5.04	202677	10.2	27	5.4	69.7	-0.3	17.7	3.4	0	0	1	70.6
149	USA	1970	32.4	19.2	29.6	26.4	73.5	1.0	7.93	5.16	205052	11.0	27	5.9	67.6	-2.8	18.1	4.8	0	0	1	68.0
150	USA	1971	32.3	18.5	29.0	24.7	74.0	1.0	7.38	5.10	207661	10.9	26	4.3	66.3	-3.4	18.0	5.8	0	0	1	66.4

OBS	COUNTRY	YEAR	GTR	G	TAX	IND	URBAN	DUMWAR	PC	PGDP	POP	XM	ORG	INFL	DIRTAX	DEFICIT	PUB	DUMPL	DUMSOC	DUMCOAL	DUMFED	STAX
151	USA	1972	32.0	18.4	30.0	24.3	74.5	1.0	7.05	4.11	209896	11.5	25	3.3	68.3	-2.0	17.7	5.5	0	0	1	66.5
152	USA	1973	31.2	17.8	30.2	24.8	75.0	0.5	7.03	5.72	211909	13.5	25	6.2	69.4	-0.9	17.2	4.8	0	0	1	67.5
153	USA	1974	32.9	18.5	31.0	24.2	75.5	0.0	8.31	8.75	213854	17.2	25	11.0	70.5	-1.7	17.3	5.5	0	0	1	68.3
154	USA	1975	35.6	19.1	29.3	22.7	76.0	0.0	9.04	9.05	215973	16.2	25	9.1	68.9	-5.9	18.0	8.3	0	0	1	66.5
155	USA	1976	34.3	18.7	30.3	22.8	76.5	0.0	6.53	5.69	218035	17.0	25	5.8	70.6	-3.9	17.6	7.6	0	0	1	67.1
156	USA	1977	33.4	19.2	30.6	22.7	77.0	0.0	6.12	5.88	220239	17.3	25	6.5	71.5	-2.6	17.1	6.9	0	0	1	67.7
157	USA	1978	32.8	17.7	31.1	22.7	77.5	0.0	7.20	7.40	222585	17.9	24	7.7	72.9	-1.7	16.7	6.0	0	0	1	69.0
158	USA	1979	33.0	17.6	29.3	22.7	78.0	0.0	7.56	8.45	225056	19.5	23	11.3	72.9	-1.3	16.4	5.8	0	0	1	68.9
159	USA	1980	35.0	18.3	29.3	22.1	78.5	0.0	9.94	8.94	227738	21.3	23	13.5	72.1	-3.0	16.7	7.0	0	0	1	68.9
160	USA	1981	35.7	18.1	29.8	21.7	79.0	0.0	9.36	9.22	230019	20.3	23	10.4	71.4	-2.6	16.5	7.5	0	0	1	69.9
161	USA	1982	37.6	19.0	28.9	20.4	79.5	0.0	6.43	6.53	232309	18.2	23	6.1	70.7	-5.6	16.7	9.5	0	0	1	68.1
162	UK	1960	33.6	16.5	27.8	34.9	80.0	0.0	4.00	1.10	52559	42.0	44	0.8	51.6	-0.8	14.8	1.6	0	0	0	90.7
163	UK	1961	34.5	16.7	29.0	34.8	79.8	0.0	4.21	3.31	52932	40.0	43	2.9	53.1	-0.7	14.9	1.5	0	0	0	91.2
164	UK	1962	34.2	17.0	29.7	34.9	79.6	0.0	3.87	3.89	53431	39.0	42	3.9	54.1	-1.1	15.1	1.9	0	0	0	89.2
165	UK	1963	35.6	16.9	28.6	34.8	79.5	0.0	3.60	2.07	53691	39.2	42	1.9	53.3	-3.9	15.3	2.3	0	0	0	88.3
166	UK	1964	33.9	16.4	28.4	34.9	79.2	0.0	4.61	3.30	54033	39.4	43	3.6	52.3	-2.2	15.5	1.7	1	0	0	88.3
167	UK	1965	36.4	16.8	30.0	35.0	79.1	0.0	6.06	4.99	54378	38.3	43	4.8	52.9	-3.0	15.7	1.4	1	0	0	88.5
168	UK	1966	35.6	17.1	31.4	34.9	79.0	0.0	5.93	4.55	54653	38.0	42	4.0	52.5	-1.1	16.1	1.5	1	0	0	88.4
169	UK	1967	38.5	17.9	32.8	34.3	78.7	0.0	4.57	2.94	54633	38.1	42	2.5	53.8	-2.0	16.9	2.3	1	0	0	88.7
170	UK	1968	39.6	17.6	34.8	34.2	78.9	0.0	5.81	4.03	55157	42.3	43	4.7	52.8	-1.6	17.4	3.2	1	0	0	89.4
171	UK	1969	41.5	17.2	34.0	34.6	78.6	0.0	6.38	5.50	55372	43.1	44	5.4	57.8	-1.7	17.6	3.0	1	0	0	89.4
172	UK	1970	39.2	17.6	36.8	34.8	78.4	0.0	10.80	7.28	55522	44.5	47	6.4	56.4	1.3	18.0	3.1	0	0	0	90.2
173	UK	1971	38.2	17.9	34.7	33.9	78.0	0.0	10.71	9.29	55712	43.9	47	9.4	57.1	0.2	18.8	3.9	0	0	0	89.5
174	UK	1972	39.2	18.4	33.2	32.8	77.9	0.0	9.38	8.26	55869	43.3	48	7.1	57.1	-3.0	19.5	4.3	0	0	0	88.6
175	UK	1973	40.8	18.3	32.5	32.2	77.7	0.0	9.41	7.11	56000	49.7	48	9.2	59.5	-4.6	19.6	3.3	0	0	0	88.0
176	UK	1974	45.0	20.0	35.8	32.3	77.5	0.0	22.34	15.05	56011	60.8	49	16.0	62.3	-5.1	19.7	3.1	1	0	0	89.6
177	UK	1975	46.6	21.9	36.7	30.9	77.4	0.0	31.00	26.87	55981	53.3	51	24.2	64.1	-6.1	21.0	4.6	1	0	0	89.6
178	UK	1976	45.8	21.4	35.7	30.2	77.2	0.0	15.35	14.70	55959	57.6	52	16.5	63.8	-6.2	21.5	6.0	1	0	0	89.8
179	UK	1977	43.8	20.3	35.4	30.3	77.1	0.0	10.45	13.99	55919	59.5	53	15.8	61.2	-4.6	21.3	6.4	1	2	0	89.9
180	UK	1978	43.4	19.9	34.4	30.0	76.9	0.0	10.41	10.93	55902	56.0	54	8.3	59.9	-5.6	21.2	6.3	1	2	0	89.9
181	UK	1979	43.2	19.8	35.7	29.3	76.8	0.0	13.99	15.09	55946	56.4	55	13.4	56.1	-4.5	21.2	5.6	0	0	0	90.3
182	UK	1980	45.4	21.4	36.1	28.1	76.6	0.0	23.53	18.99	56010	53.0	54	18.0	56.7	-4.9	21.3	6.9	0	0	0	89.9
183	UK	1981	48.0	21.9	38.0	26.2	76.5	0.0	12.84	11.59	56348	50.8	55	11.9	56.4	-5.5	22.0	10.6	0	0	0	89.0
184	UK	1982	47.4	22.0	38.9	25.3	76.3	0.5	8.62	7.15	56341	50.8	54	8.6	56.8	-3.7	22.4	12.3	0	0	0	58.6
185	ITA	1960	32.8	12.1	27.0	25.1	.	0.0	4.36	2.12	48967	26.0	32	0.9	52.5	-1.1	8.7	5.6	0	0	0	90.8
186	ITA	1961	32.3	12.7	26.5	25.1	.	0.0	5.44	2.70	49156	26.3	32	0.8	52.6	-1.8	9.0	5.1	0	0	0	89.5
187	ITA	1962	30.5	13.1	27.8	25.2	.	0.0	11.71	5.80	49563	26.6	32	5.7	54.4	-1.4	9.4	4.6	0	1	0	92.9
188	ITA	1963	31.1	13.9	27.9	25.6	.	0.0	16.80	8.63	49936	27.3	32	7.3	56.2	-1.6	9.9	3.9	0	2	0	92.3
189	ITA	1964	31.8	14.3	29.1	25.6	.	0.0	7.93	6.26	50439	26.2	32	5.2	58.1	-1.2	10.1	4.3	0	2	0	93.1
190	ITA	1965	34.7	15.1	28.9	26.0	.	0.0	9.08	3.93	50840	26.9	32	4.1	57.3	-4.2	10.5	5.4	0	2	0	90.9
191	ITA	1966	34.3	14.9	28.6	26.0	.	0.0	2.47	2.24	51227	28.4	32	2.9	57.3	-4.2	10.9	5.9	0	2	0	93.1
192	ITA	1967	33.7	14.4	30.1	26.3	.	0.0	2.26	2.77	51664	28.8	32	3.7	57.7	-2.7	11.0	5.4	0	2	0	92.2
193	ITA	1968	34.7	14.5	30.7	26.8	.	0.0	3.62	1.74	52042	29.4	32	1.4	58.7	-3.1	11.3	5.6	0	2	0	93.1
194	ITA	1969	34.2	14.2	27.8	27.9	.	0.0	5.45	4.05	52376	31.4	34	2.6	58.8	-3.5	11.5	5.6	0	0	0	92.0
195	ITA	1970	34.2	13.8	27.3	29.3	.	0.0	6.29	6.87	52771	32.5	36	5.0	59.1	-3.8	11.8	5.3	0	2	0	91.4
196	ITA	1971	36.6	15.5	27.7	29.5	.	0.0	15.88	7.19	53124	32.7	38	4.8	60.8	-5.5	12.5	5.3	0	2	0	91.4
197	ITA	1972	38.6	16.1	27.6	29.6	.	0.0	8.10	6.25	53548	34.2	41	5.7	63.2	-7.7	13.1	5.3	0	1	0	90.3
198	ITA	1973	37.8	15.5	27.2	29.6	.	0.0	12.43	11.61	53981	37.2	42	10.8	64.0	-7.4	13.5	6.2	0	2	0	93.7
199	ITA	1974	37.9	15.1	27.5	29.8	.	0.0	16.90	18.47	54541	46.9	46	19.1	64.3	-7.3	13.7	5.3	0	2	0	96.4
200	ITA	1975	43.2	15.4	28.4	29.7	.	0.0	12.22	17.52	54967	43.2	47	17.0	69.2	-12.2	14.1	5.8	0	0	0	96.9

OBS	COUNTRY	YEAR	GTR	G	TAX	IND	URBAN	DUMWAR	PC	PGDP	POP	XM	ORG	INFL	DIRTAX	DEFICIT	PUB	DUMPL	DUMSOC	DUMCOAL	DUMFED	STAX
201	ITA	1976	42.2	14.8	30.0	29.4	.	0	16.92	18.02	55325	48.3	49.0	16.8	68.0	-9.3	14.4	6.6	0	0	0	95.4
202	ITA	1977	42.5	15.3	31.3	28.5	.	0	21.91	19.08	55576	48.5	50.0	17.0	67.3	-8.2	14.8	7.0	0	0	0	95.6
203	ITA	1978	46.1	15.9	32.6	28.0	.	0	18.88	13.86	55806	48.0	52.0	12.1	69.1	-10.1	15.0	7.1	0	0	0	97.5
204	ITA	1979	45.5	16.2	32.2	27.7	.	0	21.16	15.70	56016	51.3	53.0	14.8	70.6	-9.8	15.1	7.5	0	1	0	97.5
205	ITA	1980	46.1	16.4	34.1	27.8	.	0	22.98	20.35	56121	50.2	54.0	21.2	70.5	-8.3	15.1	7.4	0	2	0	97.2
206	ITA	1981	51.2	18.2	35.5	27.2	.	0	27.28	18.33	56292	52.5	55.0	17.8	72.6	-11.9	15.3	8.3	0	2	0	97.1
207	ITA	1982	53.7	18.4	37.9	26.8	.	0	16.43	17.45	56448	51.1	57.0	16.6	73.1	-12.2	15.4	8.9	0	2	0	97.1
208	GER	1960	37.9	13.6	33.9	37.8	.	0	5.41	2.42	55433	37.4	33.0	1.8	57.9	3.5	8.0	1.3	0	1	1	67.1
209	GER	1961	34.8	14.1	34.9	37.7	.	0	6.13	4.34	56175	35.9	33.0	2.6	58.9	3.6	8.4	0.8	0	1	1	66.5
210	GER	1962	35.6	14.6	33.7	37.8	.	0	3.88	4.05	56837	36.2	33.0	3.1	58.9	1.0	8.8	0.7	0	1	1	67.3
211	GER	1963	36.4	15.5	33.8	37.7	.	0	4.32	3.07	57389	36.6	32.0	2.6	59.2	0.5	9.2	0.8	0	1	1	68.0
212	GER	1964	36.1	14.8	33.5	37.7	.	0	5.05	2.75	57971	37.9	32.0	2.4	59.2	0.3	9.5	0.8	0	1	1	68.1
213	GER	1965	36.7	15.2	32.8	38.3	.	0	7.43	3.60	58619	38.8	32.0	3.2	58.8	-1.0	9.8	0.7	0	1	1	69.1
214	GER	1966	36.9	15.5	33.2	38.2	.	0	6.77	3.54	59148	39.5	32.0	3.5	59.7	-0.7	10.1	0.7	0	1	1	69.0
215	GER	1967	38.8	16.2	33.5	37.5	.	0	2.82	1.22	59286	41.3	31.0	1.4	59.0	-1.9	10.8	2.1	0	2	1	68.9
216	GER	1968	39.2	15.5	33.3	37.8	.	0	3.93	1.59	59500	43.0	31.0	2.9	60.9	-1.2	10.8	1.5	0	2	1	68.7
217	GER	1969	38.8	15.6	35.3	38.9	.	0	7.57	3.60	60067	43.2	31.0	1.9	59.9	-0.6	10.9	0.9	0	2	1	68.2
218	GER	1970	38.6	15.8	34.4	39.4	.	0	9.28	7.05	60651	43.3	32.0	3.4	62.7	-0.3	11.2	0.8	1	1	1	69.6
219	GER	1971	40.1	16.9	35.2	37.4	.	0	12.42	7.74	61302	42.8	31.0	5.3	63.7	-0.7	11.6	0.9	1	1	1	69.4
220	GER	1972	40.8	17.1	35.8	36.8	.	0	6.51	5.57	61672	44.2	31.0	5.5	63.6	-1.0	12.2	0.8	1	1	1	67.3
221	GER	1973	41.6	17.8	38.0	36.7	.	0	9.74	5.02	61976	52.2	32.0	6.9	65.1	1.4	12.5	0.8	1	1	1	67.9
222	GER	1974	44.6	19.3	38.2	36.4	.	0	11.59	6.88	62054	50.4	33.0	7.0	67.6	-2.2	13.2	1.6	1	1	1	67.6
223	GER	1975	48.9	20.5	37.6	35.6	.	0	6.19	6.72	61829	53.2	33.0	6.0	67.4	-6.3	13.9	3.6	1	1	1	69.3
224	GER	1976	48.0	19.9	39.1	35.1	.	0	3.46	3.26	61531	53.2	33.0	4.5	68.5	-4.0	14.2	3.7	1	1	1	69.1
225	GER	1977	48.0	19.6	40.2	35.1	.	0	4.81	3.78	61400	52.7	33.0	3.7	69.0	-3.0	14.4	3.6	1	1	1	68.4
226	GER	1978	47.7	19.7	39.7	34.8	.	0	3.04	3.81	61327	51.5	33.0	2.7	67.9	-3.1	14.6	3.5	1	1	1	68.7
227	GER	1979	47.6	19.6	39.3	34.5	.	0	4.91	3.73	61359	54.2	33.0	4.1	67.3	-3.4	14.8	3.2	1	1	1	68.9
228	GER	1980	48.3	20.1	41.2	34.3	.	0	6.23	4.80	61566	58.5	33.0	5.5	68.3	-3.7	14.9	3.0	1	1	1	69.8
229	GER	1981	49.3	20.6	41.1	33.6	.	0	5.12	4.20	61682	63.5	33.0	5.9	68.8	-4.6	15.2	4.4	1	1	1	71.0
230	GER	1982	49.4	20.3	41.2	33.1	.	0	3.42	4.74	61638	64.5	33.0	5.3	69.4	-4.1	15.6	6.1	1	1	1	71.3
231	CAN	1960	30.6	13.6	24.8	24.6	69.4	0	4.15	1.46	17870	35.8	39.4	1.2	47.6	-1.9	15.2	7.0	0	0	1	67.8
232	CAN	1961	31.7	15.4	25.4	24.0	70.1	0	4.19	0.65	18238	36.6	38.6	0.8	47.7	-2.3	15.6	7.1	0	0	1	66.9
233	CAN	1962	30.0	15.2	24.8	23.6	70.8	0	2.32	1.40	18583	36.4	38.0	1.3	46.1	-3.0	16.0	5.9	0	0	1	60.6
234	CAN	1963	29.5	14.9	24.5	23.4	71.5	0	1.79	1.54	18931	36.6	37.5	1.5	46.5	-2.7	16.4	5.5	0	0	1	59.7
235	CAN	1964	28.9	14.9	25.4	23.9	72.1	0	5.88	2.76	19291	38.3	37.5	1.2	46.9	-1.1	16.8	4.7	0	0	1	60.3
236	CAN	1965	29.1	14.9	25.7	24.0	72.8	0	4.56	3.16	19644	38.3	38.0	1.9	46.3	-1.0	17.2	3.9	0	0	1	59.2
237	CAN	1966	30.1	15.5	27.0	24.5	73.6	0	6.73	4.35	20015	40.0	39.1	3.3	48.7	-0.7	17.6	3.6	0	0	1	59.5
238	CAN	1967	32.1	16.5	28.3	23.2	74.1	0	6.78	3.88	20378	40.9	38.6	3.6	50.1	-1.1	18.0	4.1	0	0	1	58.1
239	CAN	1968	33.0	17.3	29.3	22.6	74.6	0	5.72	3.25	20701	42.4	38.9	4.0	52.1	-0.6	18.6	4.4	0	0	1	57.4
240	CAN	1969	33.5	17.6	30.9	22.5	75.1	0	8.30	4.35	21001	43.9	39.2	4.5	54.0	1.0	19.0	4.4	0	0	1	58.1
241	CAN	1970	35.7	19.2	31.0	22.3	75.6	0	5.82	4.67	21297	43.6	38.5	3.4	55.1	-0.5	19.5	5.6	0	0	1	57.2
242	CAN	1971	36.6	19.2	31.0	21.8	76.1	0	6.13	3.12	21568	42.4	37.7	2.8	55.9	-1.3	20.4	6.1	0	0	1	57.2
243	CAN	1972	37.2	19.1	31.7	21.8	76.0	0	7.22	5.04	21801	43.4	38.0	4.8	56.0	-1.3	20.2	6.2	0	0	1	57.3
244	CAN	1973	36.0	18.5	31.4	22.0	75.9	0	8.55	9.23	22043	45.8	37.3	7.6	57.4	-0.4	19.8	5.5	0	0	1	57.7
245	CAN	1974	37.4	18.6	33.3	21.7	75.8	0	16.06	15.50	22364	50.0	36.9	10.9	57.9	0.4	19.8	5.3	0	0	1	60.3
246	CAN	1975	40.8	20.0	32.1	20.2	75.7	0	15.47	10.76	22697	47.6	36.8	10.8	60.0	-3.9	20.3	6.9	0	0	1	59.6
247	CAN	1976	39.4	19.7	31.6	20.3	75.5	0	13.27	9.37	22993	45.9	38.1	7.5	59.2	-3.1	20.0	7.1	0	0	1	58.7
248	CAN	1977	40.3	20.3	31.3	19.6	75.5	0	9.68	7.24	23287	47.7	37.8	8.0	58.9	-3.8	20.3	8.0	0	0	1	55.1
249	CAN	1978	40.8	20.1	30.6	19.6	75.5	0	8.18	6.44	23534	50.9	38.6	8.9	59.0	-4.6	19.8	8.3	0	0	1	53.0
250	CAN	1979	39.3	19.3	30.2	12.9	75.5	0	8.40	10.62	23769	54.4	38.0	9.2	59.4	-3.2	18.9	7.4	0	0	1	54.0

OBS	COUNTRY	YEAR	GTR	G	TAX	IND	URBAN	DUMWAR	PC	PGDP	POP	XM	ORG	INFL	DIRTAX	DEFICIT	PUB	DUMPL	DUMSOC	DUMCOAL	DUMFED	STAX
251	CAN	1980	41.0	19.6	30.7	19.7	75.5	0	12.00	10.75	24042	55.9	38	10.2	61.0	-3.90	18.8	7.4	0	0	1	55.3
252	CAN	1981	41.5	19.6	32.6	19.3	75.5	0	14.15	10.69	24342	54.0	38	12.5	59.2	-2.60	18.9	7.5	0	0	1	57.7
253	CAN	1982	45.8	21.0	32.2	18.1	75.5	0	12.24	10.07	24634	48.2	38	10.8	58.3	-6.80	19.9	10.9	0	0	1	56.0
254	NED	1960	33.3	12.8	27.4	29.7	74.5	0	6.38	2.57	11486	98.3	39	1.9	63.7	0.50	11.7	1.2	0	1	0	98.3
255	NED	1961	35.3	13.4	31.9	29.5	75.0	0	5.97	2.51	11639	96.2	39	1.4	67.7	0.00	11.7	0.9	0	1	0	98.4
256	NED	1962	35.6	13.9	31.2	29.3	75.5	0	7.27	3.72	11805	94.6	38	2.6	67.9	-1.20	11.7	0.8	0	1	0	98.1
257	NED	1963	37.6	14.7	32.1	29.1	76.9	0	7.35	4.59	11966	95.9	38	3.8	68.8	-2.00	11.6	0.9	0	1	0	98.2
258	NED	1964	37.8	14.8	32.6	28.9	78.4	0	17.04	8.38	12127	94.4	37	6.8	69.3	-2.10	11.5	0.8	0	1	0	98.4
259	NED	1965	38.7	14.8	34.1	28.6	78.4	0	9.62	6.08	12295	91.6	37	4.0	70.5	-1.40	11.5	0.8	0	2	0	98.4
260	NED	1966	40.7	15.2	35.8	28.4	78.4	0	9.68	5.89	12456	89.9	38	5.4	70.9	-1.50	11.6	1.0	0	2	0	98.4
261	NED	1967	42.5	15.3	37.1	28.2	78.4	0	9.71	4.15	12598	86.8	38	3.5	71.1	-1.90	11.9	2.0	0	1	0	98.3
262	NED	1968	43.9	15.2	38.0	28.0	78.3	0	6.04	3.90	12730	86.9	37	3.7	70.4	-1.50	11.9	1.5	0	1	0	98.5
263	NED	1969	44.4	15.3	39.1	27.7	78.1	0	9.13	6.06	12878	90.3	36	7.5	72.9	-1.20	12.0	1.0	0	1	0	98.8
264	NED	1970	46.0	15.6	39.8	27.5	77.9	0	8.61	5.40	13039	96.2	37	3.6	71.4	-1.50	12.1	1.0	0	1	0	98.9
265	NED	1971	48.0	16.0	41.7	27.2	77.8	0	12.13	8.53	13194	95.8	37	7.5	72.2	-1.20	12.4	1.3	0	1	0	99.0
266	NED	1972	48.6	15.9	42.7	26.2	77.7	0	10.85	9.43	13329	91.7	38	7.8	72.0	-0.60	12.8	2.2	0	1	0	98.9
267	NED	1973	49.3	15.6	44.0	25.8	77.4	0	11.44	8.39	13439	95.9	38	8.0	73.2	-0.50	13.0	2.2	1	2	0	98.9
268	NED	1974	51.5	16.3	44.8	25.7	77.2	0	15.86	9.32	13545	110.2	38	9.6	75.0	-0.80	13.2	2.7	1	2	0	98.8
269	NED	1975	56.5	17.4	46.2	25.0	76.8	0	13.29	11.20	13666	101.0	38	10.2	75.5	-0.34	13.5	5.2	1	2	0	99.1
270	NED	1976	56.5	17.2	45.6	23.8	76.6	0	9.09	8.89	13774	103.4	39	8.8	74.6	-3.00	14.0	5.5	1	2	0	99.2
271	NED	1977	54.6	17.4	46.3	23.2	76.5	0	6.47	6.32	13856	93.9	38	6.4	73.3	-2.50	14.4	5.3	1	2	0	99.2
272	NED	1978	55.9	17.7	47.1	23.0	76.4	0	5.79	5.20	13942	89.8	38	4.1	73.0	-3.40	14.6	5.3	0	1	0	99.3
273	NED	1979	58.0	18.1	47.6	22.3	76.3	0	5.78	4.17	14038	98.7	37	4.2	73.6	-4.30	14.7	5.4	0	1	0	99.3
274	NED	1980	59.5	17.9	46.0	21.5	76.2	0	4.50	5.25	14150	105.6	36	6.5	74.0	-4.50	14.9	6.0	0	1	0	99.3
275	NED	1981	61.1	17.8	45.4	20.9	76.1	0	2.50	5.82	14247	112.1	36	6.7	74.5	-6.10	15.4	8.6	0	1	0	99.2
276	NED	1982	63.7	17.8	45.9	20.5	76.0	0	3.37	5.64	14313	11.2	36	6.0	75.2	-7.90	15.8	11.4	0	2	0	99.1

Table A.1 The growth of government, 1960–82

Country: USA

Definition of government: G+TR/Y

Explanatory variable	Coefficient	t-ratio
For demand model		
Intercept	14.9	0.41
IND	-0.96	-2.97
URBAN	0.48	0.98
DPOP	-1.63	-0.80
PCPGDP	-16.1	-2.22
XM	-0.24	-0.66
ORG	0.60	1.59
INFL	0.27	1.74
DIRTAX	0.16	0.63
DEFICIT	-0.53	-2.77
For supply model		
Intercept		
PCPGDP		
PUBP		
UNEMPL		
DUMSOC		
DUMCOAL		
DUMFED		
STAX		

Coefficient of determination: 0.964
F-ratio: 32.4
Mean squared error: 0.46
Durbin–Watson d statistic: 2.26

Table A.2 The growth of government, 1960–82

Country: USA

Definition of government: G+TR/Y

Explanatory variable	Coefficient	t-ratio
For demand model		
Intercept		
IND		
URBAN		
DPOP		
PCPGDP		
XM		
ORG		
INFL		
DIRTAX		
DEFICIT		
For supply model		
Intercept	-89.7	
PCPGDP	18.7	6.63
PUBP	1.90	4.37
UNEMPL	1.12	7.15
DUMSOC		
DUMCOAL		
DUMFED		
STAX	0.88	3.89

Coefficient of determination: 0.922
F-ratio: 40.2
Mean squared error: 0.72
Durbin–Watson d statistic: 1.27

Table A.3 The growth of government, 1960–82

Country: USA

Definition of government: G/Y

Explanatory variable	Coefficient	t-ratio
For demand model		
Intercept	2.45	0.15
IND	-0.16	-1.10
URBAN	0.08	0.38
DPOP	-0.68	-0.74
PCPGDP	-5.55	-1.71
XM	-0.19	-1.14
ORG	0.33	1.93
INFL	0.13	1.90
DIRTAX	0.20	1.70
DEFICIT	-0.34	-3.92
For supply model		
Intercept		
PCPGDP		
PUBP		
UNEMPL		
DUMSOC		
DUMCOAL		
DUMFED		
STAX		

Coefficient of determination: 0.891
F-ratio: 9.82
Mean squared error: 0.093
Durbin–Watson d statistic: 2.17

Table A.4 The growth of government, 1960–82

Country: USA

Definition of government: G/Y

Explanatory variable	Coefficient	t-ratio
For demand model		
Intercept		
IND		
URBAN		
DPOP		
PCPGDP		
XM		
ORG		
INFL		
DIRTAX		
DEFICIT		
For supply model		
Intercept	-27.9	
PCPGDP	0.16	0.15
PUBP	1.34	8.02
UMEMPL	0.21	3.38
DUMSOC		
DUMCOAL		
DUMFED		
STAX	0.32	3.65

Coefficient of determination: 0.826
F-ratio: 16.1
Mean squared error: 0.11
Durbin–Watson d statistic: 1.76

Table A.5 The growth of government, 1960–82

Country: USA

Definition of government: TAX/Y

Explanatory variable	Coefficient	t-ratio
For demand model		
Intercept	11.5	0.54
IND	-0.83	-4.39
URBAN	-0.28	-0.97
DPOP	-0.19	-1.00
PCPGDP	6.60	1.56
XM	-0.22	-1.03
ORG	0.88	4.01
INFL	0.14	1.53
DIRTAX	0.48	3.19
DEFICIT	0.28	2.48
For supply model		
Intercept		
PCPGDP		
PUBP		
UNEMPL		
DUMSOC		
DUMCOAL		
DUMFED		
STAX		

Coefficient of determination: 0.937
F-ratio: 18.0
Mean squared error: 0.16
Durbin–Watson d statistic: 2.52

Table A.6 The growth of government, 1960–82

Country: USA

Definition of government: TAX/Y

Explanatory variable	Coefficient	t-ratio
For demand model		
Intercept		
IND		
URBAN		
DPOP		
PCPGDP		
XM		
ORG		
INFL		
DIRTAX		
DEFICIT		
For supply model		
Intercept	-32.8	
PCPGDP	12.5	5.14
PUBP	0.75	2.01
UNEMPL	-0.06	-0.41
DUMSOC		
DUMCOAL		
DUMFED		
STAX	0.51	2.60

Coefficient of determination: 0.707
F-ratio: 8.22
Mean squared error: 0.52
Durbin–Watson d statistic: 0.90

Table A.7 The growth of government, 1960–82

Country: Canada

Definition of government: G+TR/Y

Explanatory variable	Coefficient	t-ratio
For demand model		
Intercept	20.0	0.58
IND	-0.95	-1.31
URBAN	-0.07	-0.21
DPOP	0.35	0.18
PCPGDP	5.52	0.51
XM	-0.26	-2.12
ORG	0.42	1.07
INFL	0.27	1.29
DIRTAX	0.51	3.54
DEFICIT	-0.30	-1.04
For supply model		
Intercept		
PCPGDP		
PUBP		
UNEMPL		
DUMSOC		
DUMCOAL		
DUMFED		
STAX		

Coefficient of determination: 0.979
F-ratio: 68.3
Mean squared error: 0.84
Durbin–Watson d statistic: 1.25

Table A.8 The growth of government, 1960–82

Country: Canada

Definition of government: G+TR/Y

Explanatory variable	Coefficient	t-ratio
For demand model		
Intercept		
IND		
URBAN		
DPOP		
PCPGDP		
XM		
ORG		
INFL		
DIRTAX		
DEFICIT		
For supply model		
Intercept	-23.0	
PCPGDP	20.6	6.91
PUBP	0.71	3.54
UNEMPL	0.82	5.01
DUMSOC		
DUMCOAL		
DUMFED		
STAX	0.23	3.06

Coefficient of determination: 0.984
F-ratio: 205.7
Mean squared error: 0.51
Durbin–Watson d statistic: 2.16

Table A.9 The growth of government, 1960–82

Country: Canada

Definition of government: G/Y

Explanatory variable	Coefficient	t-ratio
For demand model		
Intercept	-7.89	-0.54
IND	-0.67	-2.14
URBAN	0.43	2.97
DPOP	0.25	0.29
PCPGDP	-1.12	-0.24
XM	-0.08	-1.52
ORG	0.04	0.23
INFL	-0.09	-1.00
DIRTAX	0.22	3.60
DEFICIT	-0.05	-0.39
For supply model		
Intercept		
PCPGDP		
PUBP		
UNEMPL		
DUMSOC		
DUMCOAL		
DUMFED		
STAX		

Coefficient of determination: 0.982
F-ratio: 76.7
Mean squared error: 0.15
Durbin–Watson d statistic: 2.30

Table A.10 The growth of government, 1960–82

Country: Canada

Definition of government: G/Y

Explanatory variable	Coefficient	t-ratio
For demand model		
Intercept		
IND		
URBAN		
DPOP		
PCPGDP		
XM		
ORG		
INFL		
DIRTAX		
DEFICIT		
For supply model		
Intercept	-3.2	
PCPGDP	4.11	2.43
PUBP	0.79	6.98
UNEMPL	0.29	3.06
DUMSOC		
DUMCOAL		
DUMFED		
STAX	-0.01	-0.30

Coefficient of determination: 0.974
F-ratio: 129.6
Mean squared error: 0.16
Durbin–Watson d statistic: 1.97

Table A.11 The growth of government, 1960–82

Country: Canada

Definition of government: TAX/Y

Explanatory variable	Coefficient	t-ratio
For demand model		
Intercept	0.41	0.02
IND	-0.84	-2.02
URBAN	0.43	2.23
DPOP	0.43	0.38
PCPGDP	-0.33	-0.05
XM	-0.29	-4.15
ORG	0.28	1.24
INFL	0.32	2.65
DIRTAX	0.31	3.86
DEFICIT	0.64	3.93
For supply model		
Intercept		
PCPGDP		
PUBP		
UNEMPL		
DUMSOC		
DUMCOAL		
DUMFED		
STAX		

Coefficient of determination: 0.981
F-ratio: 75.7
Mean squared error: 0.27
Durbin–Watson d statistic: 1.89

Table A.12 The growth of government, 1960–82

Country: Canada

Definition of government: TAX/Y

Explanatory variable	Coefficient	t-ratio
For demand model		
Intercept		
IND		
URBAN		
DPOP		
PCPGDP		
XM		
ORG		
INFL		
DIRTAX		
DEFICIT		
For supply model		
Intercept	-27.7	
PCPGDP	13.8	4.86
PUBP	1.17	6.14
UNEMPL	-0.43	-2.76
DUMSOC		
DUMCOAL		
DUMFED		
STAX	0.35	4.68

Coefficient of determination: 0.958
F-ratio: 77.9
Mean squared error: 0.46
Durbin–Watson d statistic: 1.97

Table A.13 The growth of government, 1960–82

Country: Australia

Definition of government: G+TR/Y

Explanatory variable	Coefficient	t-ratio
For demand model		
Intercept	90.8	1.49
IND	-1.41	-5.04
URBAN	-0.81	-0.98
DPOP	-0.01	-0.02
PCPGDP	-9.11	-0.80
XM	0.17	1.10
ORG	0.40	2.20
INFL	0.15	1.01
DIRTAX	0.47	1.70
DEFICIT	-0.21	-0.81
For supply model		
Intercept		
PCPGDP		
PUBP		
UNEMPL		
DUMSOC		
DUMCOAL		
DUMFED		
STAX		

Coefficient of determination: 0.979
F-ratio: 66.3
Mean squared error: 0.67
Durbin–Watson d statistic: 2.30

Table A.14 The growth of government, 1960–82

Country: Australia

Definition of government: G+TR/Y

Explanatory variable	Coefficient	t-ratio
For demand model		
Intercept		
IND		
URBAN		
DPOP		
PCPGDP		
XM		
ORG		
INFL		
DIRTAX		
DEFICIT		
For supply model		
Intercept	-64.9	
PCPGDP	12.2	2.67
PUBP	1.83	2.92
UNEMPL	0.41	1.44
DUMSOC	0.14	0.13
DUMCOAL		
DUMFED		
STAX	0.40	1.23

Coefficient of determination: 0.967
F-ratio: 77.5
Mean squared error: 0.85
Durbin–Watson d statistic: 1.94

Table A.15 The growth of government, 1960–82

Country: Australia

Definition of government: G/Y

Explanatory variable	Coefficient	t-ratio
For demand model		
Intercept	54.5	1.68
IND	-0.87	-5.85
URBAN	-0.36	-0.81
DPOP	-0.08	-0.30
PCPGDP	-3.03	-0.50
XM	0.05	0.62
ORG	0.09	0.93
INFL	0.04	0.45
DIRTAX	0.16	1.12
DEFICIT	-0.16	-1.18
For supply model		
Intercept		
PCPGDP		
PUBP		
UNEMPL		
DUMSOC		
DUMCOAL		
DUMFED		
STAX		

Coefficient of determination: 0.984
F-ratio: 87.2
Mean squared error: 0.19
Durbin–Watson d statistic: 2.40

Table A.16 The growth of government, 1960–82

Country: Australia

Definition of government: G/Y

Explanatory variable	Coefficient	t-ratio
For demand model		
Intercept		
IND		
URBAN		
DPOP		
PCPGDP		
XM		
ORG		
INFL		
DIRTAX		
DEFICIT		
For supply model		
Intercept	-48.2	
PCPGDP	9.44	4.18
PUBP	1.11	3.56
UNEMPL	0.12	0.85
DUMSOC	-0.05	-0.09
DUMCOAL		
DUMFED		
STAX	0.27	0.11

Coefficient of determination: 0.978
F-ratio: 118.9
Mean squared error: 0.21
Durbin–Watson d statistic: 1.54

Table A.17 The growth of government, 1960–82

Country: Australia

Definition of government: TAX/Y

Explanatory variable	Coefficient	t-ratio
For demand model		
Intercept	35.4	0.89
IND	-0.59	-3.21
URBAN	-0.33	-0.61
DPOP	0.14	0.45
PCPGDP	4.97	0.67
XM	0.30	3.08
ORG	0.06	0.47
INFL	0.08	0.84
DIRTAX	0.25	1.39
DEFICIT	-0.13	-0.78
For supply model		
Intercept		
PCPGDP		
PUBP		
UNEMPL		
DUMSOC		
DUMCOAL		
DUMFED		
STAX		

Coefficient of determination: 0.986
F-ratio: 98.5
Mean squared error: 0.29
Durbin–Watson d statistic: 2.78

Table A.18 The growth of government, 1960–82

Country: Australia

Definition of government: TAX/Y

Explanatory variable	Coefficient	t-ratio
For demand model		
Intercept		
IND		
URBAN		
DPOP		
PCPGDP		
XM		
ORG		
INFL		
DIRTAX		
DEFICIT		
For supply model		
Intercept	-60.1	
PCPGDP	18.2	5.67
PUBP	0.91	2.07
UNEMPL	0.17	0.82
DUMSOC	-0.04	-0.05
DUMCOAL		
DUMFED		
STAX	0.49	2.14

Coefficient of determination: 0.978
F-ratio: 118.9
Mean squared error: 0.21
Durbin–Watson d statistic: 1.54

Table A.19 The growth of government, 1960–82

Country: United Kingdom

Definition of government: G+TR/Y

Explanatory variable	Coefficient	t-ratio
For demand model		
Intercept	-13.1	-0.08
IND	-0.75	-1.24
URBAN	0.51	0.30
DPOP	0.38	0.23
PCPGDP	50.3	2.11
XM	0.04	0.37
ORG	-0.61	-2.00
INFL	-0.09	-0.71
DIRTAX	0.10	0.40
DEFICIT	0.12	0.41
For supply model		
Intercept		
PCPGDP		
PUBP		
UNEMPL		
DUMSOC		
DUMCOAL		
DUMFED		
STAX		

Coefficient of determination: 0.958
F-ratio: 27.2
Mean squared error: 1.71
Durbin–Watson d statistic: 1.95

Table A.20 The growth of government, 1960–82

Country: United Kingdom

Definition of government: G+TR/Y

Explanatory variable	Coefficient	t-ratio
For demand model		
Intercept		
IND		
URBAN		
DPOP		
PCPGDP		
XM		
ORG		
INFL		
DIRTAX		
DEFICIT		
For supply model		
Intercept	-24.0	-0.81
PCPGDP	32.4	2.20
PUBP	-0.03	-0.04
UNEMPL	0.30	1.51
DUMSOC	1.46	2.17
DUMCOAL	-1.05	-1.83
DUMFED		
STAX	0.27	0.79

Coefficient of determination: 0.952
F-ratio: 53.7
Mean squared error: 1.44
Durbin–Watson d statistic: 2.08

Table A.21 The growth of government, 1960–82

Country: United Kingdom

Definition of government: G/Y

Explanatory variable	Coefficient	t-ratio
For demand model		
Intercept	-81.0	-2.82
IND	-0.56	-5.08
URBAN	1.31	4.20
DPOP	-0.74	-2.50
PCPGDP	18.1	4.15
XM	-0.03	-1.60
ORG	-0.11	-1.98
INFL	0.05	2.24
DIRTAX	0.01	0.30
DEFICIT	0.04	0.74
For supply model		
Intercept		
PCPGDP		
PUBP		
UNEMPL		
DUMSOC		
DUMCOAL		
DUMFED		
STAX		

Coefficient of determination: 0.992
F-ratio: 27.2
Mean squared error: 0.06
Durbin–Watson d statistic: 2.45

Table A.22 The growth of government, 1960–82

Country: United Kingdom

Definition of government: G/Y

Explanatory variable	Coefficient	t-ratio
For demand model		
Intercept		
IND		
URBAN		
DPOP		
PCPGDP		
XM		
ORG		
INFL		
DIRTAX		
DEFICIT		
For supply model		
Intercept	-6.14	-0.58
PCPGDP	27.2	5.14
PUBP	-0.77	-2.95
UNEMPL	0.22	3.07
DUMSOC	0.09	0.36
DUMCOAL	-0.09	-0.43
DUMFED		
STAX	0.06	0.50

Coefficient of determination: 0.965
F-ratio: 73.7
Mean squared error: 0.19
Durbin–Watson d statistic: 1.79

Table A.23 The growth of government, 1960–82

Country: United Kingdom

Definition of government: TAX/Y

Explanatory variable	Coefficient	t-ratio
For demand model		
Intercept	21.6	0.16
IND	-0.03	-0.05
URBAN	-0.29	-0.20
DPOP	0.80	0.60
PCPGDP	54.2	2.79
XM	0.00	0.01
ORG	-0.44	-1.80
INFL	-0.07	-0.65
DIRTAX	-0.10	-0.47
DEFICIT	0.79	3.38
For supply model		
Intercept		
PCPGDP		
PUBP		
UNEMPL		
DUMSOC		
DUMCOAL		
DUMFED		
STAX		

Coefficient of determination: 0.942
F-ratio: 19.6
Mean squared error: 1.13
Durbin–Watson d statistic: 2.16

Table A.24 The growth of government, 1960–82

Country: United Kingdom

Definition of government: TAX/Y

Explanatory variable	Coefficient	t-ratio
For demand model		
Intercept		
IND		
URBAN		
DPOP		
PCPGDP		
XM		
ORG		
INFL		
DIRTAX		
DEFICIT		
For supply model		
Intercept	-30.2	-0.74
PCPGDP	0.37	0.01
PUBP	1.01	1.01
UNEMPL	0.17	0.61
DUMSOC	1.01	1.09
DUMCOAL	-1.37	-1.73
DUMFED		
STAX	0.48	1.03

Coefficient of determination: 0.816
F-ratio: 11.8
Mean squared error: 2.71
Durbin–Watson d statistic: 1.22

Table A.25 The growth of government, 1960–82

Country: Germany

Definition of government: G+TR/Y

Explanatory variable	Coefficient	t-ratio
For demand model		
Intercept	12.1	1.17
IND	-0.49	-3.24
URBAN		
DPOP	-0.57	-1.48
PCPGDP	9.49	2.48
XM	0.03	0.88
ORG	0.34	1.76
INFL	-0.27	-2.98
DIRTAX	0.36	2.21
DEFICIT	-0.54	-7.00
For supply model		
Intercept		
PCPGDP		
PUBP		
UNEMPL		
DUMSOC		
DUMCOAL		
DUMFED		
STAX		

Coefficient of determination: 0.996
F-ratio: 451.6
Mean squared error: 0.18
Durbin–Watson d statistic: 2.46

Table A.26 The growth of government, 1960–82

Country: Germany

Definition of government: G+TR/Y

Explanatory variable	Coefficient	t-ratio
For demand model		
Intercept		
IND		
URBAN		
DPOP		
PCPGDP		
XM		
ORG		
INFL		
DIRTAX		
DEFICIT		
For supply model		
Intercept	38.5	
PCPGDP	9.38	1.19
PUBP	1.56	2.63
UNEMPL	0.80	2.77
DUMSOC	-1.66	-1.47
DUMCOAL	-1.00	-1.54
DUMFED		
STAX	-0.39	-2.07

Coefficient of determination: 0.988
F-ratio: 179.6
Mean squared error: 0.52
Durbin–Watson d statistic: 1.39

Table A.27 The growth of government, 1960–82

Country: Germany

Definition of government: G/Y

Explanatory variable	Coefficient	t-ratio
For demand model		
Intercept	9.61	1.30
IND	-0.27	-2.52
URBAN		
DPOP	-0.33	-1.20
PCPGDP	5.16	1.88
XM	-0.02	-0.82
ORG	0.18	1.27
INFL	0.11	1.60
DIRTAX	0.09	0.78
DEFICIT	-0.24	-4.35
For supply model		
Intercept		
PCPGDP		
PUBP		
UNEMPL		
DUMSOC		
DUMCOAL		
DUMFED		
STAX		

Coefficient of determination: 0.989
F-ratio: 162.7
Mean squared error: 0.09
Durbin–Watson d statistic: 2.86

Table A.28 The growth of government, 1960–82

Country: Germany

Definition of government: G/Y

Explanatory variable	Coefficient	t-ratio
For demand model		
Intercept		
IND		
URBAN		
DPOP		
PCPGDP		
XM		
ORG		
INFL		
DIRTAX		
DEFICIT		
For supply model		
Intercept	10.79	
PCPGDP	8.60	1.64
PUBP	0.41	1.06
UNEMPL	0.28	1.44
DUMSOC	-1.02	-1.36
DUMCOAL	-0.93	-2.15
DUMFED		
STAX	-0.12	-0.97

Coefficient of determination: 0.972
F-ratio: 74.4
Mean squared error: 0.23
Durbin–Watson d statistic: 1.40

Table A.29 The growth of government, 1960–82

Country: Germany

Definition of government: TAX/Y

Explanatory variable	Coefficient	t-ratio
For demand model		
Intercept	14.4	1.14
IND	-0.56	-3.02
URBAN		
DPOP	0.75	1.58
PCPGDP	9.20	1.97
XM	0.08	1.73
ORG	0.51	2.15
INFL	-0.30	-2.70
DIRTAX	0.18	0.89
DEFICIT	0.26	2.76
For supply model		
Intercept		
PCPGDP		
PUBP		
UNEMPL		
DUMSOC		
DUMCOAL		
DUMFED		
STAX		

Coefficient of determination: 0.981
F-ratio: 88.3
Mean squared error: 0.27
Durbin–Watson d statistic: 2.51

Table A.30 The growth of government, 1960–82

Country: Germany

Definition of government: TAX/Y

Explanatory variable	Coefficient	t-ratio
For demand model		
Intercept		
IND		
URBAN		
DPOP		
PCPGDP		
XM		
ORG		
INFL		
DIRTAX		
DEFICIT		
For supply model		
Intercept	60.6	
PCPGDP	9.53	0.91
PUBP	0.48	0.61
UNEMPL	0.71	1.86
DUMSOC	-1.31	-0.88
DUMCOAL	-1.77	-2.05
DUMFED		
STAX	-0.59	-2.35

Coefficient of determination: 0.930
F-ratio: 28.4
Mean squared error: 0.91
Durbin–Watson d statistic: 1.41

Table A.31 The growth of government, 1960–82

Country: France

Definition of government: G+TR/Y

Explanatory variable	Coefficient	t-ratio
For demand model		
Intercept	125.6	8.42
IND	-2.22	-7.59
URBAN	-0.29	-1.69
DPOP	-3.90	-4.36
PCPGDP	4.87	0.34
XM	-0.04	-0.36
ORG	-0.03	-0.07
INFL	0.18	1.30
DIRTAX	-0.09	-0.29
DEFICIT	-0.78	-3.73
For supply model		
Intercept		
PCPGDP		
PUBP		
UNEMPL		
DUMSOC		
DUMCOAL		
DUMFED		
STAX		

Coefficient of determination: 0.990
F-ratio: 120.8
Mean squared error: 0.33
Durbin–Watson d statistic: 2.40

Table A.32 The growth of government, 1960–82

Country: France

Definition of government: G+TR/Y

Explanatory variable	Coefficient	t-ratio
For demand model		
Intercept		
IND		
URBAN		
DPOP		
PCPGDP		
XM		
ORG		
INFL		
DIRTAX		
DEFICIT		
For supply model		
Intercept	100.0	
PCPGDP	28.7	3.10
PUBP	-2.60	-2.10
UNEMPL	1.51	3.17
DUMSOC	1.09	1.04
DUMCOAL		
DUMFED		
STAX	-0.67	-3.26

Coefficient of determination: 0.970
F-ratio: 86.8
Mean squared error: 0.76
Durbin–Watson d statistic: 1.34

Table A.33 The growth of government, 1960–82

Country: France

Definition of government: G/Y

Explanatory variable	Coefficient	t-ratio
For demand model		
Intercept	34.3	6.96
IND	-0.49	-5.02
URBAN	-0.20	-3.56
DPOP	-0.62	-2.10
PCPGDP	3.06	0.64
XM	0.01	0.30
ORG	0.12	0.84
INFL	0.00	0.01
DIRTAX	0.01	0.14
DEFICIT	-0.13	-1.86
For supply model		
Intercept		
PCPGDP		
PUBP		
UNEMPL		
DUMSOC		
DUMCOAL		
DUMFED		
STAX		

Coefficient of determination: 0.979
F-ratio: 54.6
Mean squared error: 0.04
Durbin–Watson d statistic: 2.12

Table A.34 The growth of government, 1960–82

Country: France

Definition of government: G/Y

Explanatory variable	Coefficient	t-ratio
For demand model		
Intercept		
IND		
URBAN		
DPOP		
PCPGDP		
XM		
ORG		
INFL		
DIRTAX		
DEFICIT		
For supply model		
Intercept	10.7	
PCPGDP	-5.02	-1.68
PUBP	0.70	1.76
UNEMPL	0.42	2.73
DUMSOC	0.12	0.37
DUMCOAL		
DUMFED		
STAX	-0.02	-0.31

Coefficient of determination: 0.938
F-ratio: 40.5
Mean squared error: 0.09
Durbin–Watson d statistic: 1.69

Table A.35 The growth of government, 1960–82

Country: France

Definition of government: TAX/Y

Explanatory variable	Coefficient	t-ratio
For demand model		
Intercept	115.6	8.12
IND	-2.01	-7.17
URBAN	-0.35	-2.12
DPOP	-3.71	-4.33
PCPGDP	11.50	0.84
XM	-0.08	-0.62
ORG	0.01	0.02
INFL	0.16	1.21
DIRTAX	-0.15	0.52
DEFICIT	0.31	1.54
For supply model		
Intercept		
PCPGDP		
PUBP		
UNEMPL		
DUMSOC		
DUMCOAL		
DUMFED		
STAX		

Coefficient of determination: 0.978
F-ratio: 53.0
Mean squared error: 0.30
Durbin–Watson d statistic: 2.39

Table A.36 The growth of government, 1960–82

Country: France

Definition of government: TAX/Y

Explanatory variable	Coefficient	t-ratio
For demand model		
Intercept		
IND		
URBAN		
DPOP		
PCPGDP		
XM		
ORG		
INFL		
DIRTAX		
DEFICIT		
For supply model		
Intercept	53.5	
PCPGDP	2.22	0.26
PUBP	-0.64	-0.56
UNEMPL	1.51	3.42
DUMSOC	-0.30	-0.30
DUMCOAL		
DUMFED		
STAX	-0.16	-0.87

Coefficient of determination: 0.937
F-ratio: 39.5
Mean squared error: 0.65
Durbin–Watson d statistic: 2.30

Table A.37 The growth of government, 1960–82

Country: Italy

Definition of government: G+TR/Y

Explanatory variable	Coefficient	t-ratio
For demand model		
Intercept	25.6	2.78
IND	-0.81	-4.52
URBAN		
DPOP	-1.41	-0.87
PCPGDP	6.58	2.02
XM	-0.01	-0.11
ORG	0.42	2.47
INFL	-0.20	-2.20
DIRTAX	0.13	0.64
DEFICIT	-0.71	-3.51
For supply model		
Intercept		
PCPGDP		
PUBP		
UNEMPL		
DUMSOC		
DUMCOAL		
DUMFED		
STAX		

Coefficient of determination: 0.988
F-ratio: 143.3
Mean squared error: 0.82
Durbin–Watson d statistic: 1.28

Table A.38 The growth of government, 1960–82

Country: Italy

Definition of government: G+TR/Y

Explanatory variable	Coefficient	t-ratio
For demand model		
Intercept		
IND		
URBAN		
DPOP		
PCPGDP		
XM		
ORG		
INFL		
DIRTAX		
DEFICIT		
For supply model		
Intercept	-46.2	-2.35
PCPGDP	10.53	1.15
PUBP	0.04	0.05
UNEMPL	3.11	5.94
DUMSOC		
DUMCOAL	-0.59	-0.94
DUMFED		
STAX	0.55	2.55

Coefficient of determination: 0.967
F-ratio: 99.4
Mean squared error: 1.86
Durbin–Watson d statistic: 1.43

Table A.39 The growth of government, 1960–82

Country: Italy

Definition of government: G/Y

Explanatory variable	Coefficient	t-ratio
For demand model		
Intercept	9.68	4.35
IND	-0.24	-5.53
URBAN		
DPOP	0.30	0.78
PCPGDP	9.31	11.78
XM	-0.07	-2.54
ORG	0.03	0.60
INFL	0.02	0.69
DIRTAX	0.00	0.01
DEFICIT	-0.18	-3.58
For supply model		
Intercept		
PCPGDP		
PUBP		
UNEMPL		
DUMSOC		
DUMCOAL		
DUMFED		
STAX		

Coefficient of determination: 0.986
F-ratio: 125.9
Mean squared error: 0.05
Durbin–Watson d statistic: 1.90

Table A.40 The growth of government, 1960–82

Country: Italy

Definition of government: G/Y

Explanatory variable	Coefficient	t-ratio
For demand model		
Intercept		
IND		
URBAN		
DPOP		
PCPGDP		
XM		
ORG		
INFL		
DIRTAX		
DEFICIT		
For supply model		
Intercept	-4.70	-0.89
PCPGDP	12.69	5.18
PUBP	-0.46	-2.60
UNEMPL	0.20	1.41
DUMSOC		
DUMCOAL	-0.16	-0.95
DUMFED		
STAX	0.08	1.36

Coefficient of determination: 0.954
F-ratio: 70.9
Mean squared error: 0.13
Durbin–Watson d statistic: 1.27

Table A.41 The growth of government, 1960–82

Country: Italy

Definition of government: TAX/Y

Explanatory variable	Coefficient	t-ratio
For demand model		
Intercept	19.4	2.02
IND	-1.12	-5.95
URBAN		
DPOP	-0.68	-0.40
PCPGDP	0.60	1.95
XM	0.08	0.63
ORG	-0.03	-0.17
INFL	-0.12	-1.28
DIRTAX	0.54	2.55
DEFICIT	0.30	1.44
For supply model		
Intercept		
PCPGDP		
PUBP		
UNEMPL		
DUMSOC		
DUMCOAL		
DUMFED		
STAX		

Coefficient of determination: 0.936
F-ratio: 25.4
Mean squared error: 0.90
Durbin–Watson d statistic: 2.00

Table A.42 The growth of government, 1960–82

Country: Italy

Definition of government: TAX/Y

Explanatory variable	Cocfficient	t-ratio
For demand model		
Intercept		
IND		
URBAN		
DPOP		
PCPGDP		
XM		
ORG		
INFL		
DIRTAX		
DEFICIT		
For supply model		
Intercept	-42.1	-2.40
PCPGDP	7.72	0.95
PUBP	-1.29	-2.19
UNEMPL	2.21	4.74
DUMSOC		
DUMCOAL	0.34	0.61
DUMFED		
STAX	0.68	3.50

Coefficient of determination: 0.954
F-ratio: 70.9
Mean squared error: 0.13
Durbin–Watson d statistic: 1.27

Table A.43 The growth of government, 1960–82

Country: The Netherlands

Definition of government: G+TR/Y

Explanatory variable	Coefficient	t-ratio
For demand model		
Intercept	91.0	2.76
IND	-0.94	-1.32
URBAN	-0.96	-2.02
DPOP	3.07	0.98
PCPGDP	21.31	3.34
XM	-0.04	-1.98
ORG	-0.05	-0.12
INFL	0.20	1.06
DIRTAX	0.33	1.04
DEFICIT	-0.51	-1.06
For supply model		
Intercept		
PCPGDP		
PUBP		
UNEMPL		
DUMSOC		
DUMCOAL		
DUMFED		
STAX		

Coefficient of determination: 0.991
F-ratio: 167.1
Mean squared error: 1.23
Durbin–Watson d statistic: 2.22

Table A.44 The growth of government, 1960–82

Country: The Netherlands

Definition of government: G+TR/Y

Explanatory variable	Coefficient	t-ratio
For demand model		
Intercept		
IND		
URBAN		
DPOP		
PCPGDP		
XM		
ORG		
INFL		
DIRTAX		
DEFICIT		
For supply model		
Intercept	-225.1	-1.22
PCPGDP	23.6	8.43
PUBP	-1.86	-1.46
UNEMPL	2.03	4.09
DUMSOC	-0.23	-0.24
DUMCOAL	-0.85	-1.10
DUMFED		
STAX	2.60	1.31

Coefficient of determination: 0.991
F-ratio: 304.6
Mean squared error: 1.01
Durbin–Watson d statistic: 1.67

Table A.45 The growth of government, 1960–82

Country: The Netherlands

Definition of government: G/Y

Explanatory variable	Coefficient	t-ratio
For demand model		
Intercept	-2.76	-0.29
IND	-0.17	-0.84
URBAN	0.07	0.54
DPOP	1.40	1.56
PCPGDP	4.53	2.47
XM	0.00	0.16
ORG	0.17	1.44
INFL	-0.02	-0.54
DIRTAX	0.04	0.40
DEFICIT	-0.21	-1.52
For supply model		
Intercept		
PCPGDP		
PUBP		
UNEMPL		
DUMSOC		
DUMCOAL		
DUMFED		
STAX		

Coefficient of determination: 0.972
F-ratio: 54.6
Mean squared error: 0.10
Durbin–Watson d statistic: 2.22

Table A.46 The growth of government, 1960–82

Country: The Netherlands

Definition of government: G/Y

Explanatory variable	Coefficient	t-ratio
For demand model		
Intercept		
IND		
URBAN		
DPOP		
PCPGDP		
XM		
ORG		
INFL		
DIRTAX		
DEFICIT		
For supply model		
Intercept	58.1	0.82
PCPGDP	5.81	5.42
PUBP	0.00	0.01
UNEMPL	0.31	0.70
DUMSOC	-0.60	-1.69
DUMCOAL	0.07	0.21
DUMFED		
STAX	-0.51	-0.69

Coefficient of determination: 0.954
F-ratio: 55.0
Mean squared error: 0.15
Durbin–Watson d statistic: 1.10

Table A.47 The growth of government, 1960–82

Country: The Netherlands

Definition of government: TAX/Y

Explanatory variable	Coefficient	t-ratio
For demand model		
Intercept	-14.1	-0.65
IND	-0.44	-0.95
URBAN	-0.04	-0.12
DPOP	0.46	0.22
PCPGDP	18.2	4.33
XM	-0.01	-1.43
ORG	0.16	0.61
INFL	-0.25	-2.06
DIRTAX	0.54	2.60
DEFICIT	0.47	1.47
For supply model		
Intercept		
PCPGDP		
PUBP		
UNEMPL		
DUMSOC		
DUMCOAL		
DUMFED		
STAX		

Coefficient of determination: 0.992
F-ratio: 176.1
Mean squared error: 0.53
Durbin–Watson d statistic: 1.70

Table A.48 The growth of government, 1960–82

Country: The Netherlands

Definition of government: TAX/Y

Explanatory variable	Coefficient	t-ratio
For demand model		
Intercept		
IND		
URBAN		
DPOP		
PCPGDP		
XM		
ORG		
INFL		
DIRTAX		
DEFICIT		
For supply model		
Intercept	-115.8	-0.71
PCPGDP	23.1	9.37
PUBP	-0.99	-0.88
UNEMPL	0.48	1.10
DUMSOC	0.29	0.36
DUMCOAL	-0.30	-0.40
DUMFED		
STAX	1.34	0.78

Coefficient of determination: 0.985
F-ratio: 179.6
Mean squared error: 0.78
Durbin–Watson d statistic: 2.01

Table A.49 The growth of government, 1960–82

Country: Belgium

Definition of government: G+TR/Y

Explanatory variable	Coefficient	t-ratio
For demand model		
Intercept	-300.0	-1.42
IND	-1.82	-3.86
URBAN	5.10	2.09
DPOP	-3.44	-2.87
PCPGDP	-55.65	-4.42
XM	-0.02	-0.62
ORG	-0.01	-0.12
INFL	0.38	2.74
DIRTAX	0.19	1.47
DEFICIT	-1.14	-6.18
For supply model		
Intercept		
PCPGDP		
PUBP		
UNEMPL		
DUMSOC		
DUMCOAL		
DUMFED		
STAX		

Coefficient of determination: 0.996
F-ratio: 397.0
Mean squared error: 0.43
Durbin–Watson d statistic: 2.03

Table A.50 The growth of government, 1960–82

Country: Belgium

Definition of government: G+TR/Y

Explanatory variable	Coefficient	t-ratio
For demand model		
Intercept		
IND		
URBAN		
DPOP		
PCPGDP		
XM		
ORG		
INFL		
DIRTAX		
DEFICIT		
For supply model		
Intercept	126.1	1.27
PCPGDP	11.89	1.15
PUBP	3.38	6.65
UNEMPL	-0.22	-1.15
DUMSOC	0.42	0.43
DUMCOAL	-0.72	-1.28
DUMFED		
STAX	-1.54	-1.48

Coefficient of determination: 0.987
F-ratio: 202.8
Mean squared error: 1.26
Durbin–Watson d statistic: 1.34

Table A.51 The growth of government, 1960–82

Country: Belgium

Definition of government: G/Y

Explanatory variable	Coefficient	t-ratio
For demand model		
Intercept	-19.7	-0.24
IND	-0.59	-3.30
URBAN	0.64	0.70
DPOP	0.35	0.76
PCPGDP	-4.12	-0.87
XM	-0.04	-3.36
ORG	0.03	0.67
INFL	0.09	1.68
DIRTAX	0.03	0.65
DEFICIT	-0.17	-2.47
For supply model		
Intercept		
PCPGDP		
PUBP		
UNEMPL		
DUMSOC		
DUMCOAL		
DUMFED		
STAX		

Coefficient of determination: 0.992
F-ratio: 186.6
Mean squared error: 0.06
Durbin–Watson d statistic: 1.94

Table A.52 The growth of government, 1960–82

Country: Belgium

Definition of government: G/Y

Explanatory variable	Coefficient	t-ratio
For demand model		
Intercept		
IND		
URBAN		
DPOP		
PCPGDP		
XM		
ORG		
INFL		
DIRTAX		
DEFICIT		
For supply model		
Intercept	-9.82	-0.39
PCPGDP	6.61	2.50
PUBP	0.74	5.66
UNEMPL	-0.09	-1.83
DUMSOC	-0.03	-0.13
DUMCOAL	-0.14	-0.97
DUMFED		
STAX	0.07	0.28

Coefficient of determination: 0.988
F-ratio: 210.0
Mean squared error: 0.08
Durbin–Watson d statistic: 2.30

Table A.53 The growth of government, 1960–82

Country: Belgium

Definition of government: TAX/Y

Explanatory variable	Coefficient	t-ratio
For demand model		
Intercept	-373.7	-1.60
IND	-1.56	-2.99
URBAN	5.69	2.10
DPOP	-2.98	-2.24
PCPGDP	-52.37	-3.75
XM	-0.02	-0.64
ORG	0.01	0.04
INFL	0.29	1.88
DIRTAX	0.34	2.36
DEFICIT	-0.10	-0.50
For supply model		
Intercept		
PCPGDP		
PUBP		
UNEMPL		
DUMSOC		
DUMCOAL		
DUMFED		
STAX		

Coefficient of determination: 0.991
F-ratio: 156.4
Mean squared error: 0.53
Durbin–Watson d statistic: 1.92

Table A.54 The growth of government, 1960–82

Country: Belgium

Definition of government: TAX/Y

Explanatory variable	Coefficient	t-ratio
For demand model		
Intercept		
IND		
URBAN		
DPOP		
PCPGDP		
XM		
ORG		
INFL		
DIRTAX		
DEFICIT		
For supply model		
Intercept	111.4	1.09
PCPGDP	14.7	1.39
PUBP	3.11	5.98
UNEMPL	-1.09	-5.55
DUMSOC	-0.54	-0.54
DUMCOAL	-0.70	-1.21
DUMFED		
STAX	-1.39	-1.29

Coefficient of determination: 0.972
F-ratio: 92.6
Mean squared error: 1.32
Durbin–Watson d statistic: 1.83

Table A.55 The growth of government, 1960–82

Country: Austria

Definition of government: G+TR/Y

Explanatory variable	Coefficient	t-ratio
For demand model		
Intercept	-485.5	-5.80
IND	0.45	0.68
URBAN	10.79	6.01
DPOP	-5.48	-3.05
PCPGDP	-21.64	-2.51
XM	0.01	0.18
ORG	-0.28	-0.91
INFL	-0.18	-1.29
DIRTAX	0.03	0.18
DEFICIT	-0.82	-3.65
For supply model		
Intercept		
PCPGDP		
PUBP		
UNEMPL		
DUMSOC		
DUMCOAL		
DUMFED		
STAX		

Coefficient of determination: 0.990
F-ratio: 148.5
Mean squared error: 0.54
Durbin–Watson d statistic: 2.68

Table A.56 The growth of government, 1960–82

Country: Austria

Definition of government: G+TR/Y

Explanatory variable	Coefficient	t-ratio
For demand model		
Intercept		
IND		
URBAN		
DPOP		
PCPGDP		
XM		
ORG		
INFL		
DIRTAX		
DEFICIT		
For supply model		
Intercept	-58.2	
PCPGDP	18.00	1.93
PUBP	0.85	1.05
UNEMPL	-0.16	-0.24
DUMSOC	-2.82	-2.07
DUMCOAL	0.21	0.48
DUMFED		
STAX	0.86	2.76

Coefficient of determination: 0.983
F-ratio: 122.9
Mean squared error: 0.83
Durbin–Watson d statistic: 2.04

Table A.57 The growth of government, 1960–82

Country: Austria

Definition of government: G/Y

Explanatory variable	Coefficient	t-ratio
For demand model		
Intercept	-33.2	-2.39
IND	-0.03	-0.28
URBAN	0.67	2.24
DPOP	-0.86	-2.87
PCPGDP	3.61	2.51
XM	0.01	0.88
ORG	0.08	1.45
INFL	-0.04	-1.53
DIRTAX	0.08	2.94
DEFICIT	-0.24	-6.37
For supply model		
Intercept		
PCPGDP		
PUBP		
UNEMPL		
DUMSOC		
DUMCOAL		
DUMFED		
STAX		

Coefficient of determination: 0.998
F-ratio: 708.0
Mean squared error: 0.01
Durbin–Watson d statistic: 2.22

Table A.58 The growth of government, 1960–82

Country: Austria

Definition of government: G/Y

Explanatory variable	Coefficient	t-ratio
For demand model		
Intercept		
IND		
URBAN		
DPOP		
PCPGDP		
XM		
ORG		
INFL		
DIRTAX		
DEFICIT		
For supply model		
Intercept	-8.6	
PCPGDP	11.38	4.67
PUBP	-0.11	-0.56
UNEMPL	0.54	3.04
DUMSOC	-0.48	-1.34
DUMCOAL	0.05	0.43
DUMFED		
STAX	0.12	1.48

Coefficient of determination: 0.991
F-ratio: 238.0
Mean squared error: 0.06
Durbin–Watson d statistic: 1.92

Table A.59 The growth of government, 1960–82

Country: Austria

Definition of government: TAX/Y

Explanatory variable	Coefficient	t-ratio
For demand model		
Intercept	-249.4	-4.46
IND	0.52	1.18
URBAN	5.12	4.27
DPOP	-0.85	-0.70
PCPGDP	-4.59	-0.80
XM	-0.07	-1.22
ORG	-0.20	-0.98
INFL	0.01	0.07
DIRTAX	0.50	4.46
DEFICIT	0.09	0.61
For supply model		
Intercept		
PCPGDP		
PUBP		
UNEMPL		
DUMSOC		
DUMCOAL		
DUMFED		
STAX		

Coefficient of determination: 0.987
F-ratio: 113.5
Mean squared error: 0.23
Durbin–Watson d statistic: 2.57

Table A.60 The growth of government, 1960–82

Country: Austria

Definition of government: TAX/Y

Explanatory variable	Coefficient	t-ratio
For demand model		
Intercept		
IND		
URBAN		
DPOP		
PCPGDP		
XM		
ORG		
INFL		
DIRTAX		
DEFICIT		
For supply model		
Intercept	-15.8	
PCPGDP	-6.62	-0.72
PUBP	1.65	2.08
UNEMPL	-1.13	-1.71
DUMSOC	-0.53	-0.40
DUMCOAL	0.07	0.17
DUMFED		
STAX	0.55	1.79

Coefficient of determination: 0.952
F-ratio: 42.5
Mean squared error: 0.79
Durbin–Watson d statistic: 1.92

Table A.61 The growth of government, 1960–82

Country: Norway

Definition of government: G+TR/Y

Explanatory variable	Coefficient	t-ratio
For demand model		
Intercept	27.9	1.40
IND	-0.56	-1.56
URBAN	1.49	5.46
DPOP	-8.69	-1.93
PCPGDP	12.21	0.91
XM	-0.19	-1.93
ORG	-0.38	-2.38
INFL	0.08	0.59
DIRTAX	-0.03	-0.11
DEFICIT	-0.31	-0.84
For supply model		
Intercept		
PCPGDP		
PUBP		
UNEMPL		
DUMSOC		
DUMCOAL		
DUMFED		
STAX		

Coefficient of determination: 0.986
F-ratio: 103.7
Mean squared error: 1.18
Durbin–Watson d statistic: 1.58

Table A.62 The growth of government, 1960–82

Country: Norway

Definition of government: G+TR/Y

Explanatory variable	Coefficient	t-ratio
For demand model		
Intercept		
IND		
URBAN		
DPOP		
PCPGDP		
XM		
ORG		
INFL		
DIRTAX		
DEFICIT		
For supply model		
Intercept	-21.1	-1.20
PCPGDP	25.86	2.82
PUBP	1.54	4.00
UNEMPL	0.38	0.30
DUMSOC	2.05	1.07
DUMCOAL	1.80	0.80
DUMFED		
STAX	0.05	0.20

Coefficient of determination: 0.980
F-ratio: 133.3
Mean squared error: 1.37
Durbin–Watson d statistic: 0.87

Table A.63 The growth of government, 1960–82

Country: Norway

Definition of government: G/Y

Explanatory variable	Coefficient	t-ratio
For demand model		
Intercept	-7.45	-1.61
IND	-0.10	-1.26
URBAN	0.35	5.57
DPOP	-1.19	-1.14
PCPGDP	12.02	3.89
XM	-0.02	-0.99
ORG	-0.02	-0.41
INFL	0.10	3.01
DIRTAX	0.03	0.54
DEFICIT	-0.08	-0.93
For supply model		
Intercept		
PCPGDP		
PUBP		
UNEMPL		
DUMSOC		
DUMCOAL		
DUMFED		
STAX		

Coefficient of determination: 0.993
F-ratio: 218.2
Mean squared error: 0.06
Durbin–Watson d statistic: 1.64

Table A.64 The growth of government, 1960–82

Country: Norway

Definition of government: G/Y

Explanatory variable	Coefficient	t-ratio
For demand model		
Intercept		
IND		
URBAN		
DPOP		
PCPGDP		
XM		
ORG		
INFL		
DIRTAX		
DEFICIT		
For supply model		
Intercept	-16.7	-4.88
PCPGDP	21.2	11.85
PUBP	0.13	1.76
UNEMPL	-0.22	-0.91
DUMSOC	-1.15	-3.10
DUMCOAL	-1.15	-2.59
DUMFED		
STAX	0.11	2.27

Coefficient of determination: 0.993
F-ratio: 398.1
Mean squared error: 0.05
Durbin–Watson d statistic: 1.67

Table A.65 The growth of government, 1960–82

Country: Norway

Definition of government: TAX/Y

Explanatory variable	Coefficient	t-ratio
For demand model		
Intercept	22.2	1.14
IND	-0.28	-0.80
URBAN	1.35	5.06
DPOP	-11.09	-2.52
PCPGDP	18.55	1.42
XM	-0.20	-2.17
ORG	-0.34	-2.12
INFL	0.05	0.39
DIRTAX	-0.14	-0.59
DEFICIT	0.84	2.35
For supply model		
Intercept		
PCPGDP		
PUBP		
UNEMPL		
DUMSOC		
DUMCOAL		
DUMFED		
STAX		

Coefficient of determination: 0.985
F-ratio: 93.2
Mean squared error: 1.12
Durbin–Watson d statistic: 1.58

Table A.66 The growth of government, 1960–82

Country: Norway

Definition of government: TAX/Y

Explanatory variable	Coefficient	t-ratio
For demand model		
Intercept		
IND		
URBAN		
DPOP		
PCPGDP		
XM		
ORG		
INFL		
DIRTAX		
DEFICIT		
For supply model		
Intercept	-51.9	-2.73
PCPGDP	23.81	2.41
PUBP	0.90	2.16
UNEMPL	-0.97	-0.71
DUMSOC	1.07	0.52
DUMCOAL	0.18	0.07
DUMFED		
STAX	0.67	2.56

Coefficient of determination: 0.973
F-ratio: 96.8
Mean squared error: 1.59
Durbin–Watson d statistic: 0.99

Table A.67 The growth of government, 1960–82

Country: Sweden

Definition of government: G+TR/Y

Explanatory variable	Coefficient	t-ratio
For demand model		
Intercept	71.0	1.94
IND	-1.65	-4.23
URBAN	-0.58	-1.29
DPOP	1.37	0.04
PCPGDP	41.92	3.19
XM	0.06	0.74
ORG	0.39	2.08
INFL	0.04	0.26
DIRTAX	-0.33	-1.13
DEFICIT	-0.20	-0.83
For supply model		
Intercept		
PCPGDP		
PUBP		
UNEMPL		
DUMSOC		
DUMCOAL		
DUMFED		
STAX		

Coefficient of determination: 0.996
F-ratio: 364.1
Mean squared error: 0.88
Durbin–Watson d statistic: 2.00

Table A.68 The growth of government, 1960–82

Country: Sweden

Definition of government: G+TR/Y

Explanatory variable	Coefficient	t-ratio
For demand model		
Intercept		
IND		
URBAN		
DPOP		
PCPGDP		
XM		
ORG		
INFL		
DIRTAX		
DEFICIT		
For supply model		
Intercept	59.8	2.30
PCPGDP	-18.89	-1.06
PUBP	1.90	3.90
UNEMPL	1.02	0.68
DUMSOC	-2.35	-0.94
DUMCOAL	0.42	0.19
DUMFED		
STAX	-0.41	-2.18

Coefficient of determination: 0.977
F-ratio: 113.6
Mean squared error: 4.16
Durbin–Watson d statistic: 0.92

Table A.69 The growth of government, 1960–82

Country: Sweden

Definition of government: G/Y

Explanatory variable	Coefficient	t-ratio
For demand model		
Intercept	20.4	1.57
IND	-0.37	-2.67
URBAN	-0.31	-1.92
DPOP	-0.23	-0.40
PCPGDP	21.05	4.50
XM	-0.02	-0.61
ORG	0.14	2.16
INFL	0.04	0.80
DIRTAX	-0.02	-0.18
DEFICIT	-0.02	-0.21
For supply model		
Intercept		
PCPGDP		
PUBP		
UNEMPL		
DUMSOC		
DUMCOAL		
DUMFED		
STAX		

Coefficient of determination: 0.997
F-ratio: 451.2
Mean squared error: 0.11
Durbin–Watson d statistic: 1.80

Table A.70 The growth of government, 1960–82

Country: Sweden

Definition of government: G/Y

Explanatory variable	Coefficient	t-ratio
For demand model		
Intercept		
IND		
URBAN		
DPOP		
PCPGDP		
XM		
ORG		
INFL		
DIRTAX		
DEFICIT		
For supply model		
Intercept	13.2	2.12
PCPGDP	2.15	0.50
PUBP	0.52	4.40
UNEMPL	0.55	1.51
DUMSOC	-1.31	-2.19
DUMCOAL	0.01	0.02
DUMFED		
STAX	-0.06	-1.51

Coefficient of determination: 0.992
F-ratio: 312.5
Mean squared error: 0.24
Durbin–Watson d statistic: 1.42

Table A.71 The growth of government, 1960–82

Country: Sweden

Definition of government: TAX/Y

Explanatory variable	Coefficient	t-ratio
For demand model		
Intercept	80.8	1.72
IND	-0.54	-1.07
URBAN	-1.48	-2.57
DPOP	1.47	0.70
PCPGDP	59.43	3.51
XM	-0.03	-0.29
ORG	0.35	1.49
INFL	-0.14	-0.77
DIRTAX	-0.14	-0.38
DEFICIT	0.57	1.85
For supply model		
Intercept		
PCPGDP		
PUBP		
UNEMPL		
DUMSOC		
DUMCOAL		
DUMFED		
STAX		

Coefficient of determination: 0.982
F-ratio: 79.3
Mean squared error: 1.46
Durbin–Watson d statistic: 1.70

Table A.72 The growth of government, 1960–82

Country: Sweden

Definition of government: TAX/Y

Explanatory variable	Coefficient	t-ratio
For demand model		
Intercept		
IND		
URBAN		
DPOP		
PCPGDP		
XM		
ORG		
INFL		
DIRTAX		
DEFICIT		
For supply model		
Intercept	-21.9	-1.48
PCPGDP	38.55	3.79
PUBP	-0.09	-0.35
UNEMPL	1.07	1.24
DUMSOC	-2.16	-1.52
DUMCOAL	0.21	0.17
DUMFED		
STAX	0.20	1.85

Coefficient of determination: 0.980
F-ratio: 127.9
Mean squared error: 1.35
Durbin–Watson d statistic: 1.51

6 Constitutional constraints on the growth of government: a country survey

This chapter serves two purposes. Firstly to present the existing constitutional limitations on taxing and spending power which limits the freedom of action of Parliaments and governments in some interesting countries. Secondly to seek to summarise the discussion that has taken place within these countries on the need for constitutional reform.

This exposition will be limited to Finland and the four large countries – the United Kingdom, Germany, France and the United States. I will also limit myself largely to a discussion of the federal level and to legislation having the status of a constitution. There have of course been other attempts to slow down the growth of government. A list of medium-term budgetary objectives from the early and mid 1980s is given in Table 6.1. Such objectives, however, have turned out to be as meaningless as one could expect, since they have been proposed by exactly the same bodies unable to attain budgetary balance in the first place, namely Parliaments.

Finland

Finland is the only one of the included countries where Parliament's economic powers is subject to qualified majority rule. According to the legislation governing the procedure of Parliament, which in Finland has the status of a constitution, a qualified majority (two-thirds of the votes) is required for legislation on taxation (§68).

Table 6.1 Medium-term budgetary objectives

Country	Time scale	Objective
United States	FY1981–FY1988	Achievement of federal budget balance by 1984, amended to an FY 1988 federal deficit/GNP ratio of about 2 per cent; federal outlays to be reduced from 26 per cent of GNP in FY 1983 to 23 per cent.
Japan	1979/80–84/85	Seven-year plan to reduce public sector deficit from 11.25 per cent of GDP in 1978 to 5½ per cent, implying the elimination of deficit-financed public consumption. Subsequently revised; objective still holds but no deadline at present operative. Original intention of raising taxation altered, in 1981, to policy of restraining public expenditure through a 'zero-ceiling' on most public consumption.
Germany	1983–87	Medium-term financial plan aimed at reducing the federal deficit from DM39 billion (2.5 per cent of GNP) to DM22 billion (about 1 per cent), to be achieved by holding nominal public spending growth to about 2.75 per cent per annum.
France	1982–83	Aim to stablilise central government deficit at 3 per cent of GDP.
United Kingdom	1980/81–85/86	'Medium-term financial strategy', aimed at reducing PSBR from 5.7 per cent of GDP to 2 per cent; general government expenditure planned to fall from 47.5 per cent of GDP in 1981/82 to 43.5 per cent.
Italy	1981–83	Freezing of PSBR at 1980 level; altered to stabilising PSBR at 1982 level.
Canada	1981/82–86/87	Reduction of federal deficit to 2 per cent of GNP in 1975/76 from over 5 per cent in 1978/79; revised to cutting deficit from nearly 7 per cent of GNP in 1982/83 to 3.5 per cent in 1986/87, via a reduction in the government expenditure/GNP ratio from 26 to 23.5 per cent.
Australia	1975–82	General objective to reduce the central government deficit and size of public sector. Ceased to operate 1983.
Austria	1978–83	Reduction of central government deficit to 2.5 per cent of GDP, via expenditure restraint.
Belgium	1979–83	Reduce general government deficit by about a half, to 7 per cent of GDP, through restriction on the growth of current spending.
Denmark	1980–85	Medium-term action programme to reduce the central government deficit through restriction on the growth of public spending and revenue-raising measures.
Finland	1976–82	Growth in the volume of public consumption to be restricted to 1 per cent per annum below the annual average growth rate of GDP; tax burden to be stabilised.
The Netherlands	1978 onwards	Reduction in public sector deficit from 5.25 per cent to structural norm of 4–4.5 per cent of GDP, via expenditure restraint.
Norway	1982–85	'Long-term programme' to contain public expenditure growth and stabilise gross tax level.
Portugal	1981–84	Stabilise or reduce the central government deficit.
Spain	1979 onwards	Medium-term objective to control public sector deficit and curtail current expenditures.
Sweden	1980–90	Reduction of central government deficit in line with the achievement of external current-account balance.
Switzerland	1980–83	Establish federal government budget balance by 1984, by restricting the growth of spending; altered to achieving deficit of 0.2 per cent of GDP by 1986.

Source: OECD

But this requirement applies only in so far as it is a question of a new or increased tax which is proposed for a period exceeding one year.

Apart from these limitations it is also not obvious which laws shall be regarded as tax laws in the constitutional sense. In practice, a relatively wide definition has been used and actions such as customs duties and other import levies have been regarded as coming under the law.

A constitutional committee was set up in 1970 to propose a reform of the constitution. This committee made a proposal in 1974, but on account of disagreement so far nothing has come out of it. Most parties are agreed that the present qualified majority rule should be lessened to facilitate tax decisions but the parties disagree on how large the majority should be. The bourgeois parties have sought to retain the majority of the present legislation, while socialist parties have wanted to change the system into a pure parliamentarian system and abolish the qualified majority.

It is also of interest to note that in Finland at present there is a committee discussing the question whether the fundamental bill of rights should also be extended to include economic, cultural and social questions. Finland would in that case be the first West European country explicitly to introduce an economic bill of rights in the constitution.

United Kingdom

The institutional set-up in the UK has mostly been specified in such a way as to brake the growth of the public sector. It has not been designed to keep the budgetary deficit under control to a similar degree. Already in 1973, before the first oil crisis, the UK belonged to the countries that had a relatively large deficit in the public budget, almost 5 per cent of GDP in 1967. During the 1970s the deficit has reached all the way up to 10 per cent of GDP (OECD). The growth of public expenditures has however been somewhat slower than in other OECD countries. In 1980 the UK lay exactly on the OECD average on the income as well as on the expenditure side, which implies that the public sector as a share of GDP was smaller than in countries like Sweden, The Netherlands, Norway, Belgium, France, Germany, Austria, Italy and Ireland.

Three special conditions have contributed to this development. The first concerns the rules of decision in Parliament. Even if there is no formal constitution, there are still traditions of a constitutional character ('common law'). The distribution of powers between Parliament and government is the following. Only the government (the Crown) may suggest new expenditures. Parliament (the House of Commons) may only reject an expenditure or lower it, never increase an expenditure or propose a new expenditure. Similarly, Parliament has the power to refuse to agree to an increase in taxes which is proposed by the government or to propose decreases in taxes. Parliament cannot, however, increase taxes for instance to the purpose of covering a budgetary deficit. Nor can Parliament move individual tax rates, for instance lower one type of taxation and increase another, leaving the total tax income unchanged. The effect of this method of decision is of course that the expansion of public sector income and expenditure is kept down, but that no greater attention is directed at the budgetary balance itself.

Another characteristic feature of the British parliamentary system is that expenditures and incomes in the budget are decided upon separately. Expenditures for the present and for future years are presented in the form of a White Paper from the government in the beginning of the calendar year. The House of Commons will vote on this bill during February and March. The resulting need of taxes and the desired change in tax rates is however not discussed until March or April. The foundation is also quite different. Expenditures are discussed exclusively from a need's basis, while taxes are discussed from the need to balance the economy in a certain position given the earlier decided-upon increases in expenditures.

A third condition further impeding a focus on budget balance is that until 1980 increases in expenditures were decided upon in constant prices, while the income side was decided upon in current prices.

The British long-term budget surveys, so called PESC (Public Expenditure Survey Committee), were originally proposed explicitly to prevent a further increase in the public sector (Pliatzky 1982, p.56). PESC has been specified every year since 1959 in the form of a rolling five-year plan for public expenditures. This planning is conducted by the Treasury in co-operation with other departments. Until 1980 the forecasts were carried out in constant prices.

Despite the explicit purpose it is very doubtful whether the relatively slower rate of growth in the British public sector really can be ascribed to the planning system PESC. Firstly, it has been claimed that the system rather tends to make a change in priorities more difficult, since the most important decisions on public expenditures are taken on a two- to three-year horizon. If a department has got a certain expenditure included in the long-term survey it is quite impossible to make it reassess its needs. The budget, so to speak, has given a promise to get money to spend in the future (Heclo and Wildavsky 1974).

The other big problem concerns prices in PESC. Calculations are performed in the prices which are expected at the time of decision to be ruling in the coming years ('funny money'). Actual government expenditures in current prices will naturally come to depart from these planned figures in so far as inflation departs from forecast values. In this way a comparison of forecasts of actual expenditure volumes with plans is made almost impossible.

In later years the system has been changed with a purpose of increasing controllability of the growth of nominal government expenditures. Firstly, greater attention is directed towards the first year and much more change is made here. Secondly, calculations are now made in current prices starting from 1981. All increases in expenditures are thus specified in current prices. If inflation exceeds what is forecast, volume increases are correspondingly reduced. Inflation has also been made the cheese slicer that cuts public expenditures. It was for instance decided in the 1981 programme that inflation for the next year should be, at most, 7 per cent. From that time on the allowable amount of inflation has been decreased by one percentage point every year.

Parliamentary rules for making decisions on incomes and expenditures have so far not been changed, but a proposition has been made to coordinate expenditure and taxing decisions (see *Budgetary Reform in the UK* 1980).

Germany

The Keynesian ideas that a strict budget balance every year could be relinquished took a long time to penetrate in Germany. Until 1969 budgetary deficits at the federal level were actually forbidden according to the constitution (Grundgesetz), §115. Only in 1964 the government's Economic Council (Sachverständiger Rat) started to discuss the concept of budget deficit at all. A stabilisation policy act in 1967 (Gesetz zur Förderung der Stabilität und des Wachstums der Wirtschaft) gave the theoretical foundation for the ensuing change in the constitution two years later. According to the stabilisation policy act, underbalancing of the budget is possible in individual years but only by a cyclical evening out of the deficit. The government can freeze a certain portion of tax revenue in the central bank (Bundesbank), thereby creating a budget surplus in good times. The federal government can also, after permission from the Upper House (Bundesrat), decide that the state governments must also contribute up to 3 per cent of last year's tax revenue to such anti-cyclical reserves. The federal government has full power to decide when these funds are to be released.

In 1969 the critical §115 in the Constitution was changed to allow for temporary deficit finance. However, only after the first oil crisis in 1973/74 did a deficit in the federal budget occur. Even in the following years in the 1970s the deficits in the budget have been of a very limited amount compared to the situation in other countries. It has however not been possible, as presumed by the act, to use only previous surpluses to counterbalance deficits. The new formulation of the Constitution also allows deficit finance irrespective of earlier funds, since deficits are allowed both to finance investment and to counteract a recession. With this formulation any restraint in the form of the Constitution against a budget deficit has in practice disappeared.

There are however other limitations on the ability of Parliaments to create too large budget deficits. Firstly, there exists a coordinating committee (Finanzplanungsrat) consisting of the economic ministers at the federal level and the finance ministers of the state. The Council is supposed to co-ordinate expenditure plans, thereby preventing a too fast increase.

Secondly, the finance minister who is traditionally standing for restraint in the growth of expenditures has a very strong position in government. According to §26 in the law regulating the federal government (Geschäftsordnung der Bundesregierung) the finance minister can only be voted down in government if the chancellor is against him. The chancellor and the finance minister can together vote down all other members of government acting in unison.

Thirdly, it is prescribed in the economic law regulating the federal level (Bundeschaushaltsordnung), §27, that the German General Accounting Office (Bundesrechnungshof) has the power to supervise the proposed expenditures of government before they are passed on to the lower chamber (Bundestag).

The forms for decision in Parliament are also directed against too large deficits. According to §113 in the Constitution members of Parliament may not propose increased expenditures or decreased (!) taxes. Members of Parliament may thus very well propose increased taxes, but not decreased taxes. Compare this situation with the United Kingdom where members of Parliament may propose decreases in taxes but not increases.

France

France provides an even better example than Germany that budget balance in no way has prevented an increase in the extent of the public sector. France has had an even more conservative attitude towards budget deficits than Germany. With the exception of a couple of years after the first oil shock, the government budget has been balanced in

France in practically every year until the Mitterand regime took over in 1981. Even this socialist government has however officially bound itself to a limit for the deficit of 3 per cent of GDP, a limit which has however not been held.

Several factors give the government and the president a strong position in relationship to Parliament. In the Constitution of the Fifth Republic from 1958 there are many paragraphs that limit the ability of individual parliamentarians to propose new taxes or expenditures. These regulations have also been added to in a special Finance Regulation from 2 January 1959.

According to the Constitution article 32, the finance bill of the government must be accompanied by a national budget discussing the economic situation and also making an account for the effect on the budget deficit of the proposed expenditures and revenues.

Article 40 in the Constitution, as well as article 42 in the Finance Regulation of 1959, prevent members of Parliament from increasing the proposed budget deficit or decreasing the surplus. According to these articles, members of Parliament may not propose new increases in expenditures in relationship to the government's proposal, nor may they suggest increases in the total tax pressure. Parliamentarians may however propose decreases in some taxes provided that they also propose balance in increases in other taxes.

The Constitution's article 44 contains further restrictions on the powers of Parliament. Firstly, the government can refuse to allow Parliament to amend a bill if that amendment has not been properly discussed in a committee. Secondly, according to the same article, the government can force Parliament to vote on the entire budget proposal at the same time. In this way the government can prevent different interest groups in Parliament voting on different parts of the proposed expenditures or incomes. The government can however also define the package on which the vote is to take place, thereby effectively discarding any amendment that may have arisen in the parliamentary debate.

A further restraint on the powers of action of Parliament as well as government is the Administrative Court (Conseil Constitutionel). This court has to make an opinion concerning the consistency of various laws with the constitution. The Administrative Court has so far not put an end to any budget proposals; it succeeded however in delaying and somewhat changing the socialisation plans of the Mitterrand regime during 1981.

The United States

If France shows that it is fully possible to have a rapidly expanding public sector and yet maintain almost budget balance, the United States shows the opposite: that it is possible to maintain the size of the public sector and yet have large budget deficits.

Since the Depression in the early 1930s the federal budget has been in balance or shown a surplus for only nine of over 50 years. Since 1960 the federal budget has had a deficit in all but one year. On account of increased expenditures for defence and lowered income taxes, the budget deficit will explode in the next few years. According to the latest calculations by the Congressional Budget Office, the deficit will already in 1985 amount to about 200 billion dollars. In percentage terms it means that the United States is now rapidly surging ahead of most OECD countries with the exception of such traditional deficit countries as Belgium and Italy.

The public sector has however grown very little during this period. Between 1960 and 1980 total public expenditures as a percentage of GDP increased by only three units to be compared with 30 percentage points in a country like Sweden. At about 30 per cent of GDP, total public expenditures in 1980 are markedly lower than the OECD average of 42 per cent and among the very lowest in the OECD area. Only countries like Spain, Switzerland, Greece and Japan had public expenditures of a few percentage points lower. One must however also remember that the United States in 1960 had a relatively high share in GDP for public expenditures.

In the last decade there has been two movements in the United States to prevent a further increase of the influence of the public sector, one at the state or local level, one at the federal level.

On the state and local level there are actions to limit the incomes of the public sector such as proposition 13 in California, proposition 2½ in Massachusetts and similar actions in other states, for instance Michigan. All these actions were taken to prevent further increases in the tax revenues of the public sector. Proposition 13, for instance, prevents local authorities from charging more than 1 per cent of assessed property values in taxes. But already before this action most states had rules preventing budgetary deficits. In 1980, no less than 39 of the 50 states had various constitutional or other limitations on deficits for current expenditures.

Experiences so far would indicate that the actions taken have not been sufficient to prevent further increase of the public sector. States have shown a considerable ingenuity in finding new sources of revenue to replace those limited by the tax payers (see Danziger and Smith Ring 1982, Inman 1982, and Shapiro and Sonstelie 1982).

The federal budget, until 1974, had the same system in operation as in the UK, that is Congress discussed public expenditures and public revenues separately. Now legislation from this year (the Congressional

Budget Act) introduced several novelties specifically aimed at improving budget balance. Firstly, special budget committees were introduced with the purpose of supervising the effects on total expenditures of other committees' proposals. Secondly, an investigatory agency was introduced, the Congressional Budget Office, which was supposed to provide Congress with better information. Thirdly, several-year budget surveys were introduced for the first time (see Rivlin 1982).

At the federal level, several attempts have been made to force a balanced budget. Several bills have been introduced in both the Senate and the House of Representatives. Beginning in the 1980s, a powerful movement has arisen that attempts to force budgetary balance at the federal level by means of an amendment to the Constitution (Amendment 27). There are two ways of amending the American Constitution. Both are being attempted together in this case. One way is for state Parliaments to ask the Congress to call a special Constitutional conference with the explicit purpose in this case to write an amendment to the Constitution on budget balance. In order to force Congress to call such a conference two-thirds of the states must request it. So far 31 of the necessary 34 states have petitioned Congress and in some other states one of the two chambers have decided accordingly.

The other route is to force a decision in Congress itself. In that case two-thirds of members in both the Senate and the House of Representatives must decide favourably. In 1982 the Congress faced a bill, the text of which is given in Figure 6.1. A similar proposal was introduced in both the Senate (Senate Joint Resolution 58) and in the House of Representatives (House Joint Resolution 350). In August 1982, the bill passed the Senate with two votes over the necessary majority of 67 senators. However, in October the House of Representatives voted down the proposal. It did get a majority with 236 members out of 435, but this figure does not suffice for the qualified majority demand.*

Irrespective of whether the amendment has been accepted by a Constitutional conference or by Congress it must thereafter be ratified by the states' Parliaments. The rules specify that at least three-quarters of the number of states, that is 38 of 50, must accept the proposal for it to become an official amendment to the Constitution.

As is evident from the text of the proposed constitutional amendment, the demands for budget balance concern the expenditures and tax revenues that Congress has decided upon. There is nothing to prevent a budget deficit arising on account of the fact that tax revenues do not meet plans. It is not possible however to let expenditures exceed

* As this book goes to print, Congress itself has passed an ordinary law, the Gramm-Rudman bill, which mandates budgetary balance by 1991.

Text of the Amendment

ARTICLE—

Resolved by the Senate and House of Representatives of the United States of America in Congress assembled (two thirds of each House concurring therein), That the following article is proposed as an amendment to the Constitution of the United States, which shall be valid to all intents and purposes as part of the Constitution if ratified by the legislatures of three-fourths of the several states within seven years after its submission to the states for ratification:

SECTION 1. Prior to each fiscal year, the Congress shall adopt a statement of receipts and outlays for that year in which total outlays are no greater than total receipts. The Congress may amend such statement provided revised outlays are no greater than revised receipts. Whenever three-fifths of the whole number of both Houses shall deem it necessary, Congress in such statement may provide for a specific excess of outlays over receipts by a vote directed solely to that subject. The Congress and the President shall, pursuant to legislation or through the exercise of their powers under the first and second articles, ensure that actual outlays do not exceed the outlays set forth in such statement.

SECTION 2. Total receipts for any fiscal year set forth in the statement adopted pursuant to this article shall not increase by a rate greater than the rate of increase in national income in the year or years ending not less than six months nor more than twelve months before such fiscal year, unless a majority of the whole number of both Houses of Congress shall have passed a bill directed solely to approving specific additional receipts and such bill has become law.

SECTION 3. The Congress may waive the provisions of this article for any fiscal year in which a declaration of war is in effect.

SECTION 4. Total receipts shall include all receipts of the United States except those derived from borrowing and total outlays shall include all outlays of the United States except those for repayment of debt principal.

SECTION 5. The Congress shall enforce and implement this article by appropriate legislation.

SECTION 6. On and after the date this article takes effect, the amount of federal public limit as of such date shall become permanent and there shall be no increase in such amount unless three-fifths of the whole number of both Houses of Congress shall have passed a bill approving such increase and such bill has become law.

SECTION 7. This article shall take effect for the second fiscal year beginning after its ratification.

Figure 6.1 Proposed amendment 27

the planned level, even if revenues have risen so much that the expenditures can be increased and still budget balance maintained. A qualified majority of three-fifths of both Chambers of Congress is required to break the amendment.

Secondly, the rate of increase of federal revenues is limited to a rate corresponding to national income. The share of the total economy, measured as a percentage of national income, can therefore not increase further. There is however no rule forcing a successive decrease in the public sector. The proposal is therefore built on the supposition that the share of the public sector as of the present is just right.

Many critics have suggested that the proposed amendment is too weak to provide the necessary effect. A special citizens' movement has risen, a National Tax Limitation Committee, which wants to force not only budget balance but also a successive decrease in the share of the public sector. This is achieved by making certain additions to the Congressional proposal. If for instance inflation exceeds 3 per cent, the allowable rate of increase in public expenditures is decreased by a certain fraction of the excess of actual inflation above 3 per cent. Furthermore a budget surplus must be used to repay the existing public debt (see Wildavsky 1980, Appendix A).

Other petitioners have wanted to go even further in limiting the ability of Congress to act. Milton Friedman has for instance proposed that the Constitution should also include promises of free trade, bans against price and wage freezes, bans on progressive taxation, a demand that the money stock should increase at a predetermined rate every year and that all tax rules should be indexed for inflation (see Friedman 1980, Chapter 10).

What effects would this proposed and hotly-debated amendment have? It is evident that it proposes both to introduce permanent budget balance and to limit the rate of growth of the public sector. Calculations performed by the Congressional Budget Office also indicate that had the proposal been accepted already in 1961, the total revenues of the federal government in 1980 would have been 17 per cent of GDP as against 20 per cent in reality.

The main objection to the proposal has been that it restricts the possibility to use the federal budget as a tool for stabilisation policy. Strict budgetary balance would make counter-cyclical policy impossible. On the contrary, the budget would have a pro-cyclical effect. Public revenues would fall in the recession, since profits fall and the rate of increase in the income of individuals fall. To maintain budget balance the state is forced to lower public expenditures. This will further depress the economy with further effects on tax revenues, further decreased public expenditures and so on. The consequences for the rate of unemployment would rapidly become unacceptable. Calculations with the Wharton econometric model, for instance, has indicated that if an absolute budget balance had been introduced in 1981 unemployment would already in 1982 have risen from 8 to 14 per cent, while GDP would fall by no less than 9 per cent.

But against similar criticisms it has been objected that this is not the way the proposal is specified. It does not forbid actual deficits, only planned deficits. As a recession sets in, public revenues will decrease. But this is allowed by the amendment, which allows for an unplanned deficit. There is thus no need to curtail expenditures. Rather, the budget deficit will act as an automatic stabiliser. Expenditures can, however, not be increased to counteract the recession.

Another objection has been more technical. Politicians would be able to get around the amendment by placing expenditures outside the budget. Already about 20 billion dollars consist of so-called off-budget expenditures. Another possibility for Congress would be consciously to underestimate expenditures or overestimate tax revenues, since only planned and not actual budget balance has been prescribed. A third possibility would be to lend money to co-operations in other institutions, since loans are not counted as expenditures proper. These three possibilities imply that the amendment must be made much sharper than the present formulation (see Moore and Penner 1980).

Summary and conclusions

Judging from the four countries, it has been rather common to limit the ability of government to propose new legislation on expenditures and taxes. The absolute parliamentary system of countries like Sweden and Denmark with no limitation on the number of bills introduced by individual members of Parliament, nor their content, appears rather unique in an international comparison.

The rules have however been quite differently set out. In Finland and the UK the main purpose has been to prevent increases in the tax pressure; in France and Germany the main interest has been focused to keep the budget deficit under control. Note particularly in this context the German rule that the effect of different expenditures on the budget balance must be calculated according to the Constitution. In the United States the discussion has so far mostly concerned the influence of the state on individuals and the budget deficit. Gradually greater focus has been placed on the budget deficit. So far no change in the Constitution has been made.

The question is whether these different rules in the budgetary process have had any effect at all on the size and growth of the public sector. Earlier, in Chapter 3, the size of the public sector in France,

Germany and the UK, both in 1960 and 1982, was found to be quite similar, despite the different rules. Finland and, in particular, the United States are examples of a much smaller public sector, however. It is also difficult to draw any clear conclusions from Chapter 5 on why these countries stand out.

References

General

OECD (1982), *Budget Financing and Monetary Control* (Paris: OECD).
Tarschys, D. (1982), 'Curbing Public Expenditures: A Survey of Current Trends', Report to the OECD.

Finland

Merikoski, V. (1956), *Grunddragen av Finlands offentliga rätt, del I* (Helsingfors: Juridiska föreningen i Finland).

United Kingdom

Budgetary Reform in the UK (1980) (Oxford: Oxford University Press for the Institute for Fiscal Studies).
Heclo, H. and Wildavsky, A. (1974), *The Private Government of Public Money* (London: Macmillan).
Peacock, A. and Forte, F. (1981), eds, *The Political Economy of Taxation* (Oxford: Basil Blackwell).
Pliatzky, L. (1982), *Getting and Spending; Public Expenditure, Employment and Inflation* (Oxford: Basil Blackwell).
Wright, M. (1980), ed., *Public Spending Decisions; Growth and Restraint in the 1970s* (London: Allen & Unwin).

Germany

Dreissig, W. (1979), 'Die Technik der Staatsverschuldung', in I.F. Neumark, ed., *Handbuch der Finanzwissenschaften*, III (3rd edition).
Knott, J.H. (1981), *Managing the German Economy* (Lexington: Lexington Books).
Senf, P. (1977), 'Kurzfristige Haushaltsplanung', in F. Neumark, ed., *Handbuch der Finanzwissenschaften*, I (3rd edition).

France

Barrère, A. (1972), *Institutions Financières* (Paris: Dalloz).
Duverger, M. (1978), *Finances Publiques* (Paris: Presses Universitaires

de France).
Lafay, J.-D., 'Les democraties doivent redouter le déficit budgétaire', *Le Figaro*, 10 March 1979.
Lalumière, P. (1973), *Les finances publiques* (Paris: Armand Colin).
Paysant, A. (1979), *Finances publiques* (Paris: Masson).

USA

Congressional Budget Office (1982), *Balancing the Federal Budget and Limiting Federal Spending: Constitutional and Statutory Approaches* (Washington DC: Congress of the United States).
Danziger, J.N. and Smith Ring, P. (1982), 'Fiscal Limitations: A Selective Review of Recent Research', *Public Administration Review*, January–February.
Friedman, M. and R. (1980), *Free to Choose* (London: Secker & Warburg).
Inman, R.P. (1982), 'The Economic Case for Limits to Government', *American Economic Review*, 72 (May).
Moore, W.S. and Penner, R.G. (1980), *The Constitution and the Budget* (Washington DC: American Enterprise Institute).
Rivlin, A. (1982), 'The Political Economy of Budget Choices', *American Economic Review*, 72 (May).
Shapiro, P. and Sonstelie, J. (1982), 'Did Proposition 13 Slay Leviathan?', *American Economic Review*, 72 (May).
Wildavsky, A. (1980), *How to Limit Government Spending or how a constitutional amendment tying public spending to economic growth will decrease taxes and lessen inflation, it being in all our interest to lower outlays, provided everyone has to do it, thus increasing cooperation in society and conflict within government, which is as it should be, if resource allocation is to replace resource addition as the operating principle of a government that reflects our desires not only individually as they arise but collectively over time: a good thing in itself, and better by far than mandating balanced budgets that encourage higher taxes, or imposing drastic tax cuts, which encourage inflation* (Berkeley: University of California Press).

7 What is wrong with majority rule? A preliminary study of voting rights

This chapter serves as an introduction to the analysis in the next chapter. Many of the proposals on how the constitution can be written to prevent the further growth of government start with the finding (or assumption) that there is something wrong with having a simple majority decide. Instead such restrictions on the parliamentary majority as binding referenda, qualified majorities and so forth are suggested. This chapter discusses the underlying fundamentals of majority rule with a perspective that is largely drawn from political science, while the analysis in the next chapter is more effect-oriented and thus closer to the type of analysis performed in economics.

At the bottom of the discussion two central topics are found in political science, namely the nature of the state and the nature of the people's will. The principles chosen for collective decisions in a given society always rests on some opinion on these two fundamental questions.

One part of conservatism usually connected with names such as Novalis and Hegel wants to give the state an independent will: 'The state is a macro antropos, an independent being, analog to man, and different types of institutions and human beings carry its characteristics and abilities, just as their actions to a certain extent are to be seen as actions of the state' (Heckscher 1962, p.32). This represents what is usually called the organic view of the state. If one accepts this viewpoint, one's opinion on collective choice is also made much simpler. The state becomes an individual with a will of its own, separate from that of the citizens. There is consequently no reason to try to derive the welfare of the collective from the welfare of the individuals. Hence there is no role for a discussion of the majority versus a minority of the people.

Many of the ideas presented in this and the next chapter emanate from scientists that are usually considered to be conservative. It is therefore important to note that all of them have dissociated themselves from the organism idea as an important ingredient of the conservative ideology. Buchanan and Tullock (1962, p.13) write for instance:

> Having rejected the organic conception of the state and also the idea of class domination, we are left with a purely individualist conception of the collectivity. Collective action is viewed as the action of individuals when they choose to accomplish purposes collectively rather than individually, and the government is seen as nothing more than the set of processes, the machine, which allows such collective action to take place. This approach makes the state into something that is constructed by men, an artifact. Therefore, it is, by nature, subject to change, perfectible. This being so, it should be possible to make meaningful statements about whether or not particular modifications in the set of constraints called government will make things 'better' or 'worse'. To this extent, the approach taken in this book is rationalist.

A common trait in much of the following discussion is however the problems created by the unlimited representative democracy. In the background one can distinguish an assumption of what constitutes the people and the will of the people. Has the present generation the right to make all decisions in good democratic order or do the people constitute something more permanent, the people that existed and the people that will exist? Should the powers of the present generation be curtailed to prevent them from interfering with the rights of future generations, a 'compact' between the generations to speak with Burke. A parallel idea concerns the possibility to curtail the right of the majority to impose its will on a minority.

The starting points for the analysis can thus be found in early British conservatism rather than in the German one (cf. also Tingsten 1939, 1966). The very long-run character of the analysis has been made very clear by Hayek in his *The Constitution of Liberty* (1960, p.180). He points out that a constitutional system of government in no way interferes with the will of the people (as he defines it) but only implies that short-term goals are subordinated to more long-term ones. Although the present majority is thus partly obstructed in its use of political means, those obstructions have been erected by an earlier majority who wrote the constitution. The same point can also be formulated in such a way that the present minority has accepted the rule of the present majority on the condition that the present majority obeys certain fundamental overriding constitutional rules of the game.

Long-run considerations thus demand that the majority be subjected to certain generally-accepted rules of conduct. Democracy consists of a two-stage process. In the first step it is decided how collective decisions in society are to be made, while the actual decisions are taken in the second step. The starting point of analysis in the first step is that problems to be considered should be those of fundamental and long-run character. Secondly, and quite normally since the problems apply over longer time periods, the amount of uncertainty involved should be large. Yet the solutions must hold also in a changed future, which means that they must be given more general formulation. Thirdly, the long-run decisions also involve the more fundamental values in society. They should therefore be resolved with a qualified majority or even in unison (cf. Frey 1979).

There are however several reasons why it should be relatively easy to obtain agreement even among a vast majority of the population in constitutional matters. One reason is simply the uncertain future. An individual belonging to today's majority, who has power and influence and a good income, knows fully well that in an uncertain future it is far from certain that he and his heirs will belong to the ruling class. Thus he seeks to protect himself for the future by taking also the minority view into account. Hence solutions will be characterised by compromise and more general principles of equality than by separate group interests (Buchanan 1976). Since constitutional rules of the game take time to change, it is also most probable that today's decision-maker will look more to the welfare of future generations than to their own immediate profits (Mueller 1979, p.61).

It is hardly my task to penetrate the many ideas that have been advanced in order to create a better balance of power between the present and future generations. I would only like to take up two suggestions which have frequently been made and which have implications for the analysis in the next chapter. One is the division of Parliament into an upper and a lower house, another the demand for qualified majorities on some issues.[1, 2]

The most carefully thought-out proposal in a two-stage decision model has been made by Hayek (1979). The fundamental idea in his proposal is that decisions are to be separated into two distinct chambers in Parliament, one for constitutional issues and the other for more day-to-day issues. The first chamber, which Hayek calls the legislative, is supposed to protect the more fundamental values in society. In this assembly members of interest groups may not be represented but only individuals elected by the people and representing their views. This demand is satisfied by rules that specify that individuals who have served in the other chamber or who have worked for party (and perhaps also other interest) organisations are not eligible. To guarantee that this assembly has a more long-run approach and does not represent the temporary whims of the people, Hayek suggests that these individuals be elected for as long a period as 15 years with re-election of one-fifteenth of the legislative chamber each year. Furthermore he proposes that individuals elected must be in their 45th year so that they will be retired at 60.

Not only the conventional bill of rights come under the questions to be decided upon by the legislative assembly. Also the fundamental part of the state's taxing power should be decided here. The choice between direct and indirect taxation, the degree of progressivity in tax schedules are thus to Hayek fundamental, constitutional questions that must not be changed time and time again. Hence they must be taken away from the regular chamber of Parliament.

The other chamber, which Hayek labels the governing, corresponds in outlook and authority to the ordinary Parliaments of today. It should represent the present generation and its interests and may therefore fully well be composed of individuals representing organised interest groups in society. The government is elected by and is responsible to this chamber only. In its decisions concerning, for instance, government expenditures and taxation, this chamber is naturally bound by the decisions of the legislative assembly on constitutional issues.

It can be shown that this two-stage model of collective decision-making is efficient in the sense that the welfare of society is maximised under certain conditions (Mueller 1979). Yet it is far from certain that Hayek's proposal leads to desirable effects for society as a whole. The stress on general principles makes it very difficult to take into account the outcome of government actions. It will probably be quite impossible to change the income distribution in society – between labour and capital as well as horizontally – since the constitutional chamber has set the limits to taxation and expenditures. Still the power of the government and the Parliament may not be sufficiently curtailed. Even if the system of taxation has been fixed, the level of taxation may be raised to the lower chamber of Parliament, which will have effects on efficiency and equality in society. Another aspect not treated by Hayek concerns the possibility of deficit finance.

It should also be noted that the conditions derived by Mueller for efficiency of this two-stage democracy are very strict. The first condition is that voters maximise their expected utility. Here there may be problems of information, particularly the difference in availability of information to different groups in society. The other condition is that all voters must have the same probability distribution concerning the likelihood of actions by the government. The third condition is that all voters must have the same potential utility of a certain expenditure. All must feel as intensively on a certain question. As will be seen shortly, the intensity with which opinions are held is an important part in choosing the decision rule.

The conditions posed by Mueller are very restrictive. It appears to be hard or impossible to try to seek the distribution of tasks between parliamentary chambers that Hayek proposes.

Let us now pass to the question of simple majority versus qualified majority rule. These are of course old problems in political science.[3] The traditional claims against simple majority rule is that decisions may be too easy to make and that it allows the majority to oppress the minority.

Summarised below are the objections that have been made against simple majority as a decision rule. In his *The Constitution of Liberty* Hayek (1960) has however spelled out a more fundamental critique of majority rule irrespective of the size of the majority (p.109). One of the preconditions of democracy is that citizens form an opinion on the questions to be decided. Their votes must be able to represent the will of the people. But representative democracy presupposes that the government cannot pervert the 'true will' of the people by making propaganda for its own view. Even in societies that we consider democratic, the government usually has a strong influence on the machinery of propaganda, for instance by means of a monopoly on radio and television. For democracy to become representative, the method of decision should be a qualified majority with the degree of majority in proportion to the government's influence over opinion-making in society. The price paid for this 'true democracy' is that decisions are made more difficult and some decisions may not be made at all (cf. also Hayek 1944, p.51).[4]

Figure 7.1 shows one of the fundamental objections to simple majority rule. The discussion starts from the path-breaking book *The Calculus of Consent* by Buchanan and Tullock (1962). The purpose of a collective-decision rule is presumed to be to make the cost of decision-making in society as low as possible. This cost consists of two parts. One part is individual and is inflicted when a person does not get his will. This cost is depicted by the downward-sloping line in the figure. If a majority rule of 100 per cent is specified, that is unanimity for all decisions, obviously the individual cost is zero. The lower the limit set for decision, the larger the chance that an individual is inflicted a cost. In the society ruled by a dictator, the cost is infinite.

The positively-sloping curve shows the transaction-cost for society of coming to a decision, that is the time and resources spent to agree.

The dictatorship is obviously efficient in this dimension. The more individuals required to agree, the higher the cost of transacting the decision. Unanimity would yield infinite decision costs. The total cost for society is the sum of the individual cost and the transaction cost. The optimal decision rule is where this curve attains its minimum.

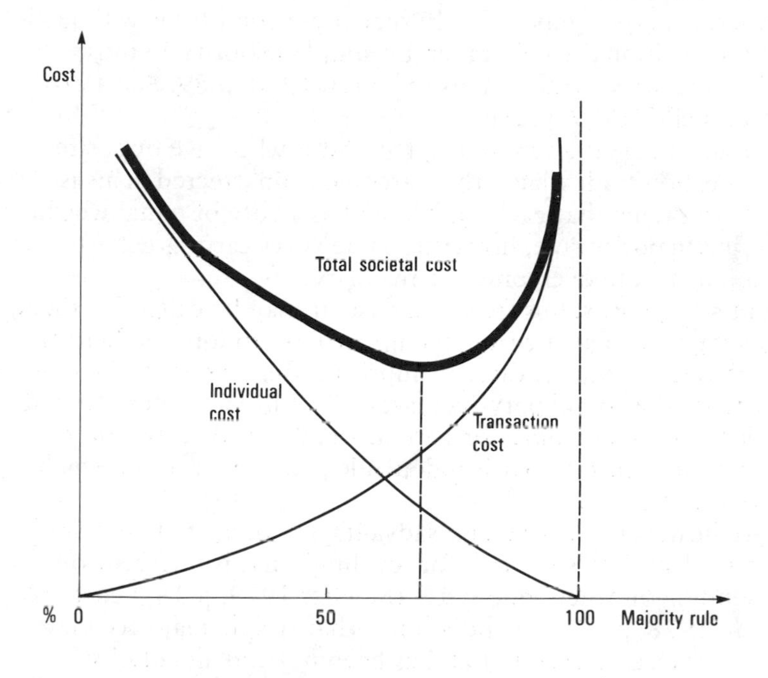

Figure 7.1 Decision costs in society

The simple fact to appear from Figure 7.1 is that there is nothing sacred about simple majority rule. It would rather be pure coincidence if the curves would happen to yield 50 per cent as the optimal-decision rule. One would rather believe that agreements will become progressively more difficult to attain with successively more individuals involved. In this case the curve has the slope indicated here and the optimal point will involve a majority greater than 50 per cent.

Naturally this way of analysing the issue can be criticised. It is far from obvious why society should prescribe a decision rule that minimises its costs. In some questions it may even be desirable to reach unanimity. If on the other hand one wants to have a decision rule that lets the individual get his will on average, then this rule can be shown to be simple majority rule (Abrams 1980, p.216).

But the conditions behind this result are strict. Firstly, there must be uncertainty about the future so that the individual does not know whether he will be a member of the minority or the majority. Secondly, voting must be independent so that A's vote does not influence B's and vice versa. Thirdly, it must not be known in advance which individuals will support or oppose a certain decision. As was the case with two-stage democracy, it is highly unlikely that these conditions will be met. Why then are decisions usually taken by simple majority in most instances? There are several reasons (cf. Frey 1978, p.89, Sen 1970, Ch. 10 and Mueller 1979, p.216).

The first advantage is anonymity; if A and B who have opposite views in a question trade places the outcome is unaffected. This is tantamount to saying that each individual has a vote of equal weight. With qualified majority rule, however, some votes carry greater power, since the minority can overcome the majority.

A second advantage stems from long use; it may be called legitimacy. A third advantage is that the rule is simple to use so long as there are two alternatives. As soon as three or more alternatives are to be compared pair-wise, the complexity increases. The outcome then depends on the order in which comparisons are made. Only with two alternatives is the rule neutral, that is independent of the order in which the alternatives are evaluated.

There are however also several disadvantages connected with simple majority rule. The first is the risk for 'cycling', that is different outcomes depending on where one starts (Mueller 1979, p.38, Sen 1970, Ch. 10, Frey 1978, p.70). The possibility that simple majority may not lead to any clear decision at all has been noticed already by Condorcet, 200 years ago. The problem is illustrated in Figure 7.2. There are three voters – 1, 2 and 3 – and three choices in society – A, B and C. The sign > means 'prefer'. Voter 1 thus prefers A to B, B to C and hence A to C. Voter 2 also prefers A to B, but he also prefers B to C and C to A. Voter 3 prefers B to both A and C but also C to A.

When the results for society as a whole are summed up, all the choices collect two votes out of three. This is an impossibility; the answer then to which alternative is chosen depends on where one starts.

So far all voters have been assumed to feel equally intensely on an issue: you either want something or you don't. Most often it is possible for intensities to vary. Let's take defence expenditures as an example. It is quite possible that a person could have a primary preference for a certain volume of expenditures. But if he cannot get this amount, he sees no point in defence at all; his preference function exhibits another peak, somewhat lower, at a completely different place on the scale.

It can be shown that a second disadvantage of simple majority rule is that it requires preference functions to be monotonic, that is they must have one peak (one desired solution) from which preferences decline in both directions. This may result for instance if all questions can be arranged on a scale from left to right (Kramer 1973). If there is another dimension, a 'green' dimension, which cannot easily be framed into the left–right scale, problems of consistency may occur. A qualified majority increases the possibility of consistency, that is that the outcome is independent of the order in which issues are voted upon.

Voters	Issues						
	A		B		C		A
1		>		>		<	
2		>		<		>	
3		<		>		>	
Society		>		>		>	

Figure 7.2 Inconsistent decisions in society with simple majorities

Shepsle and Weingast (1982) have shown that when voters are faced with many issues simultaneously, majority rule may give any result whatsoever, even when quite stringent requirements are made on the shape of the preference function. Romer and Rosenthal (1979) have shown empirically that preference functions seldom exhibit only one peak.

But the problem created by different intensities isn't over yet. We must also consider the intensity felt by the majority on a certain issue compared with the intensity felt by the minority. Again Buchanan and Tullock (1962) are the originators of the ideas presented here. The basic supposition is that on each issue there are some with strong intensities for, some with strong intensities against, while most of the population are rather indifferent. There is then a risk that a decision is taken against 49.9 per cent of the population feeling intensely against the question, while only a few of those voting for the issue may really be strongly for it.

In this case one could claim that simple majority rule is not equitable. Instead, the majority rule should be qualified depending on how intensities come out on each individual issue! One could for instance ask the minority how much they would be willing to pay members of the majority if the decision is not carried out. An example from Switzerland has however shown that, in practice, intensities appear to be quite similar. Hence simple majority would be equitable (Noam 1980).

Another objection to the objection on simple majority rule has been advanced by Downs (1961). He claims that it is not so much the decision rule itself that is at fault but the procedure. For rational decisions, voters must not be given the issues piecemeal but be able to vote on all relevant issues simultaneously (cf. also the defence of qualified majority rule by Tullock 1961).

A third set of objections that are of particular interest to the subject under consideration in this book has claimed that simple majority rule tends to bring about a too large public sector. The reason is the one noted earlier in Chapter 5, namely that expenditure decisions are taken in favour of some organised group in society, while the tax consequences are borne by all taxpayers (not to mention future generations). Every organised group in society thus feels intensely for its own area of interest, but has only a scant interest to oppose other groups' 'pet' projects. The consequence is that the public sector is expanded beyond what it would be if all groups were made to consider the whole picture at one point in time. This critique is obviously related to the one made by Downs (1961), namely that the problem is one of consistency and not so much a built-in error of the decision rule as such. The main error is that expenditure and revenue decisions are not taken at the same time (Buchanan 1977, p.284 and Brittan 1977).

Several objections have however been raised against these theories. Denzau and Mackay (1976) have shown that the demand for collective goods, as indicated by the willingness to pay, cannot bring any clear results as to the size of the public sector as such. One simply cannot say that the public sector is too large relative to what the public desires, since there is no demand for the public sector as such; there are only demands for individual goods, services and transfers produced in the public sector. Burton, Hawkins and Hughes (1981) have also shown that the model used by Brittan to show that the public sector is too large and generates inflation is subject to error. Alternative formulations of the model may give quite different results.

Among the more interesting comments are also those of Downs (1960). He claims that there is always a bias in democracies making the public sector too small! The reason is to be found in lack of information on the part of the voters as well as the government. Government/Parliament seeks to be re-elected. The strategy should then be to expand the public sector until the marginal gain of voters favourable to expansion is equal to the marginal loss of voters opposed to tax increases. But since the preferences of the voters is unknown, the government takes it easy and does not expand expenditures up to the 'optimal' level.

Downs' second point of contention is that individuals have a greater ease to evaluate the utility derived from private goods and services than from the corresponding public ones. This fact also leads to a public sector that is smaller than what is in some sense desirable.

Now Downs' argumentation builds critically on the fact that governments cannot borrow to cover expenditures. This will be one of the major contentions of one of the proposals taken up in the next chapter to counteract the tendency to 'democracy in deficit'.

To sum up, the choice of simple or qualified majority rule depends on several advantages versus disadvantages of the two alternatives. For qualified majority (and hence against simple majority) the following factors have been mentioned:

1 that the government has a greater voice in the media than the opposition;
2 that democracies have a built-in tendency to expand expenditures too much since the benefits are geared to one group while the costs are borne by all;
3 that the intensities may be stronger among those run over on an issue than among members of the majority;
4 that the total decision costs for society are lower with qualified majorities;
5 that qualified majorities decrease the risk of inconsistent decisions.

But there are several objections of both theoretical and practical nature to be made against the virtues of majority rules. The fundamental one is of course that one breaks the established rule 'one man, one vote'. More technically, it is difficult to do more than what Wicksell did 90 years ago, namely indicate qualitatively what the answer should be. What Wicksell did was to resign himself to the fact that the desired unanimity was unlikely to be met and that one had to satisfy oneself with qualified majorities. But the exact level of majority required on each issue may depend on many things. Barbosa (1978) and Nitzan and Paroush (1984) consider a few. For instance, such factors as intensities of feeling, skills of the deciding Parliament, status-quo bias of the deciding body, should be taken into account. But who is to decide and on what ground as to what the proper majority should be on each issue?

Notes

1 Frey (1981, 1983) provides more examples from the Anglo-Saxon and the German-speaking world. Among these are longer election periods as well as random elections.
2 In Sweden the indirectly elected upper house was abolished in 1970 in the partial constitutional reform, to the sorrow of many who miss its stabilising influence. A committee has been charged with the task of seeing whether some of the features of the Constitution of 1809 were not in fact superior to those of the new Constitution, now just ten years old.
3 See for instance Abrams (1980) or Mueller (1979), Chapter 3, for surveys.
4 This is of course parallel to Downs' (1960) later-discussed point that government may be too small in a democracy.

References

Abrams, R. (1980), *Foundations of Political Analysis: An Introduction to the Theory of Collective Choice* (New York: Columbia University Press).

Barbosa, A.S.P. (1978), *The Constitutional Approach to the Fiscal Process*, dissertation, Virginia Polytechnic Institute and State University.

Brittan, S. (1977), *The Economic Consequences of Democracy* (London: Temple Smith).

Buchanan, J.M. (1976), 'Taxation in Fiscal Exchange', *Journal of Public Economics* (no. 1).

Buchanan, J.M. (1977), *Freedom in Constitutional Contract* (College Station: Texas A & M University Press).

Buchanan, J.M. and Tullock, G. (1962), *The Calculus of Consent: Logical Foundations of Constitutional Democracy* (Ann Arbor: University of Michigan Press).

Burton, J., Hawkins, M.J. and Hughes, G.L. (1981), 'Is Liberal Democracy Especially Prone to Inflation', in D.A. Hibbs and H. Fassbender, eds, *Contemporary Political Economy* (Amsterdam: North Holland).

Denzau, A.T. and Mackay, R.J. (1976), 'Benefit Shares and Majority Voting', *American Economic Review*, 66 (March).

Downs, A. (1960), 'Why the Government Budget is Too Small in a Democracy', *World Politics* (December).

Downs, A. (1961), 'In Defense of Majority Voting', *Journal of Political Economy* (April).

Frey, B.S. (1978), *Modern Political Economy* (Oxford: Martin Robertson).
Frey, B.S. (1979), 'Economic Policy by Constitutional Contract', *Kyklos* (fasc 1/2).
Frey, B.S. (1981), *Theorie demokratischer Wirtschaftspolitik* (München: Verlag Franz Wahlen).
Frey, B.S. (1983), *Democratic Economic Policy* (Oxford: Martin Robertson).
Hayek, F.A. (1944), *The Road to Serfdom* (London: Routledge and Kegan Paul).
Hayek, F.A. (1960), *The Constitution of Liberty* (London: Routledge and Kegan Paul).
Hayek, F.A. (1979), *Law, Legislation and Liberty*, Vol. III, *The Political Order of a Free People* (London: Routledge and Kegan Paul).
Heckscher, G. (1962), *Svensk konservatism före representationsreformen* (Uppsala: Almquist & Wiksell).
Kramer, G.H. (1973), 'On a Class of Equilibrium Conditions for Majority Rule', *Econometrica* (March).
Mueller, D.C. (1979), *Public Choice* (Cambridge: Cambridge University Press).
Nitzan, S. and Paroush, J. (1984), 'Are Qualified Majority Rules Special?', *Public Choice*, 42 (no. 3).
Noam, E.M. (1980), 'The Efficiency of Direct Democracy', *Journal of Political Economy*, 88 (August).
Romer, T. and Rosenthal, H. (1979), 'The Elusive Median Voter', *Journal of Public Economics* (no. 1).
Sen, A. (1970), *Collective Choice and Social Welfare* (San Francisco: Holden Day).
Shepsle, K.A. and Weingast, B.R. (1982), 'Institutionalizing Majority Rule: A Social Choice Theory with Policy Implications', *American Economic Review*, 72 (May).
Tingsten, H. (1939, 1966), *De konservativa idéerna* (Stockholm: Aldus).
Tullock, G. (1959), 'Some Problems of Majority Voting', *Journal of Political Economy*, 67 (December).
Tullock, G. (1961), 'Reply to a Traditionalist', *Journal of Political Economy*, 69 (April).
Wicksell, K. (1958), 'A New Principle of Just Taxation', in R.A. Musgrave and A.T. Peacock, eds, *Classics in the Theory of Public Finance* (London: Macmillan), originally in *Finanztheoretische Untersuchungen*, Jena 1896.

8 An analysis of alternative constitutional constraints on the growth of government

Introduction

What is really meant when constitutional limitations on governments' taxing and spending powers are discussed? It should be evident from earlier that many different things may be implied. A common trait is however that the proposed action must have the sanction of a constitution (Basic Law) and that it must in some way or other limit the power of the elected politicians. Two of the norms taken up later are usually taken as economic, namely a constitutionally proscribed fixed exchange rate and a monetary norm. In this connection these two norms get quite different tasks than the stabilisational ones that they were originally prescribed for. Also discussed are budget-balance norms, ceilings on the ratio of public expenditures or incomes in relation to GDP, qualified majorities and other restrictions on Parliaments' actions, and decisive referenda.

The suggestions advanced for constitutional limitations must be examined from three separate criteria. The first must be that the rule is conducive to achieving the goal – limiting the further growth of government – but without serious negative side effects. The second criterion concerns the form of the proposed rule. Even if the rule is found to be conducive to limiting the growth of the public sector it is far from certain that it should be sanctioned by making it part of the Constitution. In a parliamentary democracy, such as Sweden, the Constitution does not contain rules and regulations of the contents of public decisions but only rules on how decisions are to be taken. For the same reason there is no constitutional court. All courts are obliged to consider whether a certain law or statute complies with the higher law. Similarly, a law cannot be challenged as unconstitutional by itself; the ruling must come when individual cases are tried.

The 1974 Swedish Constitution is specifically founded on the parliamentary system in contrast to its predecessor from 1809, which was founded on the principle of balancing powers. The rules proposed must then easily be integrated into the existing Constitution, which implies that a constitutional amendment cannot very well be proposed that goes counter to the form and spirit of the present Constitution.

The third criterion is that the rule must be easy to apply. It must be obvious to Parliament and to the government exactly what the law prescribes and what it prohibits. Similarly, it must be easy for the media and the citizenry to see when the government and Parliament break the law.

Obviously, these criteria are at once pragmatic and legalistic. They contrast sharply to the more philosophical attitude towards norms in general taken in one of the very few books to treat the need for constitutional limitations (McKenzie 1984).

In specifying the desirable constitutional limitations, the results from the previous empirical and theoretical discussions must also be kept in mind. One frequently-advanced reason for limitations on governments and Parliaments is the havoc created by politicians playing the game of the political business cycle. But it was found in Chapter 4 that the extent to which the citizens take objective economic factors into account is debatable. And at least for Sweden it is doubtful that one can write norms forbidding those actions that have had a connection with an impending election, such as a price freeze or a subsidy to a certain portion of the electorate or a 'tax rebate' given to all wage-earners, etc.

With regard to the long-run results in Chapter 5, they also do not lend themselves easily to the formulation of a constitutional norm aimed at preventing or alleviating the tendency of one specific factor to raise the share of government. To the extent that money or tax illusion is to blame, better information about the cost of an expansion of government activity could of course be required. To the extent that organised interest groups and/or government employees pressure for higher expenditures, there is a case for some constitutional reform. But as seen, these last two factors receive but qualified support. The standard public-choice arguments simply do not stand empirical tests!

As was pointed out in Chapter 1, there are presently no constitutional demands for a balanced budget in Sweden. This was not always so. The previous Constitution of 1809 stated in §62: 'After that the needs of Government have been examined by Parliament, Parliament is responsible for accepting a corresponding amount of taxation'. Even if this rule formally was not abandoned until the new Constitution of 1974, it had already been circumvented and made inoperable. The main change came in the budget reform of 1937. In this reform the government budget was divided into two parts, the current budget and the capital budget. The current budget encompassed 'real' incomes and expenditures, according to the terminology of the former budget reform act of 1911, and the means for covering the deficit of the capital funds as well as depreciation allowances. The capital budget encompassed investments on the expenditure side and a corresponding amount on the income side, showing how the expenditure was financed: partly by borrowing, partly by the depreciation allowances in the current budget.

At the same time the news was introduced that the current budget need not be balanced every year. It was still thought however that balancing should occur according to the norm proposed by Gunnar Myrdal, namely a balancing over the business cycle. Surpluses and deficits on the current budget were added to and taken out of a special budget equalisation account, which could also show a negative balance. This budget equalisation account was officially a part of the state's wealth, just as were the capital funds. These had been created by the budget reform of 1911 to correspond to the productive capital of the state, that is such capital assets that showed a real yield. This applied to investments financed through the capital budget; the defence appropriations however were counted only in the current budget and thus did not change the state net wealth.

During his tenure as Deputy Minister of Finance, Dag Hammarskjöld proposed that productive capital investments should be financed entirely by borrowing, while the current expenditures in the current budget should totally be tax financed in the longer run (Government Bill 1946:1, Appendix D). Balancing the current budget across the business cycle would, according to Hammarskjöld, lead to neutrality of the form of financing expenditures in relation to the distribution of wealth and income in society. Balancing the current budget thus was proposed mainly for distributional reasons, but the income distribution referred to was the one between generations rather than between income earners in the present generation.

Similar lines of thought have again been brought to surface by Professor Lars Werin in his objection to the White Paper of the budget reform committee of 1973. Werin writes:

> During the year when investments are made resources are taken up which could instead have been devoted to an increase in

> household consumption for that year. The revenues and effects of investments will however arise during a series of years as long as the assets are active. It could then be claimed that it is the tax payers during everyone of the years in this series who should pay for the sacrifice. Those who pay taxes during the year of investment itself should not be made to pay for the investments. They should however be made to voluntarily release a sufficient amount of resources... This type of reasoning leads to the principle that government investments should wholly be financed by borrowing and that these loans should be amortized and serviced by taxation in line with the depreciation of the assets... There may however be other stabilizational demands that may have an impact on this relationship. In practice this line of reasoning must therefore only lead to a first approximation concerning the size of total borrowing. Other arguments must thereafter be heard; the goal of equality between generations must be evaluated against other goals and the size of total borrowing adjusted in consequence.

Since the time of Hammarskjöld the official discussion of the need for a budget balance when it comes to equality between generations has been placed in the background. Already in a White Paper of 1954, it was claimed that the division of the budget into a current budget and a capital budget was of no consequence, since the regulations were written in so general terms. Instead the term total budget was gradually introduced, mentioned for the first time in the fiscal plan for 1956.

In that same White Paper of 1954 the norm proposed by Myrdal and Hammarskjöld that the current budget should balance over the business cycle was also questioned. These Keynesian thoughts that a balancing of the budget was not necessary at all were taken up again in the proposal of the stabilisational investigation of 1961 and were finally established in the budget reform act of 1973. The committee that was to write a new constitution also briefly discussed principles of budget balance and refused to allow for budget balance protected by the Constitution. There was no motivation whatsoever for this refusal.

The budget committee of 1973 produced a White Paper with two effects. Firstly, the distinction between the current and the capital budget was abolished (Bill 1976/77:130). Secondly, the committee wanted to take the whole concept of budget balance out of the discussions on economic policy. The committee wrote:

> It is however well known that the budget surplus or deficit does not give a satisfactory evaluation of the fiscal-policy effects of the budget. One fundamental reason is that these effects do not emanate from the balance as such but from each individual item

in the budget or rather from the change of each such item and that changes of the different items give rise to effects of various kinds. A certain change in the budget balance can be caused by a great number of different combinations of changes in the items of the budget, where each combination may have its characteristic effect on the economy. If one wishes to establish the effects on the total economy, it is therefore necessary to take differences in effects of the various budget items into account.

It is ironic to take notice of the fact that this committee signed its White Paper in September 1973, the month before the first oil price increase, which came to shake this ultra-Keynesian way of looking at stabilisation policy. Because, even if the quoted passage is quite correct, the budget balance also has has other effects.

While the academic debate among economists and political scientists about the motive for politics under influence of the public choice school has pushed ahead during the last 15 years, there has been virtually no discussion of constitutional norms in Sweden until this very last year, when norms in stabilisation policy have been discussed in the alternative budget proposed by the study group for co-operation between business and society (SNS). One exception is a member of Parliament by the name of Gunnar Biörck who has attempted to have a parliamentary discussion on constitutional questions. He has however not only demanded a budget balance but also discussed such actions as a limitation on the issue of currency (i.e. a monetary norm), a limitation on the powers of government and introduction of earmarking of public revenues.

The Finance Committee of Parliament made short order however of these proposals. They wrote (FiU 1980/81:21):

It is possible to view the honorable member's proposal of constitutional demands for balancing the budget as a lack of faith in the will and ability of Government to limit the expansion of Government expenditures and to find a reasonable balance between incomes and expenditures at all times. This committee may in itself have some understanding for the importance of the question. It has on several occasions warned for development where deficits in the budget and in the current account are allowed to grow. It will however rather tend to liberate Parliament from its responsibilities for the development if one were to propose constitutional changes. Such rules if they were introduced will have to be formulated in very general terms and may give rise to problems of interpretation. This committee, for its part, has full confidence in the ability of Parliament to make the right decisions to turn the development around.

The development during the four years that have passed since this was written have hardly given the common citizen any faith that government and Parliament really have the will and the ability to put an end to the continued growth of public expenditures!

The suggestions that have been made for a constitutional reform will now be discussed in turn. But before doing so, the reader should be reminded of the fundamental problem involved in the growth of public expenditures. The reason why certain norms are needed is in the standard public-choice argument expressed as follows. Every expenditure decision favours a certain category of voters, often with a strong institutional pressure group behind them. The proposal may for instance be subsidies to a firm in textiles which will otherwise go bankrupt. The expenditure thus favours a small specific group of individuals. The cost will however be spread out over all taxpayers. It does not amount to a lot per individual, who therefore have no reason to oppose any decision taken by itself. Thus the utility of the expenditure decision is much more viable than the implicit cost for the same decision. The problem is enlarged by the competition among parties of voters between the two blocs, the so-called swing voters.[1]

Exchange-rate norms

In modern times Sweden's exchange rate has mostly been fixed. From 1873 to 1931 the Swedish currency was fixed to the gold. This relationship was protected by the Constitution and was thus not formally abolished until 1974, even though in practice the fixed exchange rate had been long abandoned. During the period from the end of the Second World War until 1973, the Swedish krona was fixed to the dollar, which in turn stood in a fixed relationship to gold. During this period the value of the krona was changed only twice: revaluation in 1946 and a devaluation in 1949 in connection with the British devaluation. Even during the years after the first oil price increase Sweden tried to maintain a constant rate of exchange within the framework of the so-called snake agreement, where the krona in practice was fixed to the German mark. Since 1977 the krona is defined against a basket of foreign currency. This relationship may however hardly be characterised as a fixed one, since Sweden during the years 1976 to 1982 has devalued no less than five times with a total of over 50 per cent. Even accounting for retaliations by the other Nordic countries as well as the increase in the rate of the dollar, the effective depreciation still stands at something like 40 per cent.

There has been an extensive discussion in the whole post-war era about whether a small open economy should bind its exchange rate to a certain currency or to a basket of currencies or whether the exchange rate should be allowed to fluctuate. This discussion has however mainly had stabilisational targets in consideration. It has been maintained that by having a freely-fluctuating rate of exchange the small open economy avoids the necessity of following the economic policy of the surrounding countries. Another motivation has been that exchange rates on a free market will move more quickly and more exactly than is possible when the central bank makes decisions.

Several economists have however also warned against freely-moving exchange rates. One motivation has been the risk for relatively large fluctuations in the rate of exchange on account of speculation against a little traded currency. Another concern has been the ratchet effect on account of the fact that price levels move more easily upwards than downwards. This will imply that inflation will become faster in a system with variable rates of exchange.

This stabilisational foundation for fixed exchange rates is however a parenthesis in the historical discussion. Before the devaluation of 1931 the fixed relationship to gold was constitutionally protected. The express aim with a fixed rate of exchange was to stabilise prices (Jonung 1979). What the proponents of fixed rates of exchange were thinking of were not so much variations in the price level caused by international price movements, but to place restrictions on domestic economic policy to prevent inflation.

The main line of reasoning is the following. A developed country like Sweden cannot for a prolonged period of time have a deficit with the rest of the world; borrowing to cover deficits in the current account is only a temporary possibility. Only if the country has a currency that functions as a reserve currency (the dollar) or is an important financial market (the United States, the United Kingdom, or Switzerland) can more drawn-out deficits in the current account be tolerated. If the economic policy is given such an expensive stance that imports will surpass exports, this phenomenon leads to strains in the current account, which in turn must lead to changes in the economic policy. Similarly the fixed currency will restrict organisations in the labour market. The rate of growth of wages has to be consistent with the rate of change of productivity and the rate of change of prices in that part of the economy that is subjected to foreign competition. So long as wages are limited in this manner, the profits and the wages share of value added in the competitive sector is going to be constant. If however wage increases for a period of years surpassed this amount, a change in the exchange rate must follow sooner or later.

If a fixed rate of exchange is assumed instead, it is impossible to counteract the effects of a too fast increase in costs by means of a change in the exchange rate. This forces organisations in the labour market to accept their responsibility. But it also forces government and Parliament to conduct a more cautious economic policy. If wages rise too quickly, the government cannot take the easy way out and devalue but is forced instead to counteract with a contraction of the economy or explicit measures to bring costs down.

In order for a fixed rate of exchange to be credible it also requires that it is very difficult to change the rate of exchange. Such a credibility could be maintained with the gold standard until the First World War. A similar fixed relationship was maintained within the Britton–Woods system until 1973, where only countries with 'a fundamental disequilibrium' in the current accounts were allowed by the International Monetary Fund to devalue. Today most of the large currencies in the world float. This makes it difficult or impossible to maintain complete credibility. One way could be for countries outside the Common Market to join the European Monetary System (EMS). This would create limits on the size and frequency of devaluations and in turn give co-operation and support from other central banks. This more long-run concern for the use of norms and in particular an exchange rate norm in stabilisation policy has been well put by the Swedish social-democratic party in a parliamentary bill:

> The aims of stabilization policy may be said ultimately to be to maintain economic balance, by which is meant stabilizing the value of money, maintain full employment and equilibrium in the current account. Since the full employment target has had a superior position in Swedish post war policy ... there has all the time been a certain risk that total demand in the economy would be too large and thereby create inflation and/or a deficit in the current account. An important part in the activity to prevent such a development has been to accept certain norms for economic development. To the extent that the government has succeeded to make these norms accepted in general, they have contributed to maintain a certain discipline in the economic policy... Norms in economic policy should be simple and robust. Their most important function is of a psychological and practical-political nature. It is of the utmost importance that the norm is accepted by so many people as possible. This makes it necessary to make the norms comprehensible and meaningful as well as realistic. An economic policy that attempts to recreate and maintain economic balance, in which stabilization of prices is one of the main targets, is made more easy if it leads to the desired discipline in economic behavior. If the norms are transgressed it should be clear to everybody that the Government and Parliament are going to take the

necessary corrective actions. The norms that it is most important to restore concern a fixed rate of exchange and the amount of Government foreign borrowing. The latter should naturally stop altogether in the longer run.

Economists as well as public decision-makers have learned many lessons when it comes to the international dependence of a small open economy, as the result of the experiences of the 1970s. Firstly, that the price sensitivity in exports and imports is much larger than that previously thought. It implies that a domestic cost increase has much wider ramifications than were previously suspected. Secondly, it is known that the losses in export market shares, brought about by a too rapid expansion of costs, is not an easily reversible process.

Despite the fact the Swedish relative cost position today is substantially below the level where the problems started, only something like half of the lost market shares has been recaptured. Thirdly, it is known that the effect on domestic inflation of external shocks, be they an increase in world inflation or a devaluation, is much larger than previously thought. There is reason to suspect that the pass-through is complete in both cases in the long run and that the possibilities of economic policy only lie in postponing the pass-through of international prices on domestic ones.

A fixed rate of exchange within the framework of the EMS may contribute to giving politicians the type of support that is necessary to make them abstain from a too expansive economic policy. I can see no other fix point in the present world. However, such a connection should not be protected by the Constitution, firstly because it would mean that the Constitution would now contain a rule fixing the content of a public decision rather than the form of decision, and secondly because of uncertainties concerning the future of the world monetary system.

Monetary norm

By a monetary norm is meant a constitutional demand that the money supply in society should grow by a certain fixed percentage every year. Just as the exchange rate norm, the monetary norm also has a stabilisational and a more long-run reason.

In stabilisational policy, the demand for a constant rate of growth of money supply is usually connected with the name of Milton Friedman (see for instance his *The Optimum Quantity of Money*). Behind his demand are two opinions usually connected with the monetarist school. The first one is that only monetary policy is able to influence such variables as growth, employment and inflation. A growth in government expenditures without a corresponding growth of money supply lacks real effect. Monetary policy is thus potentially a powerful weapon in stabilisation policy. But the second reason advanced by monetarists is that this weapon should not be used. The main reason is the uncertainty concerning the structure of the economy. If politicians do not have sufficient knowledge about the working of the economy, in particular about the lags in the economy, they risk making the variability of the business cycle worse. This is the reason why Milton Friedman has proposed a rule that money supply shall, irrespective of business cycle position, grow in a certain fixed proportion every year. The actual percentage proposed has however varied. In his latest book, *Free to Choose* (1979), he has specified the rate of growth to be between 3 and 5 per cent per year. This rate of exchange should be constitutionally fixed. The percentage rate of growth is chosen with concern to the expected real increase in the economy to the aim of supplying the economy with exactly the amount of money needed for transaction purposes at this rate of growth, forcing the rate of inflation down to approximately zero.

Several theoretical and empirical objections to the prescription of Milton Friedman can however be raised. Goldfeld (1982) objects that Friedman's way of reasoning is strange in so far as it emphasises ignorance about the economic structure in the short run. Still, one presumes to have sufficient knowledge about the growth of the economy in the longer run that one can write into the Constitution a precise number for the growth of the money supply for generations to come. If the long-run rate of real growth of the economy slows down, Friedman's prescription may actually come to create inflation in the system instead of abolishing it. Another objection in a more Keynesian vein is that monetary policy is fixed irrespective of what happens to fiscal policy. A third objection concerns the possibility of controlling money supply in practice. This presupposes that there are no capital flows, creating money by increases in the foreign part of the monetary base. This in turn demands, according to the classic Friedman prescription, floating rates of exchange but we are then back to take account of the disadvantages of floating exchange rates discussed in the passage above. In a world of fixed exchange rates, money supplies cannot be guided, since foreign currency reserves float in and out of the country depending on real activity, levels of interest, etc. But even the domestic portion of the monetary base, and hence money supply, may be a difficult target. Even if the central bank is strong enough to withstand the temptations of government, refusing to hand out money for the budget deficit, choosing instead to sell bonds to the public, the banking sector enters into the picture. In economic terms we would say that even if the monetary base is manageable, there is a multiplier that is guided by the actions of the banking system. Even in systems like the Swedish one, ruled by liquidity ratios for banks and credit ceilings, it has turned out to be impossible to regulate the relationship between money supply and monetary base.

There are therefore grave objections to the use of the monetary norm as a stabilisational tool. Even empirically similar rules have turned out to create difficulties in econometric models. Cooper and Fischer (1972) have shown within the framework of the Federal Reserve Model the differences between a constant rate of growth of money supply at 4 per cent per year with a more activist rule, where the central bank reacts to variability in inflation and unemployment. The conclusion of the experiment was that inflation in the two simulations was identical, 6 per cent, while the variability in inflation was actually larger in the case of constant monetary growth. In this case unemployment is, moreover, not only higher but also more variable. Still it should be noted that these experiments have been carried out in the economy most suitable to the Friedmanian rules, namely the large and relatively closed American economy with a floating rate of exchange. In a small open economy with a larger foreign dependency and fixed exchange rates a monetary norm is irrelevant from a stabilisation point of view.

The objections to an activist monetary policy from a stabilisational point of view thus build on ignorance of politicians. A more sinister long-run interpretation is, on the other hand, that politicians have attempted to create revenues by increasing inflation. If the rate of growth of money supply is allowed to be too fast, inflation is created (in any case for a completely closed economy). These create three advantages for expansionist politicians. Firstly, the budget deficit can be used to purchase goods and services, thereby crowding out private expenditures for consumption and investment. Secondly, inflation means that the real value of outstanding bonds and currency is diminished. Bonds are therefore repaid at a lower real value. Thirdly, revenues will automatically increase faster than the real rate of growth in society if taxes are progressive and not indexed. Without having to make uncomfortable decisions to raise taxes, politicians automatically get more money to spend (Brennan and Buchanan 1981a, 1981b). Tower (1971) has calculated that the rate of inflation most suitable to the demands of politicians in this case is around 8 to 10 per cent, which corresponds rather well to the amount of inflation that has been witnessed in later years. A monetary norm would thus have as its main purpose to make politicians more disciplined, forcing back increases in expenditures and forcing politicians to make the necessary decisions on raising tax revenues. But in this case a monetary norm is equivalent to a budget norm and should be discussed as such. It should however be remembered that budget balance is not necessarily the same thing as a controlled rate of growth of money supply, since money supply in an open economy is affected both by changes in the exchange reserves and by the reactions of the banking system.

Budget-balance norm

By a budget-balance norm is meant the demand that the budget balances not only across the business cycle but every year, or at least that planned government expenditures must not exceed expected tax revenues.

Many reasons have been advanced why the budget of the government should be balanced. In the simplest version it is claimed that the state, similar to the individual household, must learn to live within its means. This moral–philosophical attitude towards the budget balance was the main reason why budgets were held balanced until the 1930s and in some countries even longer. It is ironic to note that the one frequently regarded as predecessor in applying Keynesianism in practice, Franklin Roosevelt, based his election strategy in the presidential campaign of 1932 on criticising Herbert Hoover's extravagance with the taxpayer's money. In a radio speech in July 1932, Roosevelt said (quoted by Buchanan and Wagner 1977, p.38):

> Let us have the courage to stop borrowing to meet continuing deficits... Revenues must cover expenditures by one means or another. Any government, like any family, can for a year spend a little more than it earns but you and I know that the continuation of that habit means the poor house.

When politicians and economists are pressed somewhat further on the reasons for why the budget should be balanced the main reason they mention is usually the increase in inflation that an underbalanced budget is supposed to lead to. In a small open economy, however, the relationship between budget balance and inflation is far from well-known. In the first place, the relationship between the budget balance and money supply is far from exact in a small, open economy. But even the link between money supply and inflation is not as well-known as many monetarists will have it be. The effect on inflation exerted by increasing government expenditures depends among other things on capacity utilisation in the economy. If this is low, production may be increased as the government increases its demand, without this leading to bottlenecks, increases in costs and inflation.

This applies with even greater force in a small open economy. At

fixed rates of exchange the price level is largely given from abroad, at least in the competitive side of the economy. This means that as domestic companies attempt to raise their prices, demand would instead be redirected to imports. This will lead to a deficit in the current account, speculation against the domestic currency and sooner or later a devaluation with ensuing inflation. In this case a link is found between the budget deficit and inflation but the link is not direct and the possibility to evaluate the effects of a certain budget deficit on inflation is rather small.

This simplistic way of looking at things also forgets that the state may have an influence on the rate of inflation by many other means than those visible in the budget balance, for instance by different types of regulations affecting the structure of production in an inefficient manner, raising costs. There are also many actions that the government may take like raising custom's duties or indirect taxes, with raised tax revenues, thus tending to close the budget deficit but still create inflation. As has been emphasised by, for example, Gylfason and Lindbeck (1982) attempts by income earners to compensate themselves for such increases in taxes may lead to an inflationary spiral.

A third somewhat more sophisticated argument attempts to show that a budget-balance norm is needed in order to counteract the tendency towards excessive expenditures on account of the behaviour of politicians. The next generation of taxpayers still do not possess the right to vote. Raising expenditures without raising taxes before an election is thus an easy way to win votes (Tufte 1978). But even against this thought many objections can be raised. It was shown earlier that there is little evidence that politicians really have played the game of the political business cycle. There is also little systematic relationship between the way people vote and economic events. It is also highly doubtful that the budget-balance norm really would force politicians to be more disciplined. The case of France shows for instance that it is quite possible to balance the budget at such a high level that the public share of GDP can be increased sharply even with a maintained budget balance.

There is really only one reason for a budget balance that has been advanced that is tenable (Buchanan and Wagner 1977). The argument is as follows: just as for any good, public demand for public goods and services depends on the price. The lower the price, the more goods and services demanded. If the price is held at an artificially low level by means of subsidies or regulations, demand will be correspondingly greater than it would have been at a market price. But this makes it difficult for a citizen to evaluate which price he is really paying for public services. He may possibly be aware of the fact that greater demand from him and others leads to higher taxes but, if the expenditures are deficit financed, this argument does not apply. In this case the cost that the individual believes himself to carry is much smaller because a large part of the burden is postponed, while the utility, the revenues, are reaped in the current period. In this way the demand for public goods and services will be too large, much larger than it would be if every expenditure were to be tax financed. But this creates an evil circle: deficit finance of public goods and services make these more cheap than private goods and services. This leads to a greater demand and a greater public sector and an even larger budget deficit and the merry-go-round is in full swing. Buchanan and Wagner contend that forbidding budget deficits would at least help the individual see the costs connected with a greater demand for public goods and services.

The argument makes sense, but it also demands a considerable amount of rationality and information of the individual. As long as government revenues are financed by government revenues that are not earmarked for certain supplies, it is difficult to see that individuals could separate the costs connected with various types of goods and services. On the other hand, Buchanan and Wagner are obviously right in that the costs for a public good or service must be made more visible to the individual. However, their argumentation really speaks more for earmarking of tax revenues and a larger amount of market pricing for public goods and services than for budget balance as such (see also Browning 1975 and Goetz 1968).

The advantages claimed for balanced budgets are thus frequently very diffuse and far from obvious. The motive to discipline politicians is much more easily attained by ceilings on government revenues or expenditures than by means of a budget balance. The motivation to make citizens more aware of the actual cost of the government sector is made easier by market pricing or by earmarked tax revenues than by a balanced budget. There are, however, several question-marks connected with the budget-balance norms. Some of these question-marks concern the possibilities for politicians to get round the norm. Other question-marks concern the negative effects on the economy of a binding budget-balance norm.

The first question-mark has to do with what should really be included in government expenditures. To be potent a budget balance norm must be so encompassing that the government and the Parliament cannot move expenditures outside of the norm. In American terminology one usually speaks of 'off-budget expenditures' (Bennett and Di Lorenzo 1983). In the United States a large part of housing and agriculture loans are placed outside of the budget in such authorities as the Federal National Mortgage Association, Federal Land Banks and the Federal Home Loan Mortgage Corporation. In 1983 the calculated expenditures were over 50 billion dollars, an expenditure placed outside of the government budgets. In Sweden, public authorities have so far been kept within the budget. Starting from the fiscal year 1984/85, however, a successively larger part of public authority borrowing is placed outside of the budget, as are the corresponding investment expenditures. By the stroke of a pen, the budget deficit has been decreased by almost 2 per cent of GDP!

Another problem concerns state guarantees. What prevents the government from extending a guarantee on a loan, that in reality is not expected to be repaid and which is therefore a future expenditure in hiding?

A third problem of definition concerns publicly-owned enterprises. If government expenditure proper is fixed by a budget-balance norm, one may expect that the state will move a successively larger part of its activities outside of the budget in this manner, while still retaining control.

A fourth problem concerns investment expenditures. As was pointed out above, one should calculate the stream of incomes over time yielded by a certain capital investment. The investment should not then be paid for by taxes during the same period of time. If investments also are to be covered by the rule of balanced budgets, it will not only lead to an injustice towards the present generation but also to a smaller investment activity on the part of the state.

The last and perhaps major question-mark concerns local authorities. The experiences of American legislation, in particular proposition 13, shows that the different levels of the public administration have cooperated. Thus proposition 13 did not at all have the desired effect, since the state government could supply local authorities with alternative finance. The same problem could also occur in the other direction in so far as restriction at a superior level could make this level move expenditures down to a lower level. Presumably a regulation concerning budget balance at the state level in Europe would lead government and Parliament to charge local authorities with tasks previously undertaken by the state authorities. The result is that one simply forces up local authority taxes instead.

The balanced-budget norm must thus encompass the total public sector or else the state must be prevented from moving expenditures to other levels in the public administration. The proposed constitutional amendment in the United States, discussed in Chapter 6, contained no provision to prevent such a behaviour. In an alternative formulation, which has been proposed by the National Tax Limitation Committee, a paragraph has been added, which states: 'The Government of the United States shall not require, directly or indirectly, that states or local governments engage in additional or expanded activities without compensation equal to the necessary additional costs' (Wildavsky 1980,

Appendix A).

But apart from these uncertainties of the proper definitions there are other means for government and Parliament to circumvent the norm. If the norm for instance is expressed, as was proposed in the United States, as a demand for balance between planned incomes and expenditures, a possibility is opened up for Parliament consciously to overstate the growth of revenues and understate expenditures. In order to prevent such a behaviour some independent body, for instance a constitutional court, government accounting office or an independent council of economic experts, must evaluate what shall be considered reasonable forecasts for the next year. The road is then open to almost any interpretation.

Other evasions also exist. Even a strict budget-balance norm requiring actual expenditures and incomes to agree for every year does not prevent Parliament from continuing to increase the number of regulations covering the economy. Even if legally prevented from subsidising the textile industry, the same effect can be attained by forbidding import of textile products. The effect on the voters is the same: happy textile workers. The effect on the economy is also the same: lower efficiency and higher prices. The difference is however that the budget is not affected in the second case. Nor does a demand for a balanced budget prevent Parliament and government from favouring certain groups.

But the most serious consequences would probably result if one actually succeeded in reaching an absolute budget balance every year. In this way fiscal policy would be prevented to stabilise the variations in the business cycle. But not only that: the public budget would even have a perverse effect on the economy. When the business cycle is turning down, as a result, for instance, of an international recession, public incomes will fall or at least their rate of growth will fall. But this forces Parliament to cut public expenditures in order to maintain budget balance. This leads to a further fall in public revenues, further cuts in public expenditures and so on in an evil circle.

In many of the small open economies in Europe the size of the public sector is now very large, as was pointed out in Chapter 3. In a society like the Swedish one, where total public expenditures correspond to 70 per cent of the GNP, where total public use of GDP is about 40 per cent and where public employment is also close to 40 per cent of the total, the effects on the economy of such a perverse stabilisation policy would be enormous. To this must be added a further problem, namely that it is many times more difficult to cut expenditures as fast as incomes are being diminished. This will actually force government and Parliament to plan for a continuous surplus in their activities which can be used as a buffer when revenues fall (Moore and Penner 1980).

A norm of absolute budget balance every year is therefore hardly possible; the only possibility is the US proposal of equality between planned incomes and expenditures. In this proposal nothing prevents actual expenditures from exceeding incomes. The paradox is however that actual expenditures may not exceed planned incomes, even if the economy tends to grow faster than planned. Hence in this proposal, there is a permanent tendency towards a surplus in the public budget.

But even with this milder formulation, the budget-balance norm would still have a perverse effect on the economy. There would be a possibility to use the built-in stabilising tendency in revenues to counteract the brief business cycle downturn. But calculations of state revenues for the future year must start from the revenue situation during the current year. If already in a recession, the calculations must take note of this fact and the planned revenues be made lower than at full employment. The budget-balance norm would thus prevent that a brief cyclical deficit in the budget develops into a more structural one.

A formula that binds government expenditures to planned revenues, allowing for built-in stabilisers to work only on the revenue side, may thus be said to be better for the American system than the European one. In the United States the ups and downs of the business cycle in the post-war period have frequently been very rapid, with deep but relatively brief recessions. In such a rapid downturn, state tax revenues fall quickly, and a budget deficit arises that stimulates the economy. In Europe the movement of the business cycle has been less drastic with longer but not so deep downturns. As soon as the downturn phase of a recession extends over more than one budget year, the budget-balance norm will create the perverse effect discussed earlier.

My conclusion from this analysis is that no formula for budget-balance, neither in the strict nor in its more mild form, would solve the problem at hand, namely the successively larger role that the public sector has come to play in the economy. For that the norm is too easily circumvented. At the same time an active stabilisation policy would be made more difficult or prevented altogether. The problems that the norm would create for the economy would also be much larger than the possible positive effects that such a norm would bring.

It is also interesting to note that even in the United States very few economists have backed the proposed amendment on budget-balance. Among the sceptics one may count also conservative economists that want to diminish the role of the public sector in the economy. Wildavsky (1980, p.12) writes for instance:

> I am not in favor of balanced budget amendments because they are at once too rigid and too weak. Their rigidity prevents varied

spending and taxation for counter-cyclical purposes. Their weakness permits any level of spending, however high, so long as it is matched by revenues. I want to stop government growing larger than the rest of us, not to encourage government to take more from us.

Even most economists within the government apparatus have been sceptical. The former head of the Congressional Budget Office, Alice Rivlin, is one of the active opponents, but even the conservative present and former heads of the Federal Reserve Board, Arthur Burns and Paul Volcker, have been officially negative. They both point out that they find the problem with large and rising budget deficits an acute one, but that restrictions on the balance as such do not solve the problems with a successively larger public sector. These economists would like to see as an alternative or at least as a complement to the balanced-budget norm a ceiling for the share of public expenditures or revenues in the economy.

Tax or expenditure ceilings

In order to put an immediate end to the further relative growth of the public sector it has been proposed that ceilings be placed on either public revenues or expenditures. In the version accepted by the US Senate, but rejected by the House of Representatives, total federal revenues in a certain year must not increase faster than national income during the preceding year. This is obviously the same thing as maintaining the revenue share of the public sector in national income at the existing level. There was also a rule stipulating that Congress could by a simple majority allow an increase faster than that of national income. But the decision was made more difficult in that Congress was forced to adopt special legislation for this instance.

As was seen in Chapter 3, public expenditures in the United States have not grown as much in relation to GDP as in many other countries. It is therefore hardly surprising that the proposed rule would have had no greater effect on the size of the public sector. If the constitutional amendment had been accepted in 1961, revenues would have been the same until the mid 1970s. In 1980 federal revenues would have corresponded to 17 per cent of GDP as against an actual figure of 20.

But in Europe the problem with the public sector is not so much that of revenues; the great problem lies in the fact that expenditures have exploded, creating large deficits. A ceiling for public revenues as a share of national income or GDP must therefore be supplemented by a demand for balanced budgets. An alternative is obviously to place restrictions on expenditures rather than on incomes. This is done in the alternative proposed by the National Tax Limitation Committee in the United States (see Wildavsky 1980, Appendix A). It specifies that federal expenditures for the fiscal year must not rise at a faster pace than that of the GNP in the preceding calendar year. But this proposal also contains a mechanism for diminishing the share of the public sector in the longer run. The proposal states that if inflation for the past year exceeds 3 per cent, the allowed increase in federal expenditures is reduced by one-quarter of the amount that inflation exceeds 3 per cent. If, for instance, inflation is 7 per cent, the allowed increase in federal expenditures is reduced by 1 percentage point. Taking into account the actual rates of inflation during the 1970s and early 1980s, it is apparent that the public sector would today be smaller, if this version of the amendment had been accepted.

One possible weakness in the norms would be that politicians use unexpected surpluses resulting from unexpectedly fast increases in tax revenues to build up reserve funds which can be used for an expansion of expenditures in future years. To stop such behaviour, the proposed amendment by the Tax Limitation Committee contains a clause stating that a surplus must be used to reduce the government debt.

The official amendment makes any kind of active stabilisation policy impossible. Tax revenues must not rise faster than national income and Congress is not allowed to plan for either a deficit or a surplus in the budget. The version proposed by the National Tax Limitation Committee is superior in so far as it allows for some stabilisational policy. Firstly, Congress can with simple majority allow for a faster rise of expenditures than national income. Secondly, it is permitted to lower taxes with the explicit aim of stimulating the economy. Budget deficits are thus allowed, so long as they are not caused by a too rapid increase in expenditures. The Reagan policy would thus have been allowed even under this amendment!

It is natural that one wants to write rules preventing a further relative expansion of the public sector, if one believes that the main problem is rather the size of public revenues or expenditures in relationship to the size of the economy rather than the fact that the public sector runs a large budget deficit. The advantage with the proposed ceilings is thus that the action is directed straight at the problem rather than indirectly, as is the case with the proposed norms concerning a balanced budget. Moreover, the rules may be formulated in such a way that some stabilisation policy is possible. This was not the case with the balanced-budget norms.

But ceilings on tax revenues and/or government expenditures also suffer from many difficulties. In the two versions described here they are difficult to understand for the common citizen, since they require definitions not only of government incomes and expenditures but also of the GNP or national income. This makes it difficult for the citizen as well as for the individual politician to see when the rule has been circumvented or broken. The advantage is, on the other hand, that the ceiling is placed on all government revenues or expenditures. A rule such as proposition 13 in California, which set a ceiling only on a particular category of tax revenues, has the advantage that it is easily understood and it can easily be seen when it is broken. But the rule is, on the other hand, easier to circumvent, since other taxes can be raised or additional funds borrowed.

A constitution must by necessity be written in quite general terms. It therefore remains to be seen how, in practice, a constitutional amendment should be written, preventing further growth of the public sector. All the difficulties discussed earlier under the balanced-budget norm are then encountered. In the same way as there, a ceiling on government taxation or expenditures can be made inoperative by placing government activities outside of the budget or using regulations instead of subsidies. An objection that can be made to expenditure ceilings is that they allow so-called tax expenditures, that is expenditures connected with the collection of taxes, for instance various deductions. Constitutional amendments endeavour to prevent politicians from flirting with different interest groups in society, but none of the suggested versions prevent such actions as a deduction for union fees (recently enacted in Sweden), which is expressly directed at a certain group of taxpayers.

In addition to the technical difficulties with defining revenues or expenditures, problems are also encountered in defining national income or GDP. What to do for instance when GDP fluctuates? Any attempt to limit the annual rate of growth of public expenditures to a certain fixed number is made more difficult by the fact that the base to which expenditures are to be related does not grow at a constant pace, but irregularly, even occasionally falling (Rose and Peters 1978). Even worse, the actual growth in GDP is frequently not known until several years after the event. What to do when a certain rate of growth of public expenditures has been decided upon following a believed growth rate in GDP, thereafter finding that GDP has been revised so that the now-allowed rate of growth of public expenditures is much lower? Even an upwards revision of GDP may not be a positive fact, since if politicians are suddenly given an unexpected windfall to spend, there is a great risk that it is spent inoptimally. Another important objection is that a ceiling, to be effective, must apply to all levels of government. This applies with particular force to countries like Sweden where the main growth of public demands on GDP has arisen because of local authorities and not because of the state. Thus local authorities must also be placed under the proposed ceiling. Also in countries like

Sweden the social insurance sector is formally outside the budget. Transfers from this sector is another main reason why the public sector has grown so fast. The social insurance sector must then also be placed under the ceiling, if Parliament and government are to be prevented from circumventing the ceiling on government expenditures.

The objections raised so far against the ceiling are mostly technical. Ceilings are difficult to understand and create problems of definition. But there is also a far more fundamental objection, which is more theoretical. This concerns what is to be regarded as a proper size of the public sector. To a large extent, the public sector has grown because the general public has demanded more public goods and services. The utility derived by the citizen from more public-sector services must however be weighed against the additional taxes. Technically, one would say that the size of the public sector is just right when the marginal utility of further public services corresponds to the marginal cost (disutility) from further taxation (Brennan and Buchanan 1977, 1980).

What is there to indicate that the public sector that we have today is just right? Because this is the implication of binding public revenues in relation to national income or GDP at the present level. The version proposed by the National Tax Limitation Committee has sought to take account of this criticism by forcing a diminished public sector as inflation is excessive. But in this way the public sector can only fall, never rise. Is this really what the citizens want as economies grow and become richer?

The evidence presented in Chapter 5 bears some witness to this problem. Firstly, there appears to be some illusion as to the actual size of the tax burden. This is what one may possibly get out of the arguments for inflation (INFL) and the deficit in the regressions. But on the other hand, a monetarist would also claim that a higher degree of expenditures out of a given GDP is inflationary, hence our presumed relationship may be interpreted in a directly opposite manner. Similarly, the positive relationship between expenditures and the deficit need not imply illusion on the part of taxpayers. Secondly, there is but a limited amount of evidence that organised interest groups have been able to increase the size of the public sector beyond what the public in general would like to see. Thirdly, it is found for several of the countries like the UK and Sweden that demand-oriented models explain the growth of the public sector much better than supply models. This may be some evidence for the belief that the growth of public expenditures has actually been desirable.

I have however great doubts that the normative question on the optimal size of the public sector can be meaningfully answered at all. Is it really possible to measure the marginal utility and the marginal cost of the public sector at an aggregate level? Is it not much more sensible to ask, for every clearly defined major expenditure category, if the citizens are willing to pay for an extension of this particular item by means of increased taxes. This surely must be the only meaningful way to limit the further undesired growth of government expenditures.

The conclusion is that attempts to limit the further growth of government expenditures by various ceilings in the Constitution are not only fraught with great difficulties in practice. The whole concept is theoretically of dubious value and presumably just a futile gesture.

Qualified majority rule

As was pointed out in the previous chapter there are several reasons for wanting to have a larger than absolute majority in many questions. One reason why many who believe that the public sector is already too large tend to propose qualified majorities is of course that it tends to promote status quo. Another common argument in the debate has departed from the assumption of different intensities, charging that those who are affected negatively by a decision frequently feel more strongly about it than do those in the majority. What little research exists does not tend to support this line of argumentation, which is anyway highly subjective.

There are however more objective grounds for arguing in favour of qualified majority rule. One line of reasoning that occurs frequently in the public-choice literature is that the benefits from raising government expenditures are more concentrated to individuals or groups of individuals, while the costs are spread out on all taxpayers (or even shared by future generations if the expenditures are partly deficit financed). Brennan and Buchanan (1977) also argue for qualified majorities on account of the fact that the government has a much stronger position than the opposition, for example in the form of more attention from the media.

The modern discussion of what majority should be demanded in different questions goes back to Knut Wicksell (1958). He saw clearly that government decisions in economic questions could be divided into two categories: those that concerned the supply of public goods and services and those that dealt with the income distribution. He realised that it was impossible to demand unanimity in questions regarding income redistributions. In that case redistributions would clearly never occur. But he wanted a qualified majority so that the 51 per cent would not enslave the other 49. Regarding the supply of public goods and services, however, Wicksell thought the unanimity principle more natural. Only if all citizens agree that the state or local authorities can supply a certain good or service more efficiently than the private market should this be allowed. But even when theoretical considerations support the unanimity principle, one must still have the transaction costs in mind. Even for the supply questions then, Wicksell saw himself forced to accept qualified majorities. He did not elaborate on the proper majorities.

While some arguments point in favour of qualified majorities, many others speak against it. It is firstly difficult to establish which questions should require more than absolute majority. Secondly, the rules must be so simple that both voters and parliamentarians can see when they have been transgressed. Thirdly, and most importantly, it is doubtful that qualified majorities are consistent with a parliamentary democracy. If there arises a discussion in Parliament whether a question should be decided by absolute or qualified majority, who should resolve the discussion? If Parliament can itself decide on this procedural vote with simple majority, the whole exercise is meaningless. Alternatively, there needs to be established a constitutional court, in which case we have departed from the parliamentary democracy.

Also empirical evidence points in the direction that qualified majorities tend to increase rather than decrease the rate of growth of public expenditures. This is at least the experience in the only country to use qualified majorities in tax bills, namely Finland. To get the necessary majority, the parties agreeing must each get some of their favourite issues backed by the others. No party feels it has sole responsibility for the resulting overall growth of expenditure and taxes. Similar results appear in countries like Sweden or Denmark, where the larger the coalition, the weaker it has actually been.

In Chapter 5 one of the used arguments was the existence of coalitions. The dummy variable was created to account both for coalitions within political blocs and across blocs. It is not possible however to draw any conclusions from this material as to the possible impact on expenditures of coalition governments. Only very few (three) coefficients were significant and generally the effect went both ways. In the pooled study the effect of coalitions was to raise expenditures but the coefficient was never significant.

Hence, with some regret, it must be concluded that the case for qualified majorities is not as clear as its many proponents would have it.

Limitations of government rights

An avenue so far untested is to try to limit in the Constitution what the public sector is allowed to do. Swedish local authorities are limited by legislation to 'take care of their own affairs'. As interpreted by the

Higher Administrative Court (Regeringsrätten) this has been interpreted to mean that they are allowed to run companies that supply services to the citizens of the municipality (electricity, housing, laundry services, etc.) but they are not to own companies on the excuse for instance that unemployment threatens if they do not.

Could an attempt be made to write a similar clause into the Constitution to limit the authority of the state? A limitation of the type 'take care of its own affairs' would clearly not do. Instead the question is whether goods that are truly public can be distinguished from those that are best produced in the private sphere. In the classic public finance literature, the state should only interfere with the market when the goods are truly indivisible or in case of so-called natural monopolies, when cost conditions lead to monopoly (Samuelson 1954, 1955). Later research has however not tended to share the optimism of Samuelson and others that there exists a clear distinction between private and public goods (Buchanan 1968, Davis and Whinston 1967).

The earlier discussion in Chapter 3 should also be remembered. Even if private and public production could be separated, this would not hinder an expansion of the public use of resources in the form of consumption or investment or the transfer of resources in the form of income redistribution.

If a constitutional court is again allowed to be introduced, perhaps a small start could be made by limiting the state's ownership of companies. In Figure 3.9 it was seen that this has reached formidable proportions (almost 10 per cent of employees) in countries like the United Kingdom and Germany.

Perhaps Musgrave's classic distinction could be used again to separate the causes for government take-over into allocational and stabilisational. One motivation for taking over a firm may be that the purpose of public entry is to prevent the effects of oligopoly, increasing efficiency and getting the price down. This argument has for instance been used in Sweden when the government has entered the banking and oil industries. This reason is acceptable but production must take place on the same conditions as those given other firms. Subsidies or partial monopolies are not acceptable, like the one in Sweden that the state commercial bank has a monopoly in handling the salaries of state employees.

The other motive is stabilisational, namely that a firm is at present unable to compete on the market's terms but is believed to have a potential for survival in the longer run. Again the motivation is acceptable *per se*, but in this case the company must be returned to the private sphere as soon as is feasible. And, in all likelihood, a constitutional court will be needed to decide when that is!

Stronger finance committee

A method used in other countries to combat government growth is the establishing of parliamentary committees to oversee the budget process and attempt to improve the consistency of spending and taxing decisions. In the United States a Congressional Budget Office (CBO) was introduced by the Budget Act of 1974, as well as budget committees in both chambers. The CBO in particular has tended to be an effective counterpart in the debate to the president's Office of Management and the Budget.

Proposals exist for forcing a vote on the tax and expenditure decisions in the UK Houses of Parliament simultaneously. Thus Parliament would have to face up to the resulting budget deficit.

In Germany one committee (Das Haushaltsausschuss) handles all state budget expenditures. Other committees comment on expenditure proposals to this committee which summarises these comments in its own verdict to the lower chamber (Bundestag). The lower chamber also votes on the budget *in toto* rather than on individual items. The same procedure occurs in France.

In Finland, the so-called Great Committee (Stora Utskottet) has a powerful position *vis-à-vis* other committees and tends to put on the brakes to much expansionism. Note however that questions requiring qualified majorities do not pass through this committee but are voted on directly in the chamber following committee discussion.

The Swedish finance committee was established by the partial constitutional change in 1971. According to the law governing Parliament, the finance committee should:

> prepare and discuss bills concerning the general guidelines for economic policy and the budget and those concerning the activities of the Central Bank.[3]
>
> prepare and discuss bills concerning monetary and exchange policy, and about accounting in the Central Bank and the National Debt Office. It should also supply opinion on government statistics, accounting, rationalization, about state property and procurement, and other administrative areas not dealt with by other committees. The committee shall also prepare and discuss bills concerned with budget techniques, control the calculation on state revenues and prepare the government budget (Ch. 4, §§5 and 6).

The Constitution thus supplies the finance committee with a large mandate. In practice, the other 14 parliamentary committees have not accepted the superiority of the finance committee on economic questions, however. There have been several instances of a complete neglect of co-ordination; since 1979 it even appears to be the established rule that bills are given to one committee (for example, a proposed labour-market expenditure to the labour-market committee) with no consideration to overall fiscal effect. Even consistent packages from the government have been broken into pieces and given to the various committees, which have rendered their verdict without consulting each other and with no consideration to the total effect calculated by the government.

While the lack of consistent decisions in countries like the United Kingdom or Sweden may be deplored, it is questionable whether the existence of committees with a superior mandate on economic bills would really mean very much. The United Kingdom and Germany have very similar public sectors, despite their different parliamentary treatments. And the United States is about to take the lead in having the largest budget deficit (as a share of GDP) of all the major OECD countries (except Italy) despite the existence of a strong CBO which has warned repeatedly about the development.

Stronger executive

In both France and Germany the executive have a much stronger position *vis-à-vis* Parliament than in countries like the Scandinavian democracies. In France the executive controls the package that the Parliament votes on; in Germany as well as in the United Kingdom there are restrictions on what Parliament may propose. In the United States the president can veto a decision and can only be outvoted by a qualified majority (two-thirds) of both the Senate and the House of Representatives acting together.

There are however two major objections to the introduction of these rules. One is that an argument between the Parliament and the executive must be resolved by a constitutional court. In this case it needs to be discussed how it is to be set up. Another more important objection is that one cannot possibly give the executive more power *vis-à-vis* the Parliament in a parliamentary democracy. The government is always responsible to Parliament and can be deposed by Parliament. Alternatively, it may be said in a more sinister interpretation that government always controls Parliament, since the same politicians that form the cabinet also dominate the executive committees of the parties where the nomination of candidates to Parliament takes place. The conclusion is however the same, irrespective of interpretation: in a parliamentary democracy there can never be any divergence of opinion between the government and Parliament and hence strengthening one at the expense of the other is rather futile.

Decisive referenda

For the sake of completeness the possibility to use decisive referenda as in Switzerland to slow down the expansionism of government growth should also be noted. It is however far from certain that it is the use of referenda as such that has caused Switzerland to have a public sector so much smaller than everybody else. More important is presumably the way the referenda are formulated, forcing voters to decide upon an increase in a particular expenditure and its finance at the same time.

Notes

1 Swing voters (voters changing blocs from one election to another) rose to a maximum of 7 per cent in Sweden in 1976, only to fall back somewhat in the three latest elections.
2 Inman (1982) has shown more rigorously the conditions under which quantitative restrictions on the government are superior to other forms of rule. The conditions he finds are price-inelastic demand for public goods and services, elastic supply, a monopoly bureaucracy and uncertainty as to the position of the demand curve.
3 The Swedish Central Bank (Riksbanken) and the National Debt Office (Riksgäldskontoret) are both explicitly subordinated to Parliament and not to the government. Not that the distinction makes any sense any more in a parliamentary democracy!

References

Bennett, J.T. and Di Lorenzo, T.J. (1983), *Underground government: The Off-Budget Public Sector* (Washington DC: Cato Institute).
Brennan, G. and Buchanan, J. (1977), 'Towards a Tax Constitution for Leviathan', *Journal of Public Economics*, 8 (December).
Brennan, G. and Buchanan, J. (1980), *The Power to Tax: Analytical Foundation of a Fiscal Constitution* (Cambridge: Cambridge University Press).
Brennan, G. and Buchanan, J. (1981a), 'Revenue Implications of Money Creation under Leviathan', *American Economic Review*, 71 (May).
Brennan, G. and Buchanan, J. (1981b), *Monopoly in Money and Inflation: The Case for a Constitution to Discipline Governments* (London: Institute for Economic Affairs).
Browning, E.K. (1975), 'Collective Choice and General Fund Financing',

Journal of Political Economy, 83 (April).
Buchanan, J. (1963), 'The Economics of Ear-Marked Taxes', *Journal of Political Economy*, 71 (October).
Buchanan, J. (1968), *The Demand and Supply of Public Goods* (Chicago: Rand McNally).
Buchanan, J. and Wagner, R.E. (1977), *Democracy in Deficit: The Political Legacy of Lord Keynes* (New York: Academic Press).
Budgetutredningen (1973), 'Budgetreform', *SOU*, 1973:43,44.
Congressional Budget Office (1982), *Balancing the Federal Budget and Limiting Federal Spending: Constitutional and Statutory Approaches* (Washington DC: US Congress).
Cooper, J.P. and Fischer, S. (1972), 'Simulation of Monetary Rules in the FRB-MIT Model', *Journal of Money, Credit and Banking*, 4 (May).
Danziger, J.N. and Smith Ring, P. (1982), 'Fiscal Limitations: A Selective Review of Recent Research', *Public Administration Review*, 8 (January/February).
Davis, O.A. and Whinston, A. (1967), 'On the Distribution Between Public and Private Goods', *American Economic Review*, 57 (May).
Friedman, M. (1969), *The Optimum Quantity of Money and Other Essays* (New York: Aldine).
Friedman, M. and R. (1979), *Free to Choose* (London: Secker and Warburg).
Goetz, C.J. (1968), 'Earmarked Taxes and Majority Rule Budgetary Processes', *American Economic Review*, 58 (March).
Goldfeld, S.M. (1982), 'Rules, Discretion and Reality', *American Economic Review*, 72 (May).
Gylfason, T. and Lindbeck, A. (1982), 'The Political Economy of Cost Inflation', *Kyklos* (no. 3).
Inman, R.P. (1982), 'The Economic Case for Limits to Government', *American Economic Review*, 72 (May).
Jonung, L. (1979), 'Cassel, Davidson and Heckscher on Swedish Monetary Policy', *Economy and History* (no. 2).
McKenzie, R.B., ed. (1984), *Constitutional Economics: Containing the Economic Powers of Government* (Lexington, Mass: Lexington Books).
Moore, S. and Penner, P.G. (1980), *The Constitution and the Budget* (Washington DC: American Enterprise Institute).
Musgrave, R.A. (1959), *The Theory of Public Finance* (New York: MacGraw Hill).
Rose, R. and Peters, G. (1978), *Can Government Go Bankrupt?* (Swedish edition, Stockholm: Rabén & Sjögren, 1983).
Samuelson, P.A. (1954), 'The Pure Theory of Public Expenditure', *Review of Economics and Statistics*, 36 (November).

Samuelson, P.A. (1955), 'Diagrammatic Exposition of the Theory of Public Expenditure', *Review of Economics and Statistics*, 37 (November).

Tower, E. (1971), 'More on the Welfare Cost of Inflationary Finance', *Journal of Money, Credit and Banking*, 3 (November).

Tufte, E.R. (1978), *Political Control of the Economy* (Princeton: Princeton University Press).

Weizman, M. (1974), 'Prices vs. Quantities', *Review of Economic Studies* (October).

Wicksell, K. (1958), 'A New Principle of Just Taxation', in R.A. Musgrave and A.T. Peacock, eds, *Classics in the Theory of Public Finance* (London: Macmillan). Originally published in *Finanztheoretische Untersuchungen*, 1896.

Wildavsky, A. (1980), *How to Limit Government Spending, or how a constitutional amendment tying public spending to economic growth will decrease taxes and lessen inflation, it being in all our interest to lower outlays, provided everyone has to do it, thus increasing cooperation in society and conflict within government, which is as it should be, if resource allocation is to replace resource addition as the operating principle of a government that reflects our desires not only individually as they arise but collectively over time; a good thing in itself, and better by far than mandating balanced budgets that encourage higher taxes, or imposing drastic tax cuts, which encourage inflation* (Berkeley: University of California Press).

9 Summary and implications for future research

During the post-war period there has been an intensive debate on whether the growth of government expenditures needs to be curbed and by what means. But while the political argumentation has taken place on both sides of the Atlantic, the underlying research on the normative issue has been almost exclusively centred in the United States. This means that the rules under discussion, primarily the suggestions of mandatory budget balance and ceilings for government expenditures in relation to GDP, are based on the American system. This means, in particular, a focus on a relatively closed economy and a political system subject to checks and balances between the three powers of government. It is high time that research started on how these proposed rules would fare in the open economies and the most-often parliamentary democracies of Western Europe.

Two underlying issues behind the suggestions for restrictions on politicians' spending and taxing powers can be distinguished. The first problem concerns behaviour over the electoral cycle. Is it true that politicians consciously stimulate the economy by lowered taxes and increased expenditures before an election in order to increase the chance of being re-elected? And do voters really react on economic issues in such a way that they vote out a government that has failed to bring down unemployment and inflation?

A host of studies, summarised in Chapter 4, have clearly established the connection between the polity and the economy. But it appears that the inter-relationships are much more diffuse than the public-choice school has suggested. Obviously voters do vote with regard to the success of the incumbent government. But their reaction to measurable quantities such as inflation and unemployment is unstable, both in time and across countries, because the reaction of voters to objective events is shaped by a lot of other factors, such as their basic attitude towards the government. In other words, a Social-Democratic voter naturally views the behaviour of a Social-Democratic government in a quite different manner from that of a Liberal or Conservative voter.

It also remains to be proven that governments in general tend to promote their own chances of re-election by playing the game of the political business cycle. Surely, governments will out of self-interest try to paint the economic outlook rosier than it is in order to show the success of their own policies. Surely there have also been instances where actions have been geared towards the next election. But there is scant evidence that this is a frequent phenomenon. Nor can it be shown that Socialist governments are more liberal with the taxpayers' money than Liberal or Conservative governments. The differences appear on other dimensions.

There is thus little need to focus on restrictions on the spending powers of politicians until it can be shown that there is a problem here. And whoever suggests such rules should also state how they will prevent politicians from favouring certain groups in other ways that are not subject to spending limitations, such as price freezes, tax deductions for certain taxpayers, import quotas on certain goods, etc.

It is therefore much more interesting to focus attention on the more long-run question of government growth. For the OECD area as a whole, total public expenditures in relation to the Gross National (or Domestic) Product has increased from 28 per cent in 1960 to 33 per cent in 1970 and to 42 per cent in 1982. The increase in the latter period has been somewhat faster in the small economies in comparison with the larger, 13 as against 7 percentage points. The Swedish increase is quite unique in comparison: from 31 per cent of GDP in 1960 to 45 per cent in 1973 to 68 per cent in 1982!

In 1960 the public sector in Sweden was only minutely larger than the OECD average and smaller than that in countries like Germany, France, the United Kingdom, The Netherlands and Norway. When instead 1982 is looked at, only The Netherlands is close. But Sweden clearly leads the pack.

Before attempting to discuss what should be done about it, it would seem obvious that the reasons behind this phenomenal growth in the public share of the economy should first be discussed, and also whether the increase has been in some way wanted by the electorate or whether the growth has occurred because of the combined wishes of the politicians and the bureaucrats.

Chapter 5 tried to answer these questions. A disequilibrium model for Sweden was presented in which the relative emphasis on the supply versus the demand side was made explicit. It was found that several indications pointed to the fact that the Swedish expansion had indeed been generated by the demand side. The demand equation was found to have a much better fit than the supply equation with several significant and rightly signed parameters. The supply equation gave evidence of severe mis-specification. Furthermore, in the disequilibrium framework most observations since 1975 were placed by the model in the demand regime. This does not imply however that nothing is wrong in Sweden. Rather, one of the variables on the demand side was a proxy for the interaction between voters and the interest organisations. Hence to the extent that one believes that interest articulation by organisations is not conducive to democracy, there may still be some need for intervention.

Models of individual countries as well as a model of pooled data for 12 countries was then turned to. Unfortunately, these models were incapable of giving clear-cut answers to the questions. In some cases demand appeared to have been dominant, such as in the United Kingdom. In some countries it appeared that supply had been the main force, such as in the United States. But in most countries the evidence was mixed. With the help of relative prices and some other frequently-significant variables such as the rate of unemployment, the explanatory power appeared high, until the high degree of autocorrelation was also taken account of. It appears that the same model could profitably be used for analyses of individual countries but not for cross-country analyses. Will there ever be a common model?

It thus appears that there are questionable claims made as to the desirability of constitutional restraints on governments and Parliaments. Furthermore, I find the issue of an optimal size of government a tricky one. Is it really possible for the voting citizens to make a rational choice as to the optimal size of government by balancing the marginal utility of an expanded government sector against the added disutility of extra taxes? In the aggregate I find the idea ridiculous. The most that can be said is that the demand for various aspects of government supplies of different goods and services must be considered further.

In Chapter 6 some of the existing rules in the budgetary process were surveyed. Most of them were found to centre on such aspects as the way of voting on tax and expenditure bills in Parliament. None of the surveyed countries has in its constitution restrictions of the type discussed most often, namely demands for budgetary balance and ceilings on the ratio of government expenditure or taxes to GDP.

In Chapters 7 and 8 several possible constitutional limitations on the taxing and spending powers of government were treated. But few passed muster. The budget-balance norm for instance was found to have several important drawbacks. One is that there is no restriction on raising taxes so that the budget can in principle be balanced at any level of expenditures. Other critiques centre on definitions. How can a definition of expenditures and taxes be made so encompassing that the government and Parliament cannot circumvent the restriction by, for instance, forcing more expenditures on to municipalities, and yet be simple for the common man to understand?

A more important objection is that demands for a perpetually-balanced budget would not only impede most counter-cyclical policy; it would destabilise the economy even further, since the fall of government revenues in a recession would also force a fall in expenditures, aggravating the cycle.

The ceilings on government expenditures or taxes are also subject to the same technical problems as are budget-balance demands. But the main objection is that they do not prevent politicians from favouring their constituent groups should they so desire. Far from all actions taken by politicians can be measured in direct monetary terms! And yet an outright subsidy to the textile industry may have exactly the same economic and political effects as a quota on textile imports!

The conclusion is that it appears rather meaningless to discuss limitations on the total size of the government sector. Instead, the discussion on demands of particular public goods and services and their financing should be focused on.

In writing this book I have attempted to step on as many toes as possible. I have questioned the view that an increased public sector is necessarily bad. I have attempted to show that there is little to substantiate the claim that politicians will play with the economy in order to be re-elected. I hope to have shown that there is little reason to place the fast growth of the government sector on to such variables as unions or other interest groups or public employees as a pressure group. Surely, there are some indications here and there to this effect, but the proof is hardly convincing so far. Furthermore, it appears that in countries such as Sweden where the public sector has expanded the most, the increase might actually have been wanted by the electorate.

On the normative side, I have questioned most of the proposed measures to combat the further growth of government, both because their effects on the target are dubious and because they will often have strongly negative side effects.

It is my hope that many researchers of economics as well as political science will feel that these conclusions violate their own views. In this way we may finally get some good research started on this side of the Atlantic also!

Author index

Subject index